THE MODERN STENTORS

Recent Titles in
Contributions in Economics and Economic History
Series Editor: Robert Sobel

Essays in Southern Labor History: Selected Papers, Southern Labor
History Conference, 1976
Gary M Fink and Merl E. Reed, editors

The Iron Barons: A Social Analysis of an American Urban Elite, 1874-1965
John N. Ingham

The Railroad Mergers and the Coming of Conrail
Richard Saunders

R. G. Dun & Co., 1841-1900: The Development of Credit-Reporting in
the Nineteenth Century
James D. Norris

New Directions in Political Economy: An Approach from Anthropology
Madeline Barbara Leons and Frances Rothstein, editors

Moral Revolution and Economic Science: The Demise of Laissez-Faire
in Nineteenth-Century British Political Economy
Ellen Frankel Paul

Economy and Self: Philosophy and Economics from the Mercantilists
to Marx
Norman Fischer

The Quality of Working Life in Western and Eastern Europe
Cary L. Cooper and Enid Mumford

The Politics of Organizational Change
Iain Mangham

Change Agents at Work
Richard N. Ottaway

Electricity for Rural America: The Fight for the REA
D. Clayton Brown

Commodities, Finance and Trade: Issues in the North-South Negotiations
Arjun Sengupta, editor

PHILIP T. ROSEN

THE MODERN STENTORS

RADIO BROADCASTERS AND THE
FEDERAL GOVERNMENT, 1920-1934

Contributions in Economics and Economic History, Number 31

GREENWOOD PRESS
Westport, Connecticut • London, England

Library of Congress Cataloging in Publication Data

Rosen, Philip T   1946-
   The modern stentors.

   (Contributions in economics and economic history ;
no. 31 ISSN 0084-9235)
   Bibliography: p.
   Includes index.
   1.   Radio broadcasting—United States—History.
I.   Title.
HE8698.R66   384.54'0973   79-8952
ISBN 0-313-21231-7 lib. bdg.

Library of Congress Catalog Card Number: 79-8952
ISBN: 0-313-21231-7
ISSN: 0084-9235

First published in 1980

Greenwood Press
A division of Congressional Information Service, Inc.
88 Post Road West, Westport, Connecticut 06881

Printed in the United States of America

10 9 8 7 6 5 4 3 2 1

*To Forrest, Ellen,
Jackie, and Philip*

CONTENTS

Illustrations   *ix*
Acknowledgments   *xi*

    Introduction   3
1. The Interdepartmental Contest   15
2. The Honest Broker   35
3. The Hoover Pool   47
4. Organize or Perish   61
5. The New York Solution   77
6. The Crazy Man from Chicago   93
7. Turning the Corner   107
8. The Federal Radio Commission   127
9. Network Radio   145
10. The Abortive Revolt   161
11. Consensus   179

Notes   *185*
Bibliography   *245*
Index   *257*

IllUSTRATIONS

1. WDM   6
2. Conrad's Transmitter   16
3. KDKA Transmitter, 1920   17
4. Branly Coherer   19
5. WJY Broadcast, 1921   67
6. Crystal Detector   70
7. Crosley's Two Tube Amplifier   71
8. Superheterodyne Receiver, 1922   115
9. Armstrong Receiver, 1923   115

Acknowledgments

Any manuscript is, of necessity, a collective undertaking, dependent on the cooperation, skills, patience, and good humor of the staffs of depositories, one's colleagues, friends, and family. To single out individuals among that august group meriting special thanks immediately leaves one vulnerable to the justifiable pique of contributors whose names did not happen to receive mention. On the other hand, failure to thank individually those who dedicated substantial portions of their precious time to the critique, reading, typing, or beer drinking necessary to the production of this work would be remiss. To any whom I may fail to mention, my deepest thanks and apologies.

Among foundations and institutions providing financial support to me during the time of my research and writing, I wish to thank Wayne State University, the Smithsonian Institution's Museum of History and Technology, and the Liberty Fund.

Kenneth Hagan, Loren Pennington, Stana Sukunda, and Jackie Rosen freely offered editorial comments and suggestions which proved of valuable assistance. Special thanks also go to Patricia Mavignier for typing the final manuscript.

Forrest and Ellen McDonald have guided this work from its inception. An adequate listing of the many ways in which they have aided my progress would constitute a volume in itself.

THE MODERN STENTORS

Introduction

The contours of the American broadcasting industry were established fifty years ago and have never changed fundamentally. Listener (or viewer) preference, as the executives of the networks understand that preference, stands as the ultimate arbiter of program content. The industry remains privately owned, operated for profit, sustained by the sale of airtime to advertisers, and dominated by an oligopoly of networks and their local affiliates. It is regulated, but not controlled, by an agency of the national government, the Federal Communications Commission. Dissenters to commercially owned broadcasting have criticized this scheme of things since the beginning, mainly on the grounds that the resulting programs lack cultural, intellectual, and aesthetic quality. On the other hand, this arrangement has made the product—radio and later television transmissions—available to the widest possible audience of "consumers" at an extremely low price. On negative and positive counts alike, the structure may be said to be quintessentially American.

There was, however, nothing inevitable about the way American broadcasting turned out. The system might have been very different but for the particular interplay during the crucial years 1920 to 1934 among businessmen in the nascent industry, the prospective market, politics, and bureaucrats. It might have developed into a state-owned enterprise, either of the high-quality sort for which the British Broadcasting Corporation came to be praised or of the propagandistic machinery sort for which the Nazis came to be damned; there were advocates of both in the United States. At the other extreme, it might have remained chaotic; as others advocated.

Had the U.S. Navy had its way, the medium might not have developed at all. The Naval Communications Service argued broadcasting should be banned, because it represented a frivolous use of the nation's airwaves.

The arrangements that evolved were something new in the relationship between public and private institutions in America. It was not new in the sense of an abandonment of the laissez-faire tradition; such a heritage existed as a powerful rhetorical tool in the mouths of businessmen and politicians alike but never as a tangible reality. If by laissez-faire is meant free trade between nations, it is both irrelevant to the subject at hand and a myth, for the United States had been commited to the principles of protective tariffs almost continuously since 1816. If the term has to do with supervision by government, it is indeed relevant, but laissez-faire in that sense never existed in the United States, as the studies of Oscar and Mary Handlin, Louis Hartz, and a host of others so thoroughly demonstrate. Nor did the regulated structure of broadcasting evolve as a product of efforts by "progressives" to bring a major new segment of business enterprise under the control of the people through the instrumentality of popular government. Indeed, the attempts to rationalize and stabilize the American economy through government involvement resulted from the efforts of businessmen and bureaucrats rather than from the populace. The newness of the regulatory arrangements lay elsewhere.[1]

Previously supervised economic enterprise in the United States had been of three kinds: (1) mercantilist, wherein control and inspection of the quality of production served to make the country's (or a state's or even a city's) output more marketable and thus contribute to the welfare of the whole, such as the Meat Inspection Act and the Federal Drug Administration; (2) police power, designed to protect the safety and health of the people, such as factory inspection, smoke abatement, antipollution, and child labor laws; and (3) public utilities, wherein rates and standards of service are stipulated for public necessities, such as electric, water, and gas utilities, as well as transportation companies.

By its nature, broadcasting did not lend itself to any of the older forms of government supervision. It most nearly resembled utilities, but classification as a utility was not possible for a single, insurmountable reason: to impose "standards of service" was to oversee program content, and to interfere with entertainment, newscasts, educational fare, or any other features would constitute a direct violation of First Amendment guarantees of freedom of speech and press. On the other hand, it was inherent in the technology of the medium that it could not be left unregulated, for the cacophony of competing voices on the airwaves would have made development impossible. Regulation and standardization therefore were necessary but impossible within the framework of existing institutions. This book is an effort to describe the process by which the dilemma was resolved during the crucial fourteen-year period when broadcasting came of age.

The story will tell itself, but it will not be amiss here to make a generalization or two about government, business, and technology in America. First, the introduction of a new invention or the discovery of a new use for an existing technology can disrupt the established order and threaten vested interests. Second, and equally important, technological innovations, or innovative applications of existing technology, are apt to be perceived differently by different segments of society. Ordinary citizens generally view such changes in terms of prospective benefits to society at large or to themselves as consumers. Businessmen view them both in those terms and in terms of prospective effects upon their profit and loss statements. Bureaucrats, by and large, may regard the welfare of society and the viability of business to some extent; but to them the prime reality is power, and thus their perception of technological innovation, like their view of most other changes, is shaped by its prospective effects upon existing power relations and the opportunities it creates for enlarging their share of power. Unless we understand these elements we cannot hope to understand the relationship of technology, business, and government.[2] .

The forerunner of broadcasting began innocuously enough. After its introduction in 1899, radio telegraphy principally served maritime needs. It was employed as a means of direct communication between sender and receiver (point-to-point communications), such as in traffic between ships or between ships and shore installations. It performed a valuable service by maintaining contact between ship and shore, transmitting weather information, sending navigational warnings, and coordinating rescue operations. But, since it merely presented a device for transmitting Morse code messages without wires, the system demonstrated only a limited part of its potential.

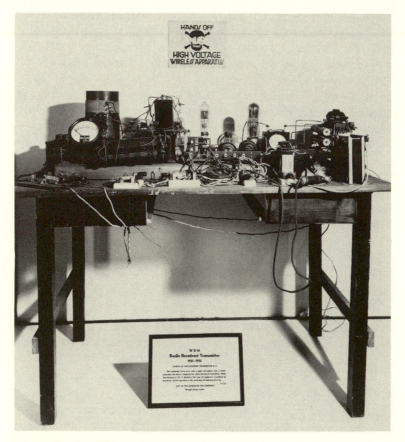

Figure 1.   WDM

A private point-to-point station assigned to the Ann Arbor Railroad Company.   *Courtesy of Smithsonian Institution, Photo No. 38, 785-D.*

For well over a decade preceding World War I, a host of individuals and commercial enterprises experimented with radio telephony (sending voice over the air). With the introduction of the three-element vacuum tube or audion, capable of producing, detecting, and amplifying electromagnetic waves, the transmission of music, news and educational information became possible. This device, together with the exigencies of mobilizing the business and scientific communities for World War I, facilitated the introduction of broadcasting, that is, the dissemination of material intended to be received by a random, anonymous, and potentially unlimited audience. Thus, by 1920, the technological obstacles to the development of a product directed toward a mass audience had been removed. On 2 November 1920, the Pittsburgh Westinghouse station, KDKA, commenced operations by transmitting the Harding-Cox election returns, thus revolutionizing communications by making radio ubiquitous, immediate, and personal.[3]

No technical development in modern American history has had more startling consequences than has broadcasting. In an era of rapid technological expansion, the new enterprise experienced phenomenal growth. In 1920-21 there were eight stations, by 1922 there were over 500, and by 1926 the number had increased to over 700 outlets. The increase offered substantial monetary rewards to those who manufactured receivers as well as to those involved in program production and merchandizing. Indeed, in less than a decade, radio sets had become a household necessity, and broadcasting had become big business.[4]

As the technology grew, proliferation of its use and overlapping of its functions caused society to question its growth and expansion. Government agencies, the industry itself, and finally Congress struggled to thrash out some form of control—either by direct domination or oblique regulation—while society struggled along with the flawed, yet extremely popular, product of intense special interest competition. In the end, conflicting policies for the organization, financing, and supervision of broadcasting, along with the confusion resulting from prolonged infighting, forced the elected representatives to take a stand and attempt to resolve the uncertainties that plagued the industry. In expressing their various motives and philosophies, each of the competing interests—bureaucrats, businessmen, educators, and legislators alike—marked American broadcasting with a unique and indelible hallmark.

By the time Warren G. Harding assumed the presidency, governmental proponents and critics of the changing role of radio based their positions on their previous use of communications and the needs and desires of their particular government agencies. Prior to 1920, wireless history had been shaped largely by naval policy. The U.S. Navy, because of its prominent position, not only disapproved of the growth of broadcasting, it also actively sought to curtail its development. As always, the navy discouraged any competing service that threatened its marine facilities, even broadcasting. Naval officials opposed the erection of transmitters and pressured the Department of Commerce to close down those stations which interfered with maritime traffic. The military considered this resource too important to be utilized for what H. L. Mencken later called "a long series of imbecile speeches by fifth-rate politicians and agitators, and an equally long series of stupid musical programmes done by fifth-raters."[5]

The Post Office and the Commerce Department opposed the navy's plans on different grounds but for the same reasons, namely their own desire for control. The Post Office advanced the general proposition that all means of electrical communications should be held by government monopoly. The agency, therefore, proposed a Bureau of Communications through which the postmaster general would supervise radio. Citing the need to consolidate facilities for increased efficiency and the Western European example of centralized management (usually through the postal service), the Post Office presented a formidable obstacle to navy designs.

The Commerce Department also seriously challenged the navy's hegemony over radio. Under the direction of Herbert C. Hoover, a technological progressive and bureaucratic imperialist, that department attempted to incorporate numerous bureaus, agencies, and functions. By bringing broadcasting within his province, Secretary Hoover not only sought to increase his power and prestige but also to secure a role in manipulating one of the most important technological innovations of the 1920s.[6]

Hoover carefully marshalled a variety of interests, including commercial companies, amateurs, engineers, scientists, and government allies, and successfully defeated both the navy and the Post Office. As a part of this strategy, he shifted the interdepartmental struggle over radio to an independent commission which he controlled, thereby outmaneuvering his rivals. In 1922–23, the Department of Commerce oversaw the creation of the Interdepartmental Radio Advisory Committee to serve as a coordinating agency for government radio.

Although the first regulatory act passed by Congress—the Radio Act of 1912—had given statutory recognition to the navy domain, Hoover methodically designed an extralegal framework to absorb its functions. While his actions clearly sidestepped the law, their success led many factions, both political and commercial, to support them. Yet Hoover spent years thereafter vainly seeking legislation to legitimize his domination of broadcasting.

The Commerce Department's initial victory in the interdepartmental struggle ensured a commercially directed industry in the United States. However much the secretary of commerce may have helped liberate the new medium from the restrictions imposed on it by the military services, he failed to control all aspects of the ensuing denouement. As the enterprise matured, the prospect of a mass audience appealed to religious and educational institutions and municipalities as well as radio manufacturers, electrical companies, and newspapers—all of whom rushed to establish stations. The most rapid proliferation occurred during Hoover's first two years as secretary of commerce. While the expansion did lead to diversity, it also generated conflicting priorities for broadcasting and its control.

Ultimately, only the large corporations and electrical companies had the experience and financial resources necessary to transcend the ensuing confusion. At the time when Hoover was focusing the major part of his activities on ways to legislate Department of Commerce supervision, the larger segments of the industry disassociated themselves from this effort. While publicly they supported Hoover and his legislative program, privately they maneuvered to organize their enterprise. In fact, American Telephone and Telegraph

(AT&T), General Electric (GE), Westinghouse, and the Radio Corporation of America (RCA) openly contended that federal regulation should be implemented only after economic and organizational stability had been achieved. Such was the impact of their insistence on the "timing" of legislation that it frustrated passage of a radio control bill for over six years.

Meanwhile, the disorder engendered by widespread signal interference served both the secretary of commerce and the industrial giants by bringing public interest and pressure to bear on the questions at hand, ushering in a new level of development. As with the final disposition of the interdepartmental struggle, resolving the managerial issues required political acumen and subtle maneuvering. David Sarnoff, general manager of RCA, guided this aspect much as Hoover manipulated the intergovernmental dispute. As the catalyst of action, Sarnoff's program portended far greater significance than might have been expected of that of any single participant. From 1921 to 1926, the radio alliance composed of General Electric, Westinghouse, and RCA and the telephone group—AT&T and its subsidiary Western Electric—battled each other for financial control of their industry. Through the efforts of Sarnoff and his counterparts, the rivals arranged a negotiated settlement which withdrew AT&T from their domain and formed the new National Broadcasting Company (NBC) to provide nationwide programming. The creation of NBC, a chain deriving its income from advertising, apexed this search for order. Founding a financially sound network system added impetus to the need for a precise government radio policy.

Although aware of the internecine struggle afoot and its potential effect on the public, politicians had intervened as little as possible. A well-calculated plan by Zenith's president Eugene McDonald induced them to confront the complicated issue of federal supervision. McDonald, following Hoover's lead, forced congressional action by violating the Radio Act of 1912. In the face of his flamboyance, Congress disregarded those who advised that broadcast legislation should be considered "only upon the recommendation of the foremost radio engineers." Instead, stung by the prospect that the secretary of commerce might use this issue to capture the 1928 Republican nomination, they responded to the challenge of presidential politics.[7]

Opposition to Hoover, not sound engineering practices, motivated the Senate to propose an alternative scheme to oversee radio. The lawmakers harkened back to the concept of placing jurisdiction under an independent commission, thereby eliminating Commerce Department domination. Separate legislative proposals suggested regulation under the secretary of commerce or under an independent agency. Bowing to the realities of political expediency, they compromised, fusing parts of both, and the Radio Act of 1927 became law.

Fifteen years after its first attempt at legislation, Congress had finally enacted a comprehensive radio law. Under the newly expanded federal jurisdiction, applicants had to secure a license, waive any claims of ownership or property rights of electromagnetic channels, and demonstrate their fitness to serve the public interest. Another segment of the measure anticipated New Deal practices by establishing the Federal Radio Commission to administer the 1927 act. Its wide ranging discretionary authority empowered the FRC to maintain order on the nation's airwaves, strengthen and safeguard facilities that served the public, and eliminate interference between radio users.

The year 1927, then, represented an important watershed in the history of broadcasting. Chaos and confusion gave way to a national system characterized by government supervision based on the commission form of regulation and syndicated network programming supported by advertising. As this occurred the political, administrative, and economic foundations characteristic of the current American system became recognizably established.

Network radio supported by advertising, the acme of industry-wide economics, considerably antedated the 1927 act. As a matter of fact, it evolved from technological and financial changes implemented in the first half of the 1920s. As advertising generated increasing revenue, broadcasters recognized the potential profit of local and national airtime sold to interconnected stations. Almost at once, businessmen throughout the United States realized the advantage of sponsoring popular national programs. As broadcasting took "its place in promotion and exploitation," the advertisers whipped out the money to support the entire commercial structure.[8]

The Radio Act of 1927 invigorated commercial radio. That year, NBC gained sufficient outlets and advertisers to expand into two networks. Almost immediately, other entrepreneurs realized the potential profit of chain hook-ups and hoped to share in the success. When their initial offers to cooperate with NBC were rebuffed, the newcomers redirected their efforts toward establishing a totally independent organization.

This upstart enterprise, under the leadership of the young maverick William S. Paley, introduced new business practices and entertainment policies that transformed and stabilized network radio. In time the financial distance between the competitors lessened, and the Columbia Broadcasting System (CBS) joined NBC to dominate national program production and marketing. Both owned several stations outright, managed others, and pervasively influenced the economic stability of independents. As the giants dominated broadcasting, their every move hinged on advertising balance sheets, profitability, and market conditions.

Added to its phenomenal expansion, the industry's internal restructuring redoubled the urgent need for outside regulation. Yet, almost immediately after its organization, the federal agency developed to provide that order was forced to contend with a host of potentially catastrophic limitations inspired by congressional ineptitude. While setting up the Federal Radio Commission, the lawmakers had failed to provide the regulatory machinery to carry out their intent; indeed, they did not even clarify that intent to the administrators. As a result, their creation suffered a series of misadventures. It managed to survive, however, by relying upon the secretary of commerce. In the process, as the FRC gained stability and more authority it commenced interpreting the Radio Act of 1927 in its own right. Using Secretary Hoover's extralegal program as its guide, the panel began to apply its own restrictions to the participants. Purposefully, the government bureau instituted measures designed to force several hundred broadcasters off the air.

In the ensuing contest for a position in the broadcast band, hundreds of stations demanded recognition. The FRC, following Hoover's recommendations at the national radio conferences, favored those with prior experience, superior equipment, and financial resources. In the drive to restore order to the airwaves, the smaller religious, educational, municipal, and private facilities suffered. In fact, the commercial advertising stations and the networks dominated the proceedings. Through its decisions, the FRC made itself an appendage of the Department of Commerce. Ultimately, those businessmen who gained favor with Secretary Hoover also fared well under the commission.

As this bias became apparent, aggrieved station owners challenged every aspect of the 1927 law as well as specific FRC rulings. During the subsequent struggle, federal judges created a solid basis of jurisprudence supporting an intricate assemblage of radio law. Over an extended period the judiciary wielded influence equal to that of the legislators and administrators. From 1927 to 1934, the federal courts unequivocally upheld the constitutionality of the 1927 legislation and the entire body of standards established by the FRC. The culminative impact of these decisions served as basic precedent for modern regulation.

As network radio and commercial advertising stations prospered, critics of American broadcasting radicalized their attacks. Indeed, those groups which suffered most from the commission's rulings led an abortive revolt in direct defiance of the system. Their reactions proved unsound and self-defeating, however. While denouncing favoritism for others, the noncommercial groups demanded special treatment for themselves. Moreover, their desire to substitute government control modeled on the British system for commercial broadcasting in the United States further undercut their position. Ironically, their paradoxical and contradictory demands, combined with their radicalism, united government bureaucrats, network executives, commercial operators, and advertisers who were anxious to preserve the existing system. Consequently, these powerful factions backed the congressional desire to unify radio, telephone, telegraph, and cables under one government agency. Their efforts resulted in the Communications Act of 1934, which created the Federal Communications Commission. One might have expected sweeping changes from it, but, as far as broadcasting was concerned, the law simply perpetuated the Radio Act of 1927. In the end, it emerged not from a struggle between hucksters, profit-motivated executives, and commercial operators against the forces of higher education, fair play, and classical music but, as always, from a perennial contest between political and economic forces. And, as always, good business turned out to be good politics, and the revolt was easily put down.

The story could have turned out differently; different decisions could have produced a totally different system. Its denouement followed a great number of legislative, judicial, and business decisions made over a fourteen-year period. In essence, the creation of the American broadcasting system represented a process and not an event. Every participant in that process—government bureaucrats, businessmen, legislators, broadcasters, network executives, and entertainers—affected it. Moreover, the story reflected the national scene, the political, social, judicial, administrative, and economic history of the 1920s and 1930s. Technological changes added to the complexity and confusion. The product, however involved it might be, emerged to be unique but not inevitable.

1

THE INTERdEPARTMENTAL CONTEST

On the night of 2 November 1920, as voters across the United States were in the process of overwhelmingly electing a Republican legislator from Ohio as the nation's new chief executive, election returns were quietly being collected in the office of the Pittsburgh *Post*. From the newspaper office they were telephoned to East Pittsburgh, where high atop one of Westinghouse's tallest buildings, a shack housing a 100-watt broadcasting station had recently been constructed. From its crude apparatus, news of the Republican landslide was transmitted to 2,000 listeners, many of them company employees, who had been provided with receiving sets. The KDKA coverage of the presidential contest that night ushered in a new epoch in the development of radio.[1]

Contemporaries viewed this innovation as a "gift of Providence," enhancing national stability and affecting the lives of the American people more profoundly than the motion picture, the automobile, the telephone, and the electric light bulb combined.[2] The immediate consequences were, in fact, rather more modest, but the KDKA transmission did bring about several significant changes. First, it disrupted the U.S. Navy's traditional domination of wireless, a service geared to marine traffic. Also, the advent of broadcasting focused attention upon the role of the federal government in communications, precipitating a bitter interdepartmental struggle for the control of radio involving three major agencies—the navy, the Post Office Department, and the Commerce Department—and a legion of less powerful interest groups as well.

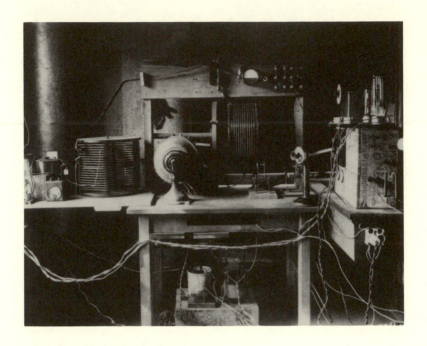

Figure 2.   Conrad's Transmitter.

Regular transmissions of music, sports, and information by Westinghouse engineer Dr. Frank Conrad's amateur station 8XK led his superiors to develop KDKA. *Courtesy of Smithsonian Institution, Photo No. 76-14664.*

The earliest significant research on radio was undertaken by James Clark Maxwell of King's College, London, who predicted the existence of self-sustaining electromagnetic waves. Building upon Michael Faraday's suggestion that "lines of force" pervade all space, Maxwell developed a comprehensive theory of wave propagation. In 1887, eight years after Maxwell died, Professor Heinrich R. Hertz of Bonn University confirmed Maxwell's theory. In a series of experiments using a Leyden jar to generate an electrical charge, he found that sparks would cross a gap between two ends of a loop of wire. With his simple apparatus, Hertz had discharged an electromagnetic current across the spark gap; thereafter he turned his attention to an analysis of the wave properties, finding many similarities to those of light.[3]

Figure 3. KDKA Transmitter, 1920.

This crude KDKA transmitter broadcast the Harding-Cox election returns in 1920 thus initiating an industry. *Courtesy of Smithsonian Institution, Photo No. 61, 017-A.*

The Italian inventor and entrepreneur Guglielmo Marconi turned these theoretical findings to practical use. What Marconi lacked in scientific background, he made up in creativity, and this (together with the help of Edouard Branly's coherer, which detected signals, and Samuel F. B. Morse's telegraph key and inker) enabled him to develop a system of communications based on the use of electromagnetic waves.[4]

In undertaking this venture, Marconi counted on several important assets. He had investment capital, for his Irish cousin, Henry Jameson-Davis, helped secure financial backers. Marconi foresaw that wireless would be of benefit in both international and marine communications. England, the maritime center where the greatest opportunity existed for exploitation of the invention, quickly became the nucleus for his activities. On 20 July 1897, the Wireless Telegraph and Signal Company was created in London to develop the Marconi equipment commercially. Soon after, it signed the first two clients, Lloyd's of London and the British Admiralty.[5]

Equally telling, Marconi understood the influential role of both the press and publicity in capturing public attention and support for his product. Indeed, he demonstrated his flair as a promoter in the summer of 1898, when the Prince of Wales (later King Edward VII) was injured, and his mother Queen Victoria wished to be kept informed of her son's condition while he convalesced aboard the yacht *Osborne*. Marconi installed a wireless telegraph outfit aboard the vessel and another at Osborne House, where the Queen was residing. The Queen thus was able to have constant communication with Edward, and, as a result, Marconi received enormous publicity. Finally, because Marconi assessed his own technical limitations realistically, he freely employed more knowledgeable consulting engineers and scientists.[6]

A dramatic demonstration of radio's efficacy took place on 28 April 1899, when the *Goodwin Sands Lightship*, severely damaged during a storm in the English Channel near Dover, successfully used the newly developed Marconi wireless apparatus to signal for assistance. Help was quickly dispatched, and, for the first time in history, wireless telegraphy played a crucial role in saving lives and property at sea.[7]

Figure 4.   Branly Coherer.

In the Branly Coherer, researched in the 1890s, enclosed metal filings, which changed their conductivity in the presence of an electric spark, formed a single detector. *Courtesy of Smithsonian Institution, Photo No. 42, 372-A.*

The use of ocean-going wireless spread. As the first practical application of radio telegraphy in the United States was also for ship-to-ship and ship-to-shore traffic, the navy logically became the government department to dominate radio prior to 1920. By 1904, the Interdepartmental Board of Wireless Telegraphy, created by President Theodore Roosevelt to examine the relationship between wireless and government, recognized the preeminence of the navy. In fact, the board opted for naval domination of coastal communications by recommending that the navy establish and operate such a system. It further suggested that private facilities be restricted so as to curtial interference with military stations, and that other federal agencies obtain the service and equipment they required from the navy. The president's approval of the report gave the navy virtually complete control of coastal radio stations in the United States.[8]

From 1904 to 1912 the navy system, initially geared to national defense and military considerations, expanded to facilitate shipping and safety at sea by transmitting weather reports, navigational warnings, and news. The extension of this system, however, created conflict between civilian operators and the navy. After their numbers began increasing rapidly, amateurs often disregarded maritime radio users and, in many instances, caused havoc with ship-to-ship and ship-to-shore traffic. One example of this interference occurred in April of 1912, when the S.S. *Titanic*, on its maiden voyage, struck an iceberg and began to sink rapidly. Rescue operations that depended upon the maintenance of communications were hampered because amateurs attempted to contact ships in the vicinity of the disaster. The navy's desire to restrict, if not eliminate, amateur operators increased in direct proportion to their interference with shipping and naval operations.[9]

At the same time, the comprehensive nature of the navy system placed it in direct competition with business firms, since many shipping interests preferred to deal with the more reliable navy system. Wireless companies dependent upon attracting shipping business naturally resented the navy's intrusion into what they considered their own special province. The limited number of channels available to radio users compounded these difficulties. The navy, amateurs, and commercial concerns had to compete for space in a spectrum that in 1912 went from 66.7 to 1,500 kHz.

There simply were not enough wavelengths to go around. Characteristically, the navy sought to impose order by demanding passage of legislation to restrict the operations of businessmen and amateurs.[10]

The law that ensued had effects quite different from what the navy had envisioned. On 24 June 1910, Congress passed the Act to Require Apparatus and Operators for Radio Communication on Certain Ocean Steamers, better known as the Wireless Ship Act. It required vessels with more than fifty persons aboard to install transmitting equipment capable of receiving and sending messages at a distance of 100 miles. The bill did not, however, solve radio problems in the United States; rather, by stimulating a rapid increase in its use, the law actually added to the existing disorder and confusion.[11]

On 13 August 1912, Congress passed the first law providing for the domestic control of radio. It favored the navy by awarding it a dominant position in the electromagnetic spectrum and by specifically protecting its stations from interference by private companies. The act reserved a band from 187.5 to 500 kHz, for government (mainly navy) use. Moreover, it relegated amateur use to frequencies above 1500 kHz, which at the time were considered unusable. Never content to restrict its operations to the government reservation, however, the navy continued to operate outside its exclusive band on specially designated wavelengths. Specifically, the department's shore stations, vessels, and apparatus sent and received on 187.5, 667, 750, 857, 1,000, and 1,200 kHz. The provisions of sections 10, 12, and 16 of the new act contained elaborate safeguards to protect naval operations from interference from those business concerns which also transmitted on these frequencies. The law also authorized the president to commandeer radio in times of national emergency or war. If national security necessitated such action, all facilities, except for government stations, were to be closed.[12]

Before Woodrow Wilson's administration, the navy's policy had centered upon protecting the coastal communications system and eliminating interference. During Wilson's tenure in office, however, it assumed a new direction. From 1913 until 1921, Secretary of the Navy Josephus Daniels actively promoted a governmental monopoly in radio under the control of the Navy Department. Secretary Daniels not only supported the administration's plans, as set forth in a document entitled "Government Ownership of Electrical Means of Communications," but also believed that federal control was necessary to preserve order, stability, and efficiency. Furthermore, he thought such jurisdiction logically should be vested in the navy, since it purchased and used most of the government's radio apparatus and since it had the most experience in operating stations. In 1914, when war broke out in Europe, the Wilson administration adopted Daniels' approach, declaring the ether essential to national defense and preparedness.[13]

In the lower echelons of the Navy Department, however, Daniels' policy met with considerable opposition. Captain William H. G. Bullard, director of naval communications, and Fleet Radio Officer Stanford C. Hooper thought exclusive naval control of the airwaves was unrealistic; consequently, they advocated navy domination only in coastal communications. Hooper had maintained since 1904 that the department should control stations on the coast for safety at sea, reduction of interference, and the training of naval personnel, but he strongly objected to overall government ownership, particularly of high-powered stations involved in trans-Atlantic transmissions. He believe these outlets, since they were still experimental, could be developed more rapidly under civilian control. In fact, he correctly postulated that private enterprise would maneuver more effectively in international competition. He continually advocated the basic premise that the government should not interfere with commercial interests; in 1916 Captain Bullard joined him in contending that the coastal system constituted the heart of naval radio.[14]

On the other hand, not all junior officers agreed with Bullard and Hooper. While Lieutenant Commander David W. Todd, head of the Radio Bureau, recognized that other opinions existed within the naval hierarchy, he nonetheless supported Daniels and argued the soundness of the principle of complete government ownership. Although he listed many reasons for supporting a federal monopoly, his primary rationale was, "The Secretary is a strong believer in it."[15]

As the specter of war in Europe loomed closer to the American continent, the United States Navy's power and influence over radio solidified and increased. In the first step on the road to eventual takeover, President Wilson issued a proclamation on 5 August 1914, to prohibit U.S. wireless stations from engaging in nonneutral conduct. This edict gave the navy complete responsibility for overseeing and enforcing such a ban. A year later, federal authorities seized several facilities owned by German firms to ensure they would not be utilized for belligerent purposes.[16]

On 6 April 1917, the president ordered the navy to commandeer apparatus that might be required for naval communications. Amateur operators received instructions to dismantle their equipment and cease operations. In effect, the proclamation gave the navy control over almost all outlets in the United States. Thus, the outcome Secretary Daniels had failed to achieve through Congress was granted to the navy as part of the national mobilization for war.[17]

Throughout World War I, Daniels urged Congress to enact legislation granting government ownership of communications to the navy. Even while attempting to utilize the crisis to secure one of his prime objectives, Daniels ensured the success of his policy by presenting Congress with a *fait accompli*. Since the majority of commercial stations belonged to only two concerns, securing them proved a comparatively simple task. In November 1918, the navy bought all the facilities in the United States owned by the Marconi Telegraph and Wireless Company, except for four high-powered stations which it already controlled; and soon afterward it bought the outlets owned by Lee De Forest. By these purchases, it effectively eliminated its leading business competition and secured ownership of all but fifteen stations in the United States.[18]

As the war drew to a close, Congress began to evince not only a hostility to many of the Wilsonian programs but also a positive rejection of Daniels' actions during the conflict. For example, James R. Mann, House Republican floor leader from Illinois, declared that the secretary of the navy should be impeached and removed from office for unlawful conduct in exceeding his authority by purchasing the Marconi and De Forest holdings. As a result of this congressional assault, the House deleted more than $4 million from a naval deficiency appropriations bill in 1919 and threatened further action. But, despite such negative congressional reaction, Daniels continued to urge governmental ownership of wireless. The head of the Radio Division of the Bureau of Engineering, Commander Stanford C. Hooper, observed that "the radio bill came to naught . . . as sentiment is thoroughly against government ownership."[19]

With Daniels under attack and many of the naval programs held in abeyance by an angry Congress, the Naval Communications Service began to disassociate itself from Daniels. Commander Hooper and Rear Admiral William Bullard masterminded this action, intending thereby to protect the naval coastal system. In the process, they hoped to bar the Marconi Company permanently from regaining its dominant position in the United States by replacing it with an American firm that would engage in long-distance transmissions, thus complementing but not competing with the naval system.[20]

With these objectives in mind, Hooper and Bullard approached General Electric, primarily because that corporation held a political trump card in the postwar radio game, namely the Alexanderson patent rights. These rights pertained to an alternator, developed by Ernst Frederick Werner Alexanderson, that had been utilized in long-distance, continuous-wave transmission during the war and, at the time, was thought to be the crucial factor in trans-Atlantic communications. Before the outbreak of the war, Marconi's recognition of the value of the patent had prompted him to try to buy it from GE, but his effort failed. In 1915, GE had seriously considered selling it. However, the war stimulated a lively interest in radio, and GE, like many other large firms, mobilized its powerful research staff and undertook a systematic and thorough investigation into radio. As a consequence, the company recognized the value of Alexanderson's alternator as a highly effective tool in long-distance communications. By 1919, GE was ready and eager to turn its wartime research into peacetime profits. The interests of the Naval Communications Service and GE coincided, albeit for different reasons, and resulted in the creation of a new GE subsidiary—the Radio Corporation of America.[21]

On 17 October 1919, RCA was incorporated in the State of New Jersey. Both the navy and GE intended for RCA to develop into a company with facilities and equipment so complete that it would be able to compete effectively in the international marketplace. In accordance with this scheme, RCA recruited its leadership primarily from the old American Marconi Company, appointing Edwin J.

Nally president and David Sarnoff commercial manager. RCA also acquired the patent rights of both American Marconi and GE. The chairman of RCA, Owen D. Young, concurred with Sarnoff and Nally in their desire to develop an industry known for "orderly and stabilized" competition.[22]

The war had clearly shown, however, that the United States lagged far behind many European nations in wireless, mainly because wasteful patent conflicts had hindered developments and resulted in time-consuming court cases. Consequently, over the next two years, RCA, GE, American Telephone and Telegraph, and Westinghouse joined in agreements to ensure that American radio would not be hindered by further such disputes. A series of cross-licensing ventures ended these patent wars and allowed RCA access to holdings controlled by the other communications firms. By 1921 it had secured access to more than 2,000 needed inventions. The company maintained a completely workable system of communications; and, with its extensive practical experience, it presented all appearances of holding an unassailable position.[23]

On the eve of the 1920 KDKA broadcast, the navy had every reason to feel firmly in control. After nearly a decade of instability and chaos, order had been achieved, and in the way the navy preferred. With the creation of an American corporation to compete internationally, the department expressed confidence that the coastal system would be safe from any further disruption. Moreover, wireless and national defense were defined in terms of naval interests, since radio was considered primarily a device for communications with ships.[24]

But the navy's position and the cross-licensing agreements coincided in one fundamental weakness. The navy, as well as the businessmen and the corporation lawyers who drew up the documents, defined radio in terms of wireless telegraphy and telephony. The KDKA election coverage shattered this definition and introduced the new dimension of broadcasting.[25]

The Post Office Department, like Secretary Daniels, accepted the general proposition that all means of electrical transmissions should be held by governmental monopoly. The Post Office contended, however, that because of both its wire and wireless interests it should assume jurisdiction over radio as well. Albert S. Burleson, the post-master general under Wilson, maintained this position throughout World War I and suggested that a prominent aspect of the transition to a peacetime economy should be the establishment of government control of communications under the Post Office.[26]

Congress recognized the Post Office Department's domain in wireless operations in 1919, when it appropriated $850,000 for the operation of radio facilities in connection with the postal Air Mail Service. On 20 August 1920, a General Post Office Order, endorsed by the second assistant postmaster general, authorized construction and installation of land radio stations at the Air Mail Service's airports, their chief function being to furnish weather reports and direction-finding information and to report the movement of planes. This appropriation gave the Post Office Department a strong claim to a share of control over radio.[27]

When Will Hays assumed direction of the Post Office in the Harding administration, a new type of managerial politician emerged. He appreciated the need for organization and the importance of the press as a disseminator of information concerning Post Office activities. In effect, he defined the role of the Post Office in much the same light as the Naval Communications Service had defined naval radio— as a public service. Hays professed a keen interest in technical developments to improve service in his domain, and toward that end he promoted the use of the airplane and other innovations as well as radio.[28]

Because of Hays' uncanny ability to reconcile conflicting interests and his cordial relationship with President Harding, the Post Office appeared to be a formidable contender in any intragovernmental rivalry for radio control. Hays was also a shrewd and not overly scrupulous advocate for the department's interests. Thus, for example, he backed broadcasting as a means to attack naval control of wireless, and he supported underlings who undertook expansionist policies. He applauded the 1921 report of the Bureau of Efficiency supporting the proposals of the Post Office for the establishment of a Bureau of Communications over which the Post Office would preside in managing government facilities in the interior. He supervised the opening of a nationwide Post Office radio system which included fifteen outlets covering a belt from the District of Columbia to the Pacific Coast and operating as an auxiliary to the Air Mail Service. This system transmitted market reports and weather information in cooperation with the Agriculture Department. Hays also supported and actively encouraged the supervisor of the Air Mail Service, James C. Edgerton, who wanted to establish Post Office supremacy by creating a network to disseminate agricultural, meteorological, and governmental information to the public. Edgerton believed that "once public demand is created for such a service, amplification of such a service would be automatically secured."[29]

There was yet another rival to the navy's hegemony over wireless. The Department of Commerce had obtained a foothold when its Bureau of Navigation was assigned the enforcement powers of the Wireless Ship Act of 1910. Since the act applied to marine services and the bureau had control of ship licenses, inspection of radio apparatus became a function of this agency. On 1 July 1911, the bureau created its own subdivision to administer the act. When Congress passed the Radio Act of 1912, it delegated supervision of all private stations in the interior of the United States to the Department of Commerce.[30]

The Bureau of Standards, another division of the Commerce Department, received regular requests from the Bureau of Navigation to investigate equipment and procedures used in the enforcement of the acts of 1910 and 1912. In 1916 appropriations bills provided the bureau with funds to carry on its work in wireless. The agency conducted experiments covering the entire realm of communications, including theoretical studies, compilations of data, and scientific research on electromagnetic phenomena.[31]

When the United States entered the war, the Commerce Department's role in radio was severely restricted, for the navy assumed control over the inspection and licensing functions of the Bureau of Navigation. Secretary of Commerce William C. Redfield, while confessing his displeasure at seeing "another step taken in the long and painful process of subtracting duties from the Department," nonetheless offered little opposition to these wartime measures; in fact, he actively supported the navy's position on the issue of government monopoly. Under Redfield, the department regarded government control of private facilities as both necessary and inevitable. Eugene T. Chamberlain, head of the Bureau of Navigation, agreed with Redfield and Daniels, asserting that federal ownership and control by the navy, rather than the Post Office, was the best policy. Both Redfield and Chamberlain urged Congress to enact legislation placing radio under naval jurisdiction.[32]

When Herbert C. Hoover assumed the office of secretary of commerce in 1921, the position was languishing in "innocuous destitude." Although traditionally his position had been considered the least prestigious in the cabinet, Hoover made it clear to President Harding that he intended to transform it from "a Department of Commerce in name only" into a government agency of foremost importance. Thus, whether Hoover is portrayed as a forgotten progressive, a Quaker humanitarian, an economic nationalist, or a "fat Coolidge," the underlying premise of his policy was the extension of the power of the secretary of commerce. What had previously been said of Lloyd George—"He did not seem to care which way he traveled providing he was in the driver's seat"—was in large measure true of Hoover as well, with one important exception. Hoover not only wanted to be in the driver's seat, he demanded to plot the route.[33]

In the midst of a postwar depression, Hoover assumed control of the department. Ready with a program more appropriate for a president than a secretary of commerce, he combatted the economic slump by waging a "new war on waste." An important aspect of his campaign centered upon the development of new industries spurred by the war. Broadcasting had an important place in this program, and Hoover wanted to have control of it.[34]

The interest of various departments in wireless intensified an already bitter U.S. Navy-Post Office quarrel. The dispute revolved around the construction of additional Post Office radio stations and the decision to designate one organization to perform broadcasting services for agencies interested in reaching the public. The navy's basic defense continued to be the 1904 Interdepartmental Board Report, which it claimed was "more sound and applicable today than when . . . it was written."[35] Commander Stanford C. Hooper contended that anytime the navy's views conflicted with those of other agencies that were "trying to get the radio under their wings," this report should be used to establish the navy's prior claim.

In effect, the Naval Communications Service argued that if additional functions were to be undertaken, the navy system, consisting of 183 shore stations and 500 ship installations, could handle the task adequately.[36]

The Post Office indignantly protested that navy radio could not even provide operations adequate for the postal Air Mail Service. In fact, its polemic continued, such inferior operations endangered pilots' lives and delayed important messages. Ignoring pleas advanced by Acting Secretary of the Navy Theodore Roosevelt, Jr., that "earnest endeavors had been made and are now being made by the Navy . . . to provide adequate facilities," the Post Office constructed numerous outlets at landing fields and cities under the pretext of remedying the situation. James C. Edgerton also argued that many of these stations could handle broadcasting for other government departments as well. The Post Office's doings struck at the very heart of the 1904 report.[37]

The navy counted on substantial supporters and allies in the contest. Groups on the West Coast, where facilities were limited, depended upon the navy for transmission of press and commercial messages. Several shipping concerns, particularly those that found private firms unreliable and interference bothersome, actively supported the navy, while many scientists saw in the navy's position the key to the development of the radio art.[38] The navy also had a strong potential ally in RCA. After the role played by Commander Hooper and Rear Admiral Bullard in creating the company, cooperation blessed the RCA-navy relationship in the first year of operations. Not only was Bullard appointed to attend company meetings, RCA frequently consulted the Naval Communications Service before implementing corporation policies.[39]

But in 1920 and 1921 the cozy relationship began to disintegrate. Initially, problems occurred over radio apparatus constructed by RCA for the navy. In a second and more serious affront, RCA began on its own initiative to construct coastal stations for commercial maritime traffic, thereby threatening to undermine the navy's position on government control of marine facilities. The Naval Communications Service had reacted previously with hostility to RCA's general manager, David Sarnoff. Sarnoff had tried to join the navy's radio bureau in World War I, but its director, Commander David W. Todd, characterized him as "distasteful" because of his East Central European ancestry—which is to say because he was a Jew. When RCA began to build its own outlets, the navy immediately labeled the firm's policies a Sarnoff innovation that would interfere with the naval coastal system. The navy's intense reaction further worsened the already deteriorating situation.[40]

By 1921, Commander Hooper was charging Owen D. Young, chairman of the board of RCA, with breach of trust and RCA with trickery and deception. To defeat the RCA program, Hooper launched an emotionally laden political attack. Exploiting a deep-seated American prejudice, he began lobbying in Congress against the RCA "monopoly" of wireless. A monopoly, in the commander's way of thinking, was not a monopoly if it was held by an agency of government. In any event, by December 1921, the special relationship between RCA and the navy had totally deteriorated, and the company gravitated toward the Commerce Department.[41]

Even before the navy and RCA parted company, the other commercial interests engaged in communications stood almost united against naval domination. American Telephone and Telegraph, for example, had encountered navy opposition to the corporation's efforts to use radio telephony as an extension of its land system. After the navy had thwarted AT&T because this undertaking threatened to interfere with the coastal system, the firm responded by inveterately opposing naval control of radio.[42]

The navy's activities in international affairs angered businessmen most, however, and forced them to turn to the Department of Commerce. On 19 March 1919, the Economic Treaties Subcommittee of the Supreme Council in Paris resolved to form the EU-F-GB-I commission to study and advise on all matters pertaining to wireless. Composed of military representatives from France, Great Britain, Italy, and the United States, the committee assembled in Washington in 1920 to amend the London Radiotelegraph Convention. The members aimed to stabilize radio by restricting private enterprise and developing unified regulation. Accordingly, they drafted a "Convention and Regulations" for a Universal Electrical Communications Union that would consolidate jurisdiction over radio, wire telegraph, and cables.[43]

American firms unanimously objected to the proposed union. They vehemently opposed a joint convention covering radio, wire, and cables on the grounds that conditions in wireless could not be equated to conditions elsewhere. They rightly supposed that any amalgamation of such diverse fields would hamper radio development. Moreover, since the union was organized by military representatives, the proposals directly implied government ownership. Dr. Alfred N. Goldsmith, secretary of the Institute of Radio Engineers, voiced the concern of all when he stated, "We object to a tendency toward government control which is felt throughout the draft." In an analogy which could be readily understood and sharply interpreted by postwar America, RCA compared the international scope of the proposal to that of the League of Nations. As a final protest, businessmen denounced any move toward an international agreement before a national policy on radio had been developed.[44]

Frustrated at having been ignored, stymied without representation, and fearful that the navy was about to establish government control, the commercial companies turned to the secretary of commerce. Hoover, seizing the opportunity, proposed that the private firms ally with the Commerce Department to oppose the navy and the Post Office. Accordingly, throughout the summer and fall of 1921, business and engineering representatives from General Electric, Westinghouse, RCA, AT&T, the Institute of Radio Engineers, the American Engineering Standards Committee, and the Radio Division of the Commerce Department held a series of meetings to plan strategy. They opted for close cooperation with Secretary Hoover to develop a national radio policy that would use supervision by the Department of Commerce to protect private enterprise. Moreover, they argued that broadcasting, the most rapidly growing use of radio, should be encouraged and protected. Gradually, a common front began to emerge as the interests of the industry and the Commerce Department intersected.[45]

Commercial concerns and government departments had other allies interested in radio control. The amateurs, their ranks enlarged by returning veterans who had received instruction in wireless during the war, constituted an important faction in any contest for domination. Their position was strengthened by the existence of the American Radio Relay League (ARRL), whose membership was almost 6,000 by 1920. Ever conscious of their influence, Hoover portrayed the Commerce Department as the "patron saint" of the amateur. He actively solicited their views on the best ways for the Department of Commerce to serve them, while making every effort to have radio inspectors attend their meetings to present the department's position on radio matters. It was no coincidence that when news of Post Office plans to administer wireless in the United States became known, the ARRL turned to the Commerce Department for information and aid to counteract the Post Office scheme.[46]

Since the navy recognized the political danger of offending the youth of the nation by appearing to oppose the American boy, it tried diligently to present the navy as the "best friend of the amateur." The secretaries of the service in both the Wilson and Harding administrations continuously attempted to maintain good relations with the ARRL. During the Harding years, Secretary Edwin Denby contended that the navy did not desire to restrict the amateurs and always considered their interests. But, having experienced navy control during the war, the amateurs responded to each military effort by moving closer to the Commerce Department.[47]

One more force worked against the navy: the postwar climate of opinion opposed continued governmental intervention. The Congress itself best expressed this attitude. Representative Edward J. King, a Republican from Illinois, summarized the prevailing mood when he contended, "in times of war we tolerated many things. . . . Now that peace has come, we should adopt the ways of peace." Both the navy and the Post Office found themselves out of harmony with what Karl Mannheim has termed the "style of thought," as the United States entered the postwar era. As if this were not enough, Hoover solicited the active support of nongovernmental interests, including amateurs, commercial groups, and scientists, to ensure that navy and Post Office intervention became and remained a thing of the past.[48]

From a variety of sources Secretary Hoover heard the call for an "honest broker," one who could rise above the conflict and arrive at a nonpartisan assessment, as the Commerce Department program gained momentum. The Bureau of Standards went as far as to contend that reliance of all American commercial and amateur interests upon the department presented the unifying force in radio. It continued, the "department is the government representative of the commercial radio companies, the amateur radio operators and those interested in the technical development of radio communications"—a classification which covered just about everyone. As the agency did not use radio, it could be billed as an unbiased body able to serve civic, commercial, and governmental concerns. What appeared to be a groundswell of opinion urging the Commerce Department to intervene had in reality, of course, been carefully orchestrated by Secretary Hoover. Against a background of interdepartmental strife and the "take-off" of commercial broadcasting, the Commerce Department stepped forward to assume control.[49]

THE HONEST BROKER

Broadcasting, as a radical radio innovation, threatened the older, more established marine services. The navy continued to maintain that no other application of wireless should be allowed to diminish the usefulness of its seemingly predestined function of maritime communications. But Hoover, labeling broadcasting as "one of the most astounding things that has come under my observation of American life," implemented several administrative policies designed to promote and protect the medium while at the same time identifying the Commerce Department with it. Consequently, at a time when military and civilian departments alike faced cutbacks and curtailed programs, the Department of Commerce, because of the enormous expansion of broadcasting, received increased appropriations as well as new responsibilities.[1]

From 1921 to 1923, Hoover planned several decisive actions to ensure the survival of broadcasting, resolve the interdepartmental dispute, and firmly establish his department in radio regulation. First, he reorganized the Department of Commerce staff by replacing key personnel with loyal supporters sympathetic to his goals and objectives. Next, he carefully marshalled a variety of interests, including broadcasters, businessmen, amateur operators, bureaucrats, and scientists, to support the Department of Commerce scheme. Finally, he chose to remain largely in the background while the navy-Post Office rivalry threatened to erupt into a full-fledged conflict. Because of the obvious power of the navy in radio matters, Hoover knew full well that a direct encounter with that venerable institution could only hurt the Commerce Department. In following this typical approach, Hoover maneuvered behind the scenes to resolve the inter-departmental conflict. Once this goal had been accomplished and spheres of interest clearly delineated, the secretary of commerce could then turn to Congress to recognize Department of Commerce pre-eminence.

In order to break the navy's stranglehold on radio, Secretary Hoover emphasized the public service aspect of commercial broad-casting's potential and opened up channels for broadcasters in the electromagnetic spectrum. Since vast numbers of amateurs were jamming the airwaves, he ordered an end to their voice transmissions. Because limiting this class could not begin to supply enough space to satisfy the needs of all those wishing to send the human voice, the Commerce Department attempted to allocate more channels for broadcasters. Next, the secretary of commerce actively intervened to settle disputes among businessmen, while relying upon coopera-tion between the industry and the department to safeguard his program. In effect, Hoover placed himself in the role of champion of private enterprise to clear the way for civilian development and control under the Department of Commerce.[2]

To bring legitimacy to broadcasting, the secretary of commerce strove to identify it as a service industry offering benefits to the public equal to those which radio provided in maritime communica-tions. The situation resulting from this change of identification and from the rapid proliferation of facilities presented Hoover with two formidable obstacles. First, he found himself denied the opportunity to select channels that were, at the time, best suited to his needs. The twenty-four-year-old marine system had already preempted a band from 300 to 550 kHz, which would have been ideal for broad-casters. Hoover was thus forced to place the new service on two wavelengths: when station managers transmitted entertainment and news they operated on 833.3 kHz; when they sent crop and weather information, or government reports, they used 618.6 kHz. Since the two frequencies lay near frequencies used in the maritime band, interference bred serious conflicts among the various interests. And since wireless apparatus aboard vessels had involved tremendous capital expenditures, shippers could not be reallocated easily to other wavelengths.[3]

The most substantial roadblock impeding Hoover's policies did not emanate from the private groups; it emerged, rather, in the tradition and patronage of the U.S. Navy. The navy also conducted ship-to-shore and ground-to-air communications above 500 kHz. The Radio Act of 1912 not only protected these services from interference but also specifically prohibited the erection of commercial stations within fifteen nautical miles of naval facilities. To circumvent this barrier, Secretary Hoover had the Commerce Department set broadcasting stations apart in a "limited commercial" class, on the ground that they did not charge directly for their programs. Many outlets that lay within the fifteen-mile limit or interfered with naval transmissions were thus able to survive.[4]

Meanwhile, the problems arising from conflicts between various private interests threatened to erupt in potentially damaging confrontations. Amateurs in several parts of the United States had never been content to limit themselves to the band above 1500 kHz established by the Radio Act of 1912. In an act of open rebellion, they began transmitting on 833.3 kHz, thereby interrupting broadcasting programs and increasing interference with other license holders. In an attempt to end the problems stemming from competition for the airwaves, the Department of Commerce ordered all amateurs to stop broadcasting in January 1922. Assistant Secretary of Commerce Claudius H. Huston authorized the insertion of the following disclaimer in all general and restricted amateur permits granted by the department: "This station is not licensed to broadcast weather reports, market reports, music, concerts, speeches, news or similar information or entertainment." Consequently, amateurs were limited to radio telephony and telegraphy above 1,500 kHz.[5]

The first amateur reaction was swift and hostile. Several organizations charged that the government had given a "monopoly of the air" to the radio trust. In the New York *Times*, Hiram Percy Maxim, president of the American Radio Relay League, denounced the policy as the direct result of pressure brought on President Harding and Secretary Hoover by the "big concerns." After further reflection, however, his group shifted its position. The ARRL, realizing that its members could not afford to antagonize the broadcast fan, adopted a more conciliatory tone. Maxim pointed out that interference with programs was of considerable concern to his association; he further stated that the ARRL would do everything in its power to curtail disruption of the airwaves. Finally, he proposed an extensive effort to appease the radio patrons. In the meantime, while the parties involved sought out the sources of interference, he advocated that the ARRL implement self-regulation.[6]

Even while a temporary resolution of the conflict between the amateurs and other radio enthusiasts took form, new complications arose. The inadequacy of only two frequencies for all broadcasting stations became painfully apparent. With over 500 facilities operating simultaneously on the same wavelengths, interference continued unabated. This condition was especially acute in the large metropolitan areas, where the increased number of licenses granted by the department resulted in overlapping signals.[7]

In the spring of 1922, businessmen and radio inspectors in the Commerce Department began to agitate for a new classification to provide another frequency for firms that maintained high technical and programming standards. During the summer the department opened a new wavelength to a select group of stations possessing efficient, expensive equipment capable of reducing harmonic interference, a disturbance characterized by production of integral multiples of the carrier frequency. Those chosen also agreed to develop new types of programming in order to give up total dependence on phonograph records, the only fare offered by most stations at the time. In exchange for these innovations the Commerce Department established a "Class B" category placing the approved stations on 750 kHz. This action, as well as strict monitoring of the participants' compliance, firmly established the Department of Commerce's right to rearrange channels. The subsequent benefit enjoyed by the class B group also affirmed a consensus that some radical changes in frequency allocation were necessary to prevent the stifling of future expansion.[8]

The administrative decisions that the Department of Commerce implemented to protect and promote the medium were based on the premise of mutual cooperation between the agency and the private sector. The department directly intervened in business disputes and problems, both by serving as a referee and by encouraging increased efficiency and standardization. It also arranged national conferences to develop a framework for reducing the disruptions inherent in broadcasting. In following this approach, Hoover pursued a method that was typical of him: believing that cooperation could eliminate waste and inefficiency, he utilized cooperation, not only as a rationale for justifying Commerce Department actions, but also as a means of gaining support for its policies.[9]

During 1922, Commerce Department personnel tried to end existing rivalries among broadcasters. In Detroit, the department threatened to divide the time between the stations of the Detroit *Free Press* and Detroit *News* if they could not agree between themselves on transmitting schedules. In Cleveland, the federal inspector arranged a division of transmission time among the Union Trust Company, Westinghouse, the Cox Manufacturing Company, and the Radio Corporation of America. His counterpart in New York successfully negotiated with seventeen interests to terminate a dispute that the magazine *Radio Broadcast* had labeled the "War Between Broadcasting stations."[10]

The Bureau of Standards' scientific research also served to cement growing cooperation between the Department of Commerce and the industry. Moreover, businessmen and engineers welcomed the studies on electromagnetic waves, signal fading, directional antennas, precise measurements, and standardization of radio apparatus. Members of the bureau participated in national conferences, published circulars on all aspects of wireless, set up a standard of frequency, and sent out signals to allow owners to adjust their own emissions. These activities linked the Department of Commerce with the broadcasters.[11]

President Harding's decision to have the First National Radio Conference gave impetus to the policy of cooperation. In an atmosphere of strife among bureaucrats, businessmen, and amateurs, fifteen official delegates representing government departments, commercial concerns, and the scientific community assembled in Washington, D.C., on 27 February 1922. The meeting had been organized to recommend possible legislative solutions to Congress after examining the problems confronting radio users. Legal, technical, and amateur committees facilitated the delegates' work.[12]

From the beginning, the Commerce Department molded and led the conference. Dr. Samuel W. Stratton, director of the Bureau of Standards, was appointed chairman, and Secretary Hoover delivered the keynote address and personally presided at a number of sessions, taking a direct interest in every aspect of the meeting. By his active participation, Hoover created tremendous publicity for broadcasting and defined the framework in which the delegates would operate.[13]

In his opening remarks, the secretary of commerce articulated the main issue before the conference: the definition and regulation of broadcasting. Throughout his speech, Hoover carefully identified the province with public interest, public right, and public welfare. His guiding principle was to preserve this new service, while carefully connecting it with the general public good and the Department of Commerce.[14]

The various committees immediately set to work proposing, among other things, the allocation of frequencies, power limitations, geographical distribution of stations, hours of operations, procedures for granting licenses, and methods to reduce interference. To emphasize the importance of its domain, the group divided broadcasting according to its government, public, private, and toll functions and defined it as a service second only to maritime communications.[15]

As deliberations continued, concepts supporting the Commerce Department emerged. Hoover cleverly exploited the general feeling against government ownership to further the cause of his own agency. By limiting the participation of the U.S. Navy and the Post Office, the secretary of commerce relegated them to the status of mere radio users and further undermined their position. Much to the chagrin of both departments, the conference reaffirmed the administrative decisions already taken by the Commerce Department to promote and protect broadcasters. In addition, the conference declared that ending the interdepartmental conflict was prerequisite to solving radio's other problems and that legislation should amend the existing laws to give the secretary of commerce adequate authority to supervise wireless.[16]

Dr. Stratton also suggested that Secretary Hoover assemble a committee of government representatives to explore the subject of federal broadcasting. In effect, the meeting officially adopted the position held by both Hoover and the Department of Commerce since the spring of 1921. Almost immediately, Hoover began to carry out the meeting's basic recommendations: to find a solution to the interdepartmental conflict and to secure legislation expanding the power of the secretary of commerce.[17]

While the conference succeeded in fulfilling many of Hoover's fondest desires, the participants had recognized that any overall settlement of the problems confronting commercial and amateur groups intimately concerned all government agencies utilizing wireless. To involve these diverse entities, the secretary of commerce invited his competitors and cohorts alike to help form what would become the Interdepartmental Advisory Committee on Government Broadcasting. (IACGB).[18]

The IACGB, like the meeting that preceded it, was a Department of Commerce function. Once again, Dr. Stratton chaired the gatherings, this time aided by J. Howard Dellinger of the Bureau of Standards, who acted as secretary. The Commerce Department took responsibility for the bookkeeping, accounting, and operating costs. As might be expected, Hoover felt that the committee would advise the secretary of commerce rather than enforce regulations or assign duties to various departments. Moreover, he stipulated that effective supervision demanded unified control of radio. It was his premise that such regulation could be achieved only by allowing one authority, one agency, to oversee all stations.[19]

J. Howard Dellinger suggested that the panel adopt two guidelines. First, radio should be ruled in the public interest. Second, since broadcasting affected a greater section of the public than did other types of wireless transmission, the channels and privileges for this class should be extended. He foresaw possible trouble with the military because of the provision that government-operated facilities should be subjected to the same requirements as those under which commercial or amateur outlets operated. He asserted, however, that such control was absolutely essential for effective supervision.[20]

While Hoover tried to secure wider advantages for broadcasters and to advance the position of the Commerce Department through the IACGB, he always anticipated a possible unfavorable reaction by the private sector. Realizing that any suspicion or distrust could severely handicap the department, he kept businessmen continuously informed of the IACGB's activities. Above all, he repeatedly stressed that this panel's efforts offered the only hope for securing the additional wavelengths necessary to curtail drastically the interference plaguing broadcasters.[21]

By the spring of 1922, the navy was suffering the difficult consequences of its past actions. The denunciations came from all sides, as business concerns demanded more frequencies, broadcast listeners complained of naval interference with programs, and the Post Office and Commerce Departments directly challenged it for control. Furthermore, Congress curtailed expenditures, forcing the navy to reduce its stations and personnel. Equally troublesome, the Naval Communications Service suffered an overburdening of its Washington, D.C., facilities because many senators and representatives deluged the department with applications to use the naval outlets to broadcast to their constituents. In April, Secretary Denby was forced to eliminate all civilian transmissions until a consistent policy could be achieved. By this time, the navy faced mounting possibility that these difficulties would produce more adverse effects in Congress. In order to avoid further incidents, the Naval Communications Service accepted Hoover's invitation to participate in the IACGB.[22]

As the navy had always promoted economy and had tried to avoid duplication, Hoover's plan to eliminate waste and inefficiency coincided with what the navy had considered its crucial programs, thus increasing its willingness to cooperate. As the date of the conference approached, the navy prepared to support only its defensible interests from the encroachments of its detractors. Secretary Denby divided the naval radio sphere into those services important in war or peace (stations along coasts, in outlying possessions, and at naval yards); those essential in time of war only (cables, time signals, and weather reports); and those of no particular military value (international radio accounting, commercial traffic, and messages handled for other government departments).[23]

To ensure protection for its crucial activities of the first and second categories, the navy launched a public relations program in the spring and summer of 1922, giving wide publicity to its position. Lobbyists from the department actively participated in "semi-political radio exhibitions" across the United States. Naval personnel attended most industrial conventions in an effort to better public relations. Moreover, in an intense endeavor to eliminate interference with broadcasting programs, the naval facilities curtailed operations during peak listening times. During the radio conference, the navy did its utmost to prevent embarrassing incidents likely to damage the navy's new image by carefully supervising its personnel and installing new apparatus. Finally, the last step of the campaign chronicled the exploits of the Naval Communications Service for the American people in newspapers, magazines, and special radio programs. By the time the IACGB began, the navy had adjusted to changing circumstances and felt fully prepared to protect its position.[24]

The intransigence of the Post Office posed a sharp contrast to the naval program of adaptability. The Post Office protested that the IACGB was a temporary solution to the problem of government radio and advanced a "logical" and "permanent" solution, using the 1921 efficiency report as justification for the establishment of a Bureau of Communications within the Post Office. Its position claiming all rights for the transmission of government materials effectively isolated the postal service from the navy and the Commerce Department and drastically curtailed any effect it might have on the committee.[25]

Throughout the spring and summer of 1922, the IACGB held numerous meetings to develop a definite policy. By July the membership of the panel had grown to twelve, including representatives of ten departments and two agencies. In one of the first decisions made after its initial organization, the body ruled that only perishable material, such as market prices and data, standard radio signals, executive announcements, statistics, weather and hydrographic news, and educational matter, could be transmitted by government personnel. In a further effort to coordinate federal activities, it proposed to establish an experimental system of eight stations to send out material by continuous-wave telegraphy for rebroadcast by local concerns. The naval outlet at Arlington, Virginia, received the sole authorization in this scheme to broadcast such information. It was becoming apparent that the board would have to expand its role to include all questions of interdepartmental relations to promote efficiency and avoid duplication.[26]

Despite the IACGB's success, the Post Office continued to advocate its own plan. In May, Postmaster General Hubert Work prepared to circumvent the committee by introducing in Congress a "Joint Resolution to Regulate Radio Broadcasting," whereby the Post Office was to be given "exclusive jurisdiction over all government broadcasting." Work and James C. Edgerton of the Air Mail Service also attempted to gain the support of the Department of Agriculture for their project by funding a joint study on the feasibility of the Post Office's transmitting farm market prices of cotton, corn, wheat, livestock, and dairy products.[27]

In a counter attempt to ensure the success of the panel, the navy tried to outflank the Post Office. The outcome of its efforts hinged on army-navy cooperation, for by now both the postal service and the navy had recognized their need to placate the army. Postmaster General Work arranged for the free transmission of official War Department materials between Washington, D.C., and San Francisco. The navy parried by placing army traffic over the same route on the same basis as navy dispatches. In March, the Signal Corps and the Naval Communications Service implemented a reciprocal agreement , which provided that messages would be handled on an equal basis over both departments' circuits. The aim of this accord was to drive the Post Office out of radio. The War Department supported the navy's position because the army felt that Work and Edgerton were making every effort to gain ascendancy over all military stations in the United States. The military services could ill-afford a failure resulting in victory for the Post Office.[28]

The army-navy arrangements ensured success for Hoover's committee and opened the way for resolution of the interdepartmental conflict. In January 1923, the IACGB attempted to eliminate the difficulties among the various federal agencies by extending its activities. It received, along with its new responsibilities, a new name, the Interdepartmental Radio Advisory Committee (IRAC), a new chairman, Acting Secretary of Commerce Stephen B. Davis, and five subcommittees to handle the reassignment of frequencies, details of operating procedures, and policy matters.[29]

In the spring, the IRAC boldly declared the Roosevelt Board Report of 1904 obsolete; in a policy statement intended to replace that document, it proclaimed, "Government interest in radio communications is paramount for national defense." Furthermore, the panel declared that since wireless rendered a public service it should be carefully regulated at the national level. The system most suitable for the country's needs was deemed to be one of privately owned and managed facilities that would be available to the government in times of emergency or war.[30]

The statement further recognized a host of agencies, including the State Department, the Treasury Department, the Navy Department, the Interior Department, the Department of Labor, and the Interstate Commerce Commission, that wished to disseminate information by broadcasting. To ensure that the diversified activities of these groups proceeded efficiently, the paper declared that they should be carefully coordinated and that the president, aided by the IRAC, should supervise their organization.[31]

The appearance of this committee marked the resolution of the fierce interdepartmental struggle that had characterized the initial phase of broadcasting. The Naval Communications Service, while aware that the IRAC's existence posed some danger to navy-controlled radio, supported the changes. The department reluctantly agreed that "the policy it endeavored to maintain must be modified." The IRAC reciprocated by agreeing to the navy's assertion that "military control of radio communications in times of war is a proper objective." The IRAC also strove to emphasize those goals that had always been of primary interest and importance for the navy, including the consolidation of radio facilities, economical administration, elimination of interference, and standardization of both apparatus and frequency allocation. In early November, Stanford C. Hooper concluded that not only had naval policies been vindicated, they had actually been strengthened by the IRAC. By cooperating closely with the army within the framework of the IRAC, the navy protected its shore system, provided excellent service for other government departments, and dislodged the Post Office's grip on radio.[32]

Although the Post Office Department saw naval success in the IRAC, it continued to urge those schemes that were geared toward establishing its own preeminence. In February 1923 the postmaster general introduced House Resolution 14196 to launch a legislative program projecting an ultimate monopoly of electrical means of transmission under postal auspices. The measure had little support. Meanwhile, on 2 February, the IRAC began the final erosion of Post Office power by transferring all broadcasting duties for the Agriculture Department from the Post Office to the navy. These two changes shattered all Post Office dreams of controlling radio.[33]

By the end of 1923, James G. Harbord, president of RCA, could state confidently that the "heresy of government ownership, especially in radio matters," no longer persisted in the federal bureaucracy. In the context of a government commission, the secretary of commerce had advanced the methods by which the interdepartmental conflict could be resolved. Hoover's eventual triumph over the Post Office and the navy, from which he emerged the main figure in ending the interdepartmental contest, owed great thanks to the navy's realistic attitude. Both the secretary of commerce and the Naval Communications Service adopted completely pragmatic approaches during their struggle for power. Perceiving that any attempt by one agency to obliterate the other would be disadvantageous to both, they strove to avoid an all-out encounter and to safeguard those vital interests that could be protected. In time, while both realized important objectives, radio supervision became a province of the stronger of the two, the Commerce Department.[34]

The Hoover Pool

That Herbert Hoover succeeded in molding the hesitant, turbulent development of radio regulation was a tribute to his administrative ability. In addition, it represented a tribute to the dedicated, anonymous civil servants who worked for him. Their efforts represented a crucial aid to Hoover because he, like some others of his time, epitomized the bureaucratic organizer. Hoover used the committee; he understood its complexities. He knew how to marshal and delegate authority, and, more importantly, he knew what authority to retain and to what degree to exercise it. Coaxing legislation from a reluctant Congress has tested the mettle of many bureaucrats. Hoover and his staff dedicated many long sessions to exactly that—but when enticement, persuasion, logic, and cajoling failed, Hoover then took the issue and acted independently.

Using many of the same skills that had allowed him to manipulate the interdepartmental controversy, Secretary Hoover moved forcefully into the legislative arena where he encountered a number of insurmountable obstacles. Unlike their bureaucratic counterparts, congressmen possessed neither vast technical knowledge nor great pragmatism concerning radio issues. Consequently, in the legislative debates and hearings, the complexities of radio technology completely overwhelmed most senators and representatives. Hoover's behind-the-scenes tactics, therefore, worked less efficiently in the Congress.

To further compound the secretary's difficulties, at the same time that he faced legislative roadblocks, the courts decided that his office possessed little legal power to administer broadcasting. Under these circumstances, Hoover was forced to formulate an alliance among the stronger of the commercial companies, nonprofit groups, technical and scientific associations, professional organizations, and government bureaus. This coalition was somewhat similar to the pool concept, which reached its heyday in the 1920s. In its usual sense, a pool represented a collective agreement among railroads or other businesses to fix prices and divide profits. The Hoover pool resembled these arrangements in that it was a mutual banding together of broadcast interests for self-protection through adherence to a group of extralegal arrangements formulated by Secretary Hoover. It differed from the usual concept in that this pool did not seek to set or fix prices; instead, by pooling interests those involved sought to eliminate the disorder and chaos that threatened to destroy the industry.

The first legislative effort to secure the secretary of commerce's domination of radio began in April 1921. House Resolution 4132 was introduced by Representative Wallace White, a Republican from Maine, who opposed military power over wireless. Although the bill wasn't enacted, it initiated regulatory legislation concerning broadcasting and also served as a guide for the Legislative Committee of the First National Radio Conference.[1]

At the conference, White chaired the committee, which proposed that the Radio Act of 1912 be amended to give the secretary of commerce adequate authority to supervise radio and cope with the continuing expansion of broadcasting. In drafting this legislation, White relied heavily on the Commerce Department for advice and assistance. The meeting recommended the enactment of a new bill placing Secretary Hoover in charge of radio.[2]

In June, as a direct result of the committee's work, Representative White and Senator Frank Kellogg, Minnesota Republican, introduced identical bills (House Resolution 11964 and Senate Resolution 3691) for control of radio. The measures amended the Radio Act of 1912, which had been passed before the advent of broadcasting and which Secretary Hoover characterized as "a weak rudder to steer so powerful a development." Both lawmakers agreed that since broadcasting was a recent innovation, it would be unwise to adopt inflexible legislation. Consequently, they recommended placing control and wide discretionary powers in the hands of the secretary of commerce. In addition, the measure proposed the creation of an advisory committee to whom Hoover could refer such matters as the administration of the law or the study of scientific problems. Also, the plan gave the Department of Commerce jurisdiction over government stations when they were not transmitting federal business. Secretary Hoover assured his followers that the bill's success would ensure additional wavelengths for commercial concerns and would reduce interference.[3]

Over the course of the next year the supporters of the legislation increased in both numbers and diversity. President Harding not only backed his secretary of commerce but also urged the "effective regulation" of wireless. The National Radio Chamber of Commerce, while opposed to a naval monopoly, favored federal supervision. Because he felt that his association agreed that the Department of Commerce was the logical agency to exercise authority, Alfred Goldsmith, secretary of the Institute of Radio Engineers, contended that the measure would be approved by his professional organization. *Radio Broadcast*, declaring that the "greatest crisis in radio history is at hand," urged readers to write their congressmen demanding passage of the bill. Secretary Hoover enthusiastically observed that this was "one of the few instances on record in which the people of the United States were united in their desire for more regulation." Moreover, he stated, there was "little or no objection to the bills"; in fact, the industry was "unique in that everyone is unanimous in the common desire for legislation and regulation."[4]

Despite wide-ranging support for Hoover's repeated warning that "anarchy in the ether" was the only alternative to new legislation, Congress, according to Wallace White, "remained in a state of wise and masterly inactivity." Part of the blame for the lack of congressional action should be placed on Wallace White, himself. After he had begun his campaign for reelection in July of 1922, he had not devoted much time to radio matters. Moreover, Congress relegated it to a secondary position, since the tariff took precedence over other considerations. Furthermore, because Hoover had stated that the voluntary system of government-industry cooperation had been working well, the lawmakers assumed there was little need for immediate action.[5]

Some businessmen rejoiced at Congress's indifference, for they remained unconvinced that this was the time for the passage of legislation. Indeed, this dissent represented the first crack in the Commerce Department program of cooperation. John W. Elwood, secretary of RCA, observed that legislative success is often dependent "upon timeliness." Despite the growing demand for congressional action to relieve the chaos in broadcasting, he was a firm believer "in letting things get worse so that you can make them better." Owen D. Young had affirmed that he would not object to supervision, but "regulation in advance of profits by people unfamiliar with the business. . . will assuredly result in no profits at all, "a situation which he would indeed oppose. The lack of organization in broadcasting concerned both Young and Elwood. They argued that until broadcasting could be placed on a solid economic basis the industry could not be regulated properly.[6]

In addition to the concerns of Elwood and Young, another negative possibility vexed many of those most closely identified with the industry. Businessmen and radio journalists alike protested that the proposed legislation gave tremendous authority to an administrative official, power that might possibly be misused by some future secretary of commerce. Arthur Batcheller, the federal inspector for New York, reported to the department that this question had been privately raised by prominent business interests. Because of such foot dragging, Wallace White observed that the "radio folks as a whole" were not behind the legislation; he concluded that until they could decide on what they wanted, the bill had little chance of success. By the end of 1922, it had become apparent to Secretary Hoover that passage of the act during that session would be impossible.[7]

The next year, using his success in resolving the interdepartmental conflict as a springboard, the secretary of commerce advanced boldly in the congressional arena. On 2 and 3 January 1923, the Committee on Merchant Marine and Fisheries of the House of Representatives held hearings on House Resolution 11964, another measure introduced by Wallace White. The chief provisions of the White bill revised sections 1, 2, and 3 of the Radio Act of 1912. The legislation strengthened Hoover's position by bestowing wide discretionary powers upon the Department of Commerce. In addition, the proposal placed federal stations, when transmitting commercial messages, under the jurisdiction of the secretary of commerce. White, reflecting the feeling of the committee, indicated that many agencies had misused wireless by appropriating desirable wavelengths and by disregarding the rights of the broadcast listener.[8]

In a statement calculated to placate further the private sector, David B. Carson, director of the Bureau of Navigation, assured businessmen that the enactment of this legislation would allow the Department of Commerce to reallocate frequencies, thereby affording a wider distribution for broadcasting stations. In short, House Resolution 11964 was aimed directly at the navy: its provisions would place military oulets, when transmitting nongovernmental maritime messages, under civilian authority. In addition, it proposed to eliminate the government band from 187.5 to 500 kHz. In effect, the passage of House Resolution 11964 would have placed the Department of Commerce in a position of supremacy.[9]

Throughout the hearings, the navy objected most vehemently to paragraph C of section 1, which remanded naval stations to the control of the secretary of commerce when they were engaged in the transmission of nongovernmental material. Hoover asserted that the navy, like any other group, should be regulated while undertaking commercial work. He declared that the moment the navy entered the private sector "it ought to yield" to Department of Commerce supervision. He further postulated that without such authority it would be impossible to set up any systematic control.[10]

The navy countered that it was often difficult to separate the official from the private part of its duties. It also complained that strict interpretation of the bill would necessitate the licensing of all naval personnel by the Department of Commerce. After numerous conferences with the secretary of the navy, White and Commander Hooper of the Naval Communications Service agreed to circumvent the problem. They accepted a navy proposal that the president, acting on the advice of the IRAC, would assign channels to government stations conforming to the general rules and guidelines developed by the secretary of commerce. By shrewd maneuvering and by involving the IRAC in the regulatory process, the navy was able to avoid direct Department of Commerce jurisdiction.[11]

On 11 January 1923, White submitted to Congress a new bill (House Resolution 13773), similar to House Resolution 11964 but containing the necessary concessions to the navy. The measure passed the House of Representatives on 31 January and arrived before the Senate Committee on Interstate Commerce on 8 February. The navy supported the resolution before the House committee and subsequently urged Senate enactment. Because of this backing, the Bureau of Navigation felt so certain of the bill's success that it had prepared for the secretary a list of members to serve on the advisory committee to be created by the legislation. Secretary Hoover, however, took no chances: he prepared a draft letter supporting the proposal for President Harding to send out to various members of Congress.[12]

The White bill evoked a flood of correspondence advancing many partisan hopes and ideas. The American Radio Relay League continued to demand that the law define the amateur's domain and specify such matters as wavelengths and power. *QST*, the ARRL magazine, observed that even though the present "Secretary of Commerce and present Commissioner of Navigation are all friendly toward the amateur . . . they won't be in office always, and we ask you to imagine a Daniels as head of the Department of Commerce." At the same time, universities and colleges with broadcasting stations urged the lawmakers to give the academic outlets preferential treatment. Harry P. Davis, vice president of Westinghouse, suggested a public service commission be established to rule radio. In addition to these recommendations, such groups as the IRAC, citizen and listener associations, and businessmen proferred widespread support for the project. The House committee concluded that all witnesses and interests concurred that the confusion in the air could be relieved only through expanded and strengthened federal supervision.[13]

Yet, despite the seeming preponderance of support for the legislation, the Senate Committee on Interstate Commerce took no action. Alabama Senator Oscar W. Underwood, like many of his colleagues, hesitated to move the bill out of committee, stating that the proposition was too important to be rushed through in the closing days of the session. The IRAC saw less innocent forces at work: its subcommittee on policy and legislation observed that several business groups had opposed the plan in the Senate. The committee reported that, among others, RCA had urged Senator Underwood to proceed cautiously on the radio question. RCA voiced concern about the organization of broadcasting and reiterated its former position that legislation could come only after the business had gained a solid economic basis.[14]

AT&T joined RCA in its objections to the bill. While admitting that the measure might improve conditions slightly, the firm challenged several aspects of the plan. It pointed out that the proposal did not provide sufficient protection for capital. Under its provisions one would be required to secure a construction permit to erect a station. Having obtained permission, construction could begin, but it was not mandatory that the Department of Commerce issue a license for operation, even if the company had adhered strictly to the provisions assigned it. AT&T suggested that the secretary be required to follow through if all stipulations of the permit were fulfilled. Furthermore, the firm opposed the wording of the monopoly clause, which prohibited the secretary of commerce from approving applications for any corporation that engaged in monopoly. The telephone company urged that the word "unlawful" be inserted into the clause. Finally, as no right to appeal the decisions of the secretary of commerce was provided, AT&T contended that the bill gave too much power to an administrative official and stated that it found it impossible to support the measure. By the middle of February, Secretary Hoover regretfully conceded that the proposal would not become law.[15]

Still smarting from his failure to achieve a legislative mandate, Hoover suffered a judicial setback. Two years earlier, on 23 May 1921, Assistant Secretary of Commerce Claudius H. Huston had revoked the license of the Intercity Radio Company for seriously menacing legitimate wireless activities by willfully interfering with government, commercial, and amateur stations in the vicinity of New York City. Intercity had taken the matter to court, and the Supreme Court of the District of Columbia had ruled in the firm's favor, ordering the secretary of commerce to issue the application. Secretary Hoover appealed the case, but in February 1923, the Court of Appeals also decided for Intercity and declared that while the secretary of commerce might designate the channels upon which the corporation had to operate—that being left to administrative discretion by the Radio Act of 1912—the issuance of a license was mandatory. Hoover appealed the case to the U.S. Supreme Court, but after several delays the Intercity Radio Company went out of business, and the question remained moot.[16]

Secretary Hoover reacted to legal obstacles in a traditionally American way, namely, by going around them, ignoring them, or subverting them. Like early counterfeiters on the Western frontier, like corporations in his own time, and like most ambitious Americans at most times, Hoover simply refused to allow the law to stand in his way. A number of policies he implemented to regulate radio were either prohibited by the Radio Act of 1912 or fell outside his jurisdiction. In order to achieve his objective, he sought the compliance of his own department, the support of other government agencies, and the approbation of the press and the industry.[17]

The Bureau of Navigation and the radio inspectors had long recognized that it would be desirable to reallocate frequencies and allow businessmen to enter the government reservation. But without new legislation the secretary of commerce, hampered by court restrictions, could not do so. Sections 2 and 4 of the Radio Act of 1912 provided for definite wavelengths for commercial stations, specifically excluding them from 187.5 to 500 kHz. Article 2 of the Service Regulations, affixed to the International Radio-Telegraph Convention and ratified by the United States on 8 July 1913, further protected the federal band from intrusion by limiting private operators to assignments outside 187.5 to 500 kHz. In a memorandum to the secretary of commerce, Commissioner of Navigation David B. Carson observed that the clear intent of both the domestic act and the international convention was to restrict use of this band of channels to military purposes.[18]

Throughout 1922, Commissioner Carson had worked for passage of the White bill allowing private groups to use the federal reservation. By December of 1922, with congestion and interference prevalent above 500 kHz and no hope of congressional activity on the measure, he argued that it would be desirable to ignore the existing statutes and remove restrictions on the government band and to implement a general rearrangement of frequencies, even without new legislation. Without such drastic action, congestion and chaos would continue to hinder broadcasting.[19]

This change of attitude within the higher echelons of the Department of Commerce reflected the activities of radio inspectors in the field, who were forced by their lack of legal authority to improvise when faced with many of the difficult situations and problems inherent in their task. The officials often "took the law in their own hands without consultation or due process." At virtually all levels within the Department of Commerce, extemporization became the norm in efforts to counter the chaos created by the broadcasting boom.[20]

Sure of support within the department, Secretary Hoover then turned to other government divisions. He received encouragement from additional agencies to take action after the failure of the White bill. Some, including James C. Gilbert of the Department of Agriculture, mentioned the need to revise the Department of Commerce's procedures, in spite of the failure of the congressional program. Captain H. P. Perrill of the Office of the Chief Coordinator of the Bureau of the Budget suggested that Secretary Hoover proceed as if the new legislation had been enacted.[21]

With the backing of these bureaucrats, Secretary Hoover moved to protect his flank by cementing his relationship with the press. In the early years of his secretaryship, Hoover had developed ties with public relations personnel and the news media, while at the same time constructing an elaborate apparatus for popular appeal that could be utilized to manipulate national opinion. As he moved to skirt the legal barriers to effective radio control, the machinery went into high gear. Skillfully utilizing personal conferences and press contacts, he began to interpret his department's new policy to the American people. To supplement these activities, the Department of Commerce issued a weekly press summary that included an impressive compilation of clippings dealing with all aspects of communications. As the department implemented its plans, officials were instructed to send all incorrect or adverse commentary directly to Hoover's personal secretary. Corrections and additional material concerning the Commerce Department's scheme were emitted continuously to clarify and prevent unfavorable or inaccurate reporting.[22]

Finally, to provide legitimacy for the extralegal measures implemented by the Department of Commerce and as a finale to his press campaign, Secretary Hoover assembled the Second National

Radio Conference in Washington, D.C., on 20 March. The meeting was convened to consider the rampant chaos in radio, which had worsened after congressional inactivity and the Intercity case. As it had dominated the first gathering, the Commerce Department painstakingly arranged every detail of the second one. Well before the delegates assembled in Washington, the department had carefully prepared the program that would become the conference's recommendations.[23]

The agenda provided for consideration of the commercial use of the wavelengths reserved for the government between 187.5 and 500 kHz, the general reallocation of frequencies, reclassification of stations, and consideration of silent periods whereby amateurs would cease their activities during peak listening hours. Businessmen's urgent demands for relief from interference monopolized the considerations. In order to resolve this issue, the department suggested a rearrangement of wavelengths and the opening of the military reservation to private radio users. Secretary Hoover felt that in lieu of the required legal sanction, such cooperation would ensure the authority to achieve these aims.[24]

The Second National Radio Conference (closely following the Department of Commerce stratagem) urged a radical departure from past policy. Previously, all broadcasting had been conducted on 618.6, 750, and 833.3 kHz. This assembly advocated that the bloc principle in frequency allocation be applied to this service and a band from 550 to 1365 kHz be established. Stations were to be classified in this scheme according to their power, the character of program transmitted, and general operating method. The delegates also urged that three groups of broadcasting stations be created: Class A, equipped to use power not exceeding 500 watts and assigned wavelengths from 999.4 to 1365 kHz; Class B, authorized to use from 500 to 1,000 watts and operated on channels from 550 to 800 kHz and 870 to 999.4 kHz; and Class C, placed on 833.3 kHz.[25]

The members advised the secretary of commerce that, because technological advances since World War I had widened the electromagnetic spectrum, those marine, mobile, and aircraft services displaced by the creation of the broadcast band now could be reallocated elsewhere. For example, ship-to-shore communications on 666.3 and 999.4 kHz could be moved to 429 kHz. Such a displacement raised the possibility of resistance from the maritime sector, of course. While marine interests rarely used the 999.4 kHz channel assigned under the international convention, these same groups did rely heavily on the popular 666.3 kHz frequency. To encourage shippers to start using the 429 kHz wavelength, the delegates proposed that all traffic cease using 666.3 kHz between the hours of 7:00 and 11:00 P.M. and instead operate on frequencies between 375 and 500 kHz. A silent period during these hours supposedly would cut interference with broadcasting programs.[26]

In addition, other spectrum blocs were designated for maritime and point-to point communications, including 190, 235–85, 315–550, and 999.4 kHz. Radio compass and radio beacon stations were to conduct their essential maritime navigation functions on 300 and 375 kHz. Finally, ground-to-air transmissions crucial for aircraft safety were to be carried on 375 to 550 and 1300 to 1350 kHz. The convention at long last had begun to deal with some of the radio's more salient problems. Finally after nineteen years, the federal reservation was to be opened partially to businessmen.[27]

The delegates asserted that, in spite of judicial and legislative setbacks, the secretary of commerce had ample authority to implement the conference's program. They further believed that under the law he could rearrange stations, regulate hours and wavelengths, and revoke or withhold licenses. Secretary Hoover, while recognizing some potential difficulties in instituting the plan, called these recommendations "a step in the ideal development of measures for the prevention of interference in public broadcasting." On 15 May, he began to introduce the scheme proposed by the conference. He assigned channels, although the Radio Act of 1912 neither made nor authorized any distribution of frequencies to individual stations. He placed commercial operators in the band from 187.5 to 500 kHz, although both domestic and international law protected the government reservation. He reallocated channels, although the same laws specified wavelengths for certain groups of radio users. As *Radio Broadcast* observed in an article entitled "Secretary Hoover Acts," the situation was "suddenly remedied" without the passage of the White bill.[28]

The Second National Radio Conference's recommendations and the Commerce Department's implementation of these measures received widespread support. The acceptance of these extralegal actions by businessmen and bureaucrats made them, in effect, law. Broadcasters uniformly approved the creation of a band and envisioned a resultant reduction of interference among radio users. In an attempt to co-ordinate federal services with civilian groups, the IRAC announced that only those channels designated by the conference for public business would be assigned to government stations.[29]

The military also approved the new policies. The army agreed that since the electromagnetic spectrum had been enlarged by technological developments the maintenance of a government band in times of peace was unjustified. The Signal Corps added that the acceptance of this new plan would improve the army's reputation with broadcast listeners. While insisting that there were more important services than broadcasting, the Signal Corps nonetheless recognized that a very large proportion of the public was interested in the medium and therefore demanded its proper protection from interference by the military.[30]

Because it was the largest user of radio, the navy sacrificed much more than any other group by acquiescing to the creation of a broadcasting band. The Naval Communications Service diplomatically agreed to what Stanford C. Hooper labeled the "sensible thing" and endorsed both the recommendations of the second conference and the IRAC policy.[31]

Although its actions might appear overly generous, the navy recognized that it no longer could justify maintaining the federal reservation. By bending, it could discard outdated apparatus and modernize naval equipment. Under this new arrangement, naval fleet operations used 95 to 120 kHz, 190 to 230 kHz, 250 kHz, and 2,005 to 2,995 kHz. When necessary, wavelengths from 1,030 to 1,285 kHz and 3,005 to 3,815 kHz were possible substitutes. In addition, shore facilities received authorization to operate either below 150 kHz or above 4,000 kHz. In sum, the navy utilized seventy-five specific frequencies allocated in the following manner: five low-frequency channels with low or high power; fourteen medium-frequency channels with high power; thirty high-frequency channels with low power; twenty high-frequency channels with low power; and six high-frequency channels with low power. Equally important, the new arrangement revitalized naval programs set aside prior to the conference by congressional cutbacks of military expenditures following World War I. In order to operate on the new wavelengths, the department needed modern apparatus. Because of the new rules and procedures, the Naval Communications Service was able to justify replacing outdated equipment that was inoperative at the new frequencies and receive increased appropriations to facilitate the conversion. Again, by displaying adaptability and maintaining limited objectives, the navy not only lived with the new policy but actually prospered from it.[32]

The RCA Annual Report for 1923 observed that "radio broadcasting promises permanency." To a large extent this promise resulted directly from the policies implemented by Secretary Hoover in the spring and summer of 1923. In spite of legislative inactivity and a judicial decision undermining his authority, Hoover insituted several extralegal measures destined to establish the supremacy of the secretary of commerce. With the collusion of bureaucrats and businessmen, he created an informal pool whereby the business community and the Department of Commerce could combat the disorder and chaos that surrounded broadcasting.[33]

In addition, the Second National Radio Conference's allocation program effectively dealt with the major difficulties that plagued radio users. Since its resolutions placed most amateur, ship, and land stations outside the broadcasting band, interference was drastically curtailed. Moreover, by creating a separate band of wavelengths for broadcasting outlets, the conference assured the continued development and survival of the medium. This action, in essence, confined the principal problems and administrative difficulties to broadcasters. From 1923 until the passage of the Radio Act of 1927, they suffered from a lack of organization, the absence of federal regulation, and a scarcity of channels as more and more individuals erected facilities. Henceforth, the broadcasting issue would become the dominant problem on the radio scene.[34]

In time, however, the Department of Commerce policy produced an environment conducive to the creation of a viable business establishment which would assert a position distinct from that of Secretary Hoover. The department's primary goal—to control and stabilize radio—actually resulted in complications unforeseen by the secretary of commerce. Ultimately, a number of private firms emerged to utilize the Hoover pool to secure their own objectives.

4

Organize or Perish

Under the protection of the secretary of commerce, broadcasting development spurted. In the nine months after Herbert C. Hoover's appointment as secretary of commerce, the new industry blossomed into a rapidly expanding national craze. In December 1921, twenty-three stations were issued licenses by the Department of Commerce; another eight were licensed in January, twenty-four in February, seventy-seven in March, seventy-six in April, and ninety-seven in May. By 1923, there were 579 operational outlets in the United States. Not only had the secretary of commerce aided in the creation of a new industry, he had also identified the Department of Commerce with its success. Hoover's policies had been so effective that Americans seemed to many to be preoccupied with nothing but crystal sets and programs.[1]

Because of the needs and distinctive structure of the broadcasting industry, its plans and policies coincided to some extent with those of the Department of Commerce. Moreover, Secretary Hoover used the renewed chaos and disorder caused by the lack of legislation to strengthen an alliance between businessmen and his department in the hope of promoting his own endeavors. But the relationship did not disintegrate into a government dictatorship. On the contrary, Hoover's attempts to implement the extralegal arrangement, by which he aimed to secure protracted control, required a secure identification between his agency and the business community. In the process of establishing this felicitous proximity, Hoover became increasingly dependent upon the industry, thereby relinquishing part of his own command of the situation. A single challenge, a single court case questioning the secretary of commerce's legal position, would have toppled Hoover's carefully constructed program. In the tenuous stalemate that resulted, the initiative shifted from the Commerce Department to corporate interests.

As a whole, however, the commercial operators were unable to exploit Hoover's vulnerability, for they were neither united nor able to formulate common objectives. In its amalgamation of large and small companies, religious institutions, colleges and universities, and municipalities, the industry lacked a core. Moreover, all broadcasters were struggling to place their business on a sound structural and economic basis. In these circumstances, the large corporations and electrical firms emerged as the leading force in the enterprise, for only they had the organizational experience and financial resources necessary to take command during the impasse.

In 1923 and 1924, while the entire industry was still grappling with its many problems, the charge of monopoly brought a sensationalism that was to overshadow the more pressing issues at hand. In fact, the fear of exclusivity had been expressed in congressional hearings even in the earliest days of communications. During the current round of inquiries on radio legislation, mere mention of the word would touch off lengthy battles and prolong debate. The specter of illegal combinations assumed the forms of ownership of stations, patent rights pertaining to the manufacturing of tubes and sets, and political censorship of minority candidates. On 17 February 1923, Representative Wallace White succumbed to the pressure for action against the "radio trust" by introducing a resolution in the House of Representatives calling for a full Federal Trade Commission investigation into agreements that had provided exclusive rights to (1) transmission and reception, (2) the sale of radio equipment, and (3) the control and ownership of patents for the development of wireless apparatus.[2]

In actuality, the industry was characterized not by monopoly but by its opposite—competition, instability, disorder, and a state of flux of obscure origin and equally uncertain future. Business concerns representing all aspects of communications were expanding their activities to include participation in broadcasting. Of the 550 outlets in operation in 1923, almost half were associated with radio manufacturers and electrical establishments, who aimed to perpetuate and expand a market for their products. Electrical companies became involved in order to promote the use of electricity and to engage in public relations, while manufacturers hoped to sell more receiving sets. Journalists were also attracted to the medium because of its promotional values. The pioneer newspaper station, WWJ, of the Detroit *News*, was quickly imitated by a host of followers, among them WDAF (Kansas City *Star*), KSD (Saint Louis *Post-Dispatch*), WGN (Chicago *Tribune*), WSB (Atlanta *Journal*), and WFAA (Dallas *News*). Two years after the KDKA transmission, over 100 dailies had erected their own facilities.[3]

The proliferating interest was by no means confined to commercial firms; religious institutions, universities, and even municipalities vied to exploit the promise of great audiences. Aimee Semple McPherson, a West Coast evangelist, compared broadcasting to a Biblical miracle. She observed that it was now "possible to stand in the pulpit and speaking in a normal voice reach hundreds of thousands of listeners." Such church outlets as WMBI, owned and operated by the Moody Bible Institute, and WCBQ (We Can't Be Quiet), of the First Baptist Church in Nashville, commenced operations with an evangelistic zeal. Not content to leave the rewards of influencing large numbers of people to the business and religious interests, Chicago (WBU), Dallas (WRR), and New York City (WNYC) boasted municipal stations to transmit public addresses, lectures, and police messages. In addition, educators gravitated to broadcasting. At the end of 1922 seventy-three educational institutions were sending news, lectures, weather reports, and music from such schools as the University of Wisconsin, Ohio State University, and the University of New Mexico.[4]

As the need to find solutions to the numerous problems confronting the industry became more acute, many of the smaller and independent businessmen themselves tried to find the answers. On 25 and 26 April 1923, broadcasters, radio manufacturers, and journalists assembled in the Drake Hotel in Chicago in response to a call initiated by Thorne Donnelley and Elliot Jenkins of WDAF (Kansas City), Dr. Frank Elliot of WOC (Davenport), William Hedges of WMAQ (Chicago), Powell Crosley of the Crosley Manufacturing Company and owner of WWI (Cincinnati), and Eugene McDonald, Jr., of Zenith and WJAZ (Chicago). The meeting gave birth to the National

Association of Broadcasters (NAB). Even though the participants realized that a trade association was vital to the survival of their new and expanding industry, they perceived that their need to "organize or perish" stemmed from the even greater necessity for a coordinated effort to pass national legislation. In addition, they met in order to answer the challenge posed by the American Society of Composers, Authors, and Publishers (ASCAP). ASCAP was demanding royalties in return for the privilege of transmitting copyrighted songs, the basic ingredient of most programming. While many of the businessmen were ostensibly willing to recognize ASCAP's legal rights, their precarious financial situation precluded any serious thought of conciliation. Thus the NAB quickly became the voice for many of the independent broadcasters in their struggle for survival.[5]

The NAB did not, however, provide a quick answer for all problems confronting the medium. Members of the business community continued to struggle among themselves and with outside forces. Ironically, at the very time that the charge of monopoly was being leveled against the corporate giants, the "Four Horsemen of the Air —AT&T, GE, Westinghouse, and RCA" were fighting one another for control of broadcasting. Their internecine bickering resulted from a breakdown in the postwar cross-licensing agreements, which was in turn, the result of the phenomenal mushrooming of stations and the rapidly growing market for receiving sets. As Captain Ridley McLean, U.S. Navy, correctly observed, the contestants "were in general in a different frame of mind to what they had been in the past."[6]

The continuing dissension polarized the various factions according to their functions. Because of its ownership of patents, its engineering staff, and its long-lines department, the telephone group, composed of AT&T and its subsidiary Western Electric, achieved such strategic importance that for a time it threatened to overshadow the opposition completely. AT&T contended that the cross-licensing accords endowed it with exclusive rights to produce radio telephone transmitting equipment. It further argued that since one-way transmission of sound for a mass audience was really an extension of its telephone service, this too was an exclusive preserve of AT&T. Acting on this premise, the corporation demanded that all broadcasters acquire licenses under the company's patents. Its counterpart, the radio group, representing GE, Westinghouse, and their protégé, RCA, countered that broadcasting concerned only those who manufactured and sold receivers. Thus the battle lines were sharply drawn. The radio alliance found it advantageous to maintain broadcasting outlets in order to increase the sale of sets. The telephone association continued to emphasize that its position as a public service corporation endowed it with special aptitude to manage broadcasting.[7]

The absence of legislation allowed these two combinations great maneuverability. J. J. Carty, vice-president of AT&T, observed, "The new part of any business is always difficult. . . the rules of the game are not developed." In these circumstances, AT&T moved to exploit every opportunity by instituting several policies aimed at organizing broadcasting. Because of its patents for the manufacture of radio telephone transmitting equipment, AT&T received innumerable requests for the purchase of electronic hardware. Believing that the outright sale of transmitters would increase congestion, it decided to implement stabilizing policies. In order to eliminate the indiscriminate proliferation of outlets, the company constructed high-quality facilities to transmit the messages of those willing to pay for the service. Since messages were transmitted for a fee, the action heralded the advent of "toll" broadcasting. The telephone associates had been forced to search for such a new revenue source in order to compete with their broadcasting rivals, who had always been able to rely on sales of receiving sets to provide needed capital. To implement its plans, the corporation received a license for WEAF from the Department of Commerce on 1 June 1922. It conducted the station as a toll facility available for hire by those wishing to send programs. By 1923, WEAF had attracted a long list of sponsors simply by utilizing the talent available in the New York City area.[8]

AT&T's efforts to organize the medium on a nationwide basis reinforced its total approach. The company insisted that the maximum benefit of this new undertaking would be realized only if developed on a national level and furnished by one interest. At first, the firm unsuccessfully proposed to bridge the continent with fifty stations using superior equipment and famous entertainers. The purpose of the policy was, of course, to eliminate small companies employing inferior apparatus and local talent. In the prevailing environment of disorder and chaos, the overwhelming effort and organization necessary to establish a monopoly quickly disabused AT&T of its pretensions. After this preliminary flirtation with a national organization, the firm changed its methods somewhat. It inaugurated network radio by transmitting a program simultaneously over WEAF and the Boston station WNAC. In its subsequent attempt at a larger hook-up, the telephone associates even joined with the opposition; on 7 June 1923, AT&T interconnected WEAF with several radio group facilities (KDKA, WGY in Schenectady, and KYM in Chicago) to provide the second chain transmission. By the summer of 1923, the first continuous network system was implemented between WEAF and WMAF AT South Dartmouth, Massachusetts. In January of 1924, to enhance these experiments, WEAF began operating with an increased power of 5,000 watts.[9]

The radio confederation used all its assets in the corporate battle with AT&T. As the chief sales outlet for GE and Westinghouse receivers, RCA held a highly lucrative position in the manufacture and sale of receivers. It exploited patents that it held not only by producing sets but also by claiming royalties from other firms. In addition, the coalition controlled several strategically located affiliates, including the pioneer KDKA, other Westinghouse facilities, and GE's WGY, KGO in Oakland, and KOA in Denver.[10]

Ever on the alert for some innovation to attract public attention, the group experimented with combined New York stations to provide the public with a choice in entertainment. The *American Mercury* heralded the "most ambitious project of municipal magnification since Babylon—Radio Broadcast Central in Aeolian Hall," which housed two transmitters operating simultaneously on different frequencies under its one roof. WJZ dealt in serious programs and classical music, and WJY developed lighter entertainment and jazz, thus introducing specialization in station operations.[11]

Under these circumstances, David Sarnoff's leadership of RCA provided an asset equal to the financial and organizational advantages available to the radio alliance. He promoted broadcasting in much the same way that Samuel Insull championed electricity. Whether Sarnoff spoke before a local chamber of commerce, a government committee, an engineering society, a college audience, or a listener association, he continually fulfilled his intent to glorify

Figure 5.   WJY Broadcast, 1921.

With 1921 broadcasts from WJY in Newark, New Jersey, RCA attempted to follow the KDKA lead.   *Courtesy of Smithsonian Institution, Photo No. 75, 815.*

the medium. Sarnoff's facility at promoting and representing the industry was surpassed only by his aptitude in corporate intrigue, a blessing which served RCA's interest countless times. He had the uncanny ability to keep the opposition off balance and to strike from several directions at once. His movement up through the ranks of the American Marconi Company had endowed him with an understanding of corporate politicking as well as with a grasp of technology which proved crucial in his struggle with AT&T. In short, Sarnoff had few equals in broadcasting, and his tactics were reminiscent of those of the nineteenth-century financier, investment banker, and promoter, Jay Gould, who has been characterized as a son of a bitch, but an effective son of a bitch.[12]

The radio coalition strove to place broadcasting on a national basis but suffered a serious disadvantage because the telephone company refused to allow its competitors the use of its wire system except on special occasions. Therefore, RCA, GE, and Westinghouse reluctantly relied on lines leased from the Western Union Telegraph Company, which provided inferior service as they were not designed for voice transmissions. The radio partners were, of course, eager to gain full access to efficient wire facilities. After it became obvious that such access was not forthcoming, Sarnoff began to seek out AT&T's weaknesses. As a tactical maneuver, he contended that the new service should not be debased by advertising but rather that it deserved endowment by wealthy individuals. He further postulated that such support would allow the development of "Super Power" stations, which, once established throughout the United States, would transmit superior programming simultaneously to "every city, every town, every village, every hamlet."[13]

Harry P. Davis, vice-president of Westinghouse, suggested a counterproposal involving the construction of a three-tiered system. The most prestigious grouping, a superior cluster of "National Stations," would furnish programming from centers where talent was available. Repeating facilities scattered across the United States would relay the features. At the local level, less powerful community outlets would select material to fit their needs from the regularly scheduled fare. Both Sarnoff and Davis recognized that the public highly regarded those stations interconnected with the telephone company because they could receive superior programs. To combat this detriment to RCA, GE, and Westinghouse, the three had to find some way to gain comparable wire service for their allies.[14]

By 1924, the two combinations had developed a basic accord. They had always felt that broadcasting should be organized on a nationwide basis. The radio associates agreed with the telephone group that national advertising should underwrite operating costs. (On 1 July 1924, the Board of Directors of RCA resolved to permit the sale of air time, thereby putting them on the same basis as WEAF). Both also concurred that the power of outlets would have to be increased to reach large audiences and to overcome interference. Finally, they agreed that the large number of facilities was only a transitory phenomenon impossible to sustain because of the prohibitive cost of managing stations. The two industrial combinations maneuvered for stronger positions while using these four premises as the basis for the future organization of broadcasting.[15]

The developments in radio sets, programming, and audience maturation reinforced these trends in industrial organization. At first, the majority of listeners used home-altered, if not homemade, receivers. The earliest of these were inexpensive crystal detectors capable of bringing in programs only at a distance of twenty-five miles or less from the transmitter. Superior equipment using the three-element tube quickly followed, however. When the tube set succeeded the crystal apparatus, the storage battery came into its own; then, with the advent of the so-called peanut tubes, it became possible to utilize the dry battery. In 1923, RCA took the radio out of the basement and attic and placed it in the living room by introducing the Radiola Super-Heterodyne receiver in a "handsome cabinet." Incidentally, after the widespread acceptance of the ready-made outfits, the demand for those parts which had been sold previously to the enthusiasts constructing their own sets declined drastically. From 1922 to 1924, the number of families with radios increased from 2 to 10.1 percent of the population. Their sales value grew from $5 million in 1922 to $100 million in 1926 and increased even more rapidly thereafter. In effect, the radio console had become a household necessity, and transmitting antennas proliferated.[16]

Figure 6.   Crystal Detector.

The crystal detector, a simple, inexpensive rectifier
of radio frequency, brought any handy radio fan the
means to build a crystal set, the simplest form of
radio receiver by combining this detector, a tuning
coil, and earphones.   *Courtesy of Smithsonian Institution, Photo No. 72, 132.*

Figure 7. Crosley's Two Tube Amplifier.

A two tube amplifier promoted by Powell Crosley, Jr. as the model A of radio. *Courtesy of Smithsonian Institution, Photo No. 38,966-A.*

While the number of stations mushroomed in the first two years of broadcasting, the refinement of programs was a more gradual process. Initially, programs were designed largely by chance and conducted in a haphazard fashion, mainly utilizing phonograph records and amateur talent. Even though outlets were operating only a few hours a day, businessmen foraged with increasing resourcefulness to maintain a steady flow of entertainment. While in the early days listeners had been satisfied with the thrill of picking up distant voices and were not overly concerned with program quality, the novelty of the medium had worn off by 1923, and operators responded to public interest in better transmissions by producing more lively fare. As audiences became more sophisticated, programming underwent important changes. It became apparent that for broadcasters to render genuine service they had to be ready to implement full-time scheduling geared to continuous operations. In the process, management became more specialized, for the work force was divided into departments concerned with devising programs, broadcasting them, and obtaining publicity. In order to attract audiences, businessmen began seeking out famous entertainers to provide public appeal. In turn, the cost of utilizing such talent forced them to turn to advertising to finance their shows. Each of these developments reinforced the concept of national service, sponsored entertainment, and continuous operations.[17]

Secretary Hoover supported the policies implemented by the large corporations because he recognized that these innovations would benefit both the industry and the public. Given his tenuous legal position, he probably could not have reacted otherwise. He encouraged experimentation in the name of progress. In the matter of high power and interconnection, for example, the Commerce Department granted experimental licenses to Westinghouse, GE, AT&T, and RCA. The department justified its action by predicting that the results would be decreased static, better service to those listeners in isolated areas, and increased selection of stations for the owners of inexpensive receiving sets. Moreover, Secretary Hoover supported the concept of national service and particularly wanted to provide coverage for political events, such as conventions and speeches by leading government officials. Happily for many businessmen, the

Commerce Department did not oppose the sale of air time. In fact, Hoover recognized that advertising, whether direct or indirect, was the principal motive for establishing outlets; in addition, he opposed license fees as a means of meeting the cost of station expenses. Administratively, the Commerce Department encouraged continuous operations by voiding licenses of those concerns which did not transmit regularly.[18]

Although Hoover felt that the charge of monopoly was bogus, he recognized that the issue had vast political ramifications, and therefore he voiced loud opposition to any restraint of trade. Such a stance was necessary if he was to achieve his major objective, the passage of legislation establishing the Commerce Department's supremacy in radio. Toward that end, the secretary of commerce worked closely with Representative Wallace White and the Inter-departmental Radio Advisory Committee while reviewing the congressional problem and drafting a new bill to introduce in the first session of the sixty-ninth Congress. To forestall the objections that had been raised against the earlier proposal, the Department of Commerce suggested the inclusion of a provision containing the right of appeal from decisions of the secretary of commerce to the Court of Appeals of the District of Columbia. On 28 February, White introduced House Resolution 7357, "A Bill to Regulate Radio Communications." It contained provisions almost identical to those of the measure that had passed the House of Representatives in the preceding Congress, except that it included an appeals clause.[19]

Hearings were held in March before the House Committee on Merchant Marine and Fisheries. White indicated that the issue of monopoly had become the "most troublesome question" confronting the lawmakers. To overcome the objections to the "radio trust," he inserted a section that applied the antitrust statutes to radio, directing the secretary of commerce to deny a license to any applicant who he believed was seeking an illegal restraint of trade. Notables from the business community, amateur groups, listener associations, and the bureaucracy paraded before the committee urging passage of House Resolution 7357. In his presentation, Secretary Hoover noted that the issue was one of the most complex problems before Congress and reiterated the pressing need for legislation to establish order in the ether.[20]

As in the past the committee viewed a deceptive display of unanimity. Backstage, however, a variety of interests were at work in opposition to giving an administrative official the amount of power proposed in the bill. P. R. Scheverin of the Federal Telegraph Company wrote that his company opposed "clothing the Secretary of Commerce with regulatory powers as complete and absolute as there were conferred by the radio bill." The American Radio Relay League took a similar position, albeit on different grounds. Charles Stewart, the league's secretary, observed that the broad authority delegated to Secretary Hoover could be dangerous to the interests of the amateur. The radio inspector in New York correctly projected in early March that the bill probably would fail because it vested too much power in an administrative official. Equally telling was the concern of the larger segment of the industry, which again insisted that supervision should come after broadcasting had been organized, not before. Eugene S. Wilson, vice-president of AT&T, argued that it could be disastrous to pass a law that might not be appropriate in a year or two. He observed, "It is a mistake to build a cage for an animal until you know the size and characteristics of the animal." Finally, passage of the bill was impeded by the strain between Congress and the White House in 1924: the Republican lawmakers refused to act on a single proposal that President Coolidge advanced in his annual message.[21]

In sum, radio legislation failed again—because differences of opinion separated broadcasters and radio users, because many people feared granting too much power to the secretary of commerce, and because problems existed between a Republican-dominated Congress and the nation's chief executive. It is not surprising then that what the Chicago *Tribune* called "the most important legislation that had been introduced in a decade" stood little chance of passage.[22]

Unable to arouse the first session of the Sixty-ninth Congress to action, Secretary Hoover resorted to what by now had become virtually a ritual with him: he called a meeting. In the months preceding the Third National Radio Conference, the Department of Commerce carefully prepared for the gathering by holding discussions with members of the IRAC and businessmen and by soliciting the views of various bureaucrats. Out of these efforts, the department developed an agenda for delegates, including such matters as the interconnection of stations, the limitation of power, the reclassification of outlets, and the revisions of wavelengths to reduce interference. Failure to achieve a legislative mandate had begun to reflect unfavorably on the Commerce Department; so the underlying premise of the conference was to shore up Hoover's position.[23]

The meeting convened in Washington, D.C., on 6 October with ninety delegates—more than four times the total of those participating in the two previous gatherings—in attendance. They divided their work among eight subcommittees that dealt with the rearrangement of wavelengths, allocation of frequencies to broadcasting stations, marine communications, amateurs, interference, interconnection, and coordination. In Hoover's address to the delegates, he called the meeting "an experiment in industrial self-government," which would enable bureaucrats, businessmen, and listeners to cooperate on radio matters. *Radio Broadcast* observed that across the conference table "the lambs and the wolves have lain down . . . and progress in the radio field had been constructively guided."[24]

The delegates advanced the usual quota of recommendations, and once again their deliberations were condensed into a report published by the Department of Commerce. For the most part, however, little new ground was broken; instead, the proceedings recognized and supported previously implemented government policies. On interconnection, for example, the subcommittee urged its further development to create an important national service. In the matter of "Higher Power for Broadcasting Stations" the report suggested continued experimentation under appropriate safeguards. The subcommittee on "Public Broadcasting" recognized the need for additional wavelengths and accepted the decisions of the Commerce Department for the creation of a broadcasting band from 135 to 550 kHz. In only two instances did the delegates improvise: they wished to substitute numeral classifications for the letter designations in use (replacing Class A, B, C with Class 1, 2, 3), and they also requested creation of a new zone system, but the Department of Commerce chose not to implement these proposals.[25]

Unlike the First National Radio Conference, which established the precedent for these annual affairs, and the second one, which provided legitimacy for the extralegal policies implemented by the secretary of commerce, the third assembly, despite the congenial atmosphere and Washington's balmy October weather, lacked much significance other than one of catharsis. At least all the delegates felt relieved afterward and assured themselves that they had accomplished great deeds. Unfortunately, the appearance of action was no substitute for concrete policies designed to meet the needs of the industry, the government, or the public.

Moreover, nothing was done to resolve the legislative impasse or to provide help for the users of the overcrowded broadcast spectrum. At the time of the meeting, there existed over 530 operational stations arranged as: 387 Class A outlets with low power; forty-seven Class B facilities with power from 500 to 1,000 watts; and eighty-six Class C broadcasters with low power and transmitting on 833.3 kHz. The chief problem concerned the Class B stations. Congestion prevailed and grew throughout the forty-four available wavelengths, especially in such metropolitan areas as New York City and Chicago. Goodwill, self-regulation, and cooperation did not offer any possible solution; for in the twilight of 1924, as legislation lagged, the industry began to establish its own priorities separate and distinct from the Commerce Department and began to support an alternative approach to control under an administrative official.[26]

The New York Solution

In the winter of 1924–25, outside forces took exception to the foundation of the Hoover pool and roiled its apparently tranquil surface for the first time. Initially, a public challenge to the White bill unleashed the clamor of special interests, as educators, small broadcasters, large corporations, the military, and labor groups batled to protect their place in the electromagnetic spectrum. The divisions of opinion that had always existed among them claimed more than their usual attention with so many voicing public disgust.

A second difficulty, equally important but less visible, stemmed from opposing priorities of the Commerce Department and the industry. While Secretary Hoover continued to define the key issue facing business as the lack of federal supervision, many broadcasters emphasized that the need to place the medium on a solid organizational and financial basis took priority over the passage of regulatory legislation. As the large corporations began tackling what David Sarnoff labeled the "unprecedented tasks of organization," it became evident that many of the issues could not be resolved by parliamentary debate or congressional hearings. To a large extent these problems remained outside the jurisdiction of the Commerce Department; in essence, it was the businessmen's task to resolve them.[1]

The breakdown of the legislative consensus was, to some degree, brought about by Secretary Hoover himself. On 4 December 1924, he publicly suggested to Wallace White that the congressman introduce a "very short bill" prepared by the Commerce Department to clarify the jurisdiction of the secretary of commerce, thereby enabling the latter to control the rapidly fluctuating broadcasting situation. This seemingly innocuous step would grant Hoover the right not only to fix the wavelengths of every transmitter but also to set the time of operation, determine the character of apparatus, and specify power. If enacted, this "small bill" would deliver all the discretionary authority that the secretary of commerce had sought to secure in the passage of the original White bill.[2]

Reaction to Hoover's proposition came swiftly. On 24 December 1924, Eugene F. McDonald, Jr., president of the National Association of Broadcasters, openly challenged the secretary of commerce for the first time. While indicating that he had "unbounded confidence in Mr. Hoover," McDonald nonetheless argued that the passage of the proposed law "would vest any secretary of commerce with Napoleonic powers." McDonald did not stop there. He suggested that an independent agency, similar to the Interstate Commerce Commission, be created to exercise jurisdiction over cables, telephone, and telegraph, as well as radio. McDonald's stand received widespread publicity and support from the National Association of Broadcasters, the Chicago City Council, and *Radio Broadcast*. In addition to dealing a publicly embarrassing blow to the secretary of commerce's prestige, McDonald's pronouncement made the actions of the Department of Commerce fair game for a plethora of groups that previously never would have dared utter criticism.[3]

Hoover, having momentarily stumbled, attempted to regain his composure—but to no avail. On 30 December, Harold Philip Stokes, assistant to the secretary of commerce, contended in defense of the new plan that it contained far less drastic stipulations than the original White bill. He emphasized that its only purpose was to allow Secretary Hoover to curtail interference until a more comprehensive solution could be devised. Unfortunately, this and each successive defense of the act served to discredit it further. Such doings definitely were not to Hoover's liking. The door had been forced open, and the privileged position he had created for the Commerce Department was undermined. As the members of the Sixty-ninth Congress departed for an early spring vacation, Hoover was clearly on the defensive.[4]

The obviously discomfiting situation represented only a fraction of Hoover's woes because the Department of Commerce was running out of space in the electromagnetic spectrum. Following the Third

National Radio Conference, the secretary of commerce implemented a new allocation scheme to improve reception for listeners. Under this new arrangement, he eliminated Class C licenses. Those transmitters, which had operated on 833.3 kHz, were reclassified and placed in the Class A group. After this move, the secretary of commerce had eighty-six wavelengths available, as signals were spaced ten kilocycles apart and staggered geographically to prevent overlapping. Thirty-nine channels were allocated to 455 Class A stations. These broadcasters, owing to their limited power and irregular programming, did not present many difficulties. Essentially, the wasteland already had arrived for them. Class B operators, however, because of their regular hours and increased power, experienced greater problems of interference. In their case, forty-seven frequencies had to be divided among 108 facilities. Compounding this situation was the fact that the Department of Commerce had on file 425 applications for new licenses. Added to the 563 stations already operating, approval of these requests would have produced a grand total of 988 outlets. Such a result, as Wallace White indicated, would have meant the complete breakdown of broadcasting.[5]

To head off this prospect, the Commerce Department began to notify all prospective applicants in April 1925, that all Class A and B wavelengths were in use. It further stipulated that it could offer no assurance of available channels for any newly completed transmitters. By May, in spite of this new allocation program, Secretary Hoover realized that because of the limited number of frequencies the Commerce Department would be unable to continue licensing private concerns who wished to go on the air.[6]

In the early summer, Hoover launched an extensive campaign to gather support for curtailing expansion, an act clearly beyond his authority to implement. At the same time, he hoped to gain needed publicity to parry the McDonald thrust. His initiative culminated in the Fourth National Radio Conference. From May through September of 1925, the press, the Interdepartmental Radio Advisory Committee, and the National Association of Broadcasters vigorously discussed the desirability of yet another meeting to examine restricting the number of broadcasters. A full month before the conference assembled in Washington, it was the consensus that since the number of stations had reached a "saturation point" some method of limiting their ever-increasing numbers was a top priority.[7]

The meeting convened on 9 November 1925, at the U.S. Chamber of Commerce building. Some 500 delegates, over five times the number present at the third conference, attended. As in the past, committees were created to handle advertising, interference, legislation, licensing, amateurs, copyright matters, allocation of frequencies operating regulations, and marine problems. The Department of Commerce released the proceedings of these committees, guaranteeing them wide circulation and publicity.[8]

The assemblage confined its deliberations to those issues of paramount importance: licensing procedures, an expanded electromagnetic spectrum, and legal support for the secretary of commerce. In view of the overcrowding, the delegates declared that the Department of Commerce should withhold further licenses. Secretary Hoover eagerly embraced this proposal; on 13 November, the day after the conference closed, he announced that no more broadcasting applications would be accepted. In December of the same year, the department subsequently declared that all petitions for increased power would be treated as requests for new stations, thereby effectively eliminating any avenue of escape from the fourth conference's pronouncements.[9]

Next, the delegates rejected a move to expand the broadcast range from 1,500 to 2,000 kHz. This decision was prompted by strident amateur opposition to usurpation of their wavelengths and strengthened by the recognition that most receiving sets were incapable of covering this range. The defeat of this proposal to invade the amateur domain reinforced Hoover's relationship with their national organization, the American Radio Relay League, and solidified his resolve to curtail the licensing of stations.[10]

Finally, employing the rhetoric of the 1920s, the group declared that "public interest, as represented by service to the listener, should be the basis for the broadcasting privilege." In order to ensure the success of this policy, the delegates recommended that Congress authorize the secretary of commerce to assign call letters, wavelengths, power, hours of operation, location, and character of emissions and also enable him to revoke licenses. In effect, the suggestion was to give the federal government full control over traffic and wide authority in policing interference. More importantly, this proposal put the members squarely behind Secretary Hoover's program as stipulated in the White bill.[11]

The public euphoria generated by the gathering lasted well into December. Owen D. Young, respected chairman of the board of RCA, termed the meeting a "great success." Reflecting the spirit of the occasion, the New York *Times* optimistically predicted that the Sixty-ninth Congress "will unquestionably pass a new radio bill" containing a provision for the secretary of commerce to limit the number of stations. It further observed that Secretary Hoover, "anticipating Congressional action . . . had already put this into effect." While publicly contending that enacting the program proposed by the conference would be a "great step in radio progress," privately Hoover conceded that the "real work of obtaining the necessary legislation to protect radio development has only begun."[12]

In spite of the favorable press and manifestations of goodwill offered in the aftermath of the meeting, developments in December were indicative of future controversies. The *Crosley Radio Weekly* charged that Secretary Hoover had been designated the "dictator" and "czar" of the industry by the Fourth National Radio Conference. This accusation generated sufficient adverse publicity to cause Hoover to spend a distressing amount of his time refuting it. Almost simultaneously, the Department of Commerce was drawn into a public dispute occasioned by the transmissions of the RCA affiliate, WJZ, in Bound Brook, New Jersey. The residents of the surrounding communities claimed that WJZ, operating with a power of fifty kilowatts, disrupted their reception. New Jersey lawmakers, inundated by a deluge of thousands of angry letters and petitions demanding action against RCA, threw the whole affair into Hoover's lap. Since the situation was to a large degree insoluble, once again Hoover's policy elicited a great deal of unfavorable commentary.[13]

Secretary Hoover hoped to outmaneuver the growing chorus of criticism by requesting prompt bicameral action to provide legitimacy for his position. In December, Representative White and Senator Clarence C. Dill, the newly elected Democrat from Washington, introduced in their respective chambers similar bills to control radio. These measures included many of the recommendations advanced at the Fourth National Radio Conference. Instead of stipulating the creation of an advisory committee, however, the new proposals specified the establishment of a national radio commission. This panel, which in reality the Department of Commerce had suggested to White, was to advise and assist the secretary of commerce in administering the law, studying scientific problems, and evaluating international communications treaties. The body also would hear appeals of Commerce Department decisions from aggrieved parties. By introducing a national commission and an appeals provision Secretary Hoover hoped simultaneously to disarm his critics and gain passage of a measure firmly establishing regulation as a duty of the Department of Commerce.[14]

The White bill, which began as House Resolution 5589, underwent two evolutionary changes before its passage by the House of Representatives. On 9 February, it was amended and reintroduced as House Resolution 9108. This new effort encompassed a strengthened appeals section and an adjustment of nomenclature from national radio commission to the Federal Radio Commission (FRC). The FRC would consist of five members appointed by the president from five regional zones. In House Resolution 9108 the secretary of commerce would have administrative charge of radio and would refer difficult matters to the FRC for their advice and assistance.[15]

In considering the new proposal, the House Committee on Merchant Marine and Fisheries confronted another problem. House Resolution 9108 entered the confusing domain of patent law with a section declaring it unlawful to import foreign wireless tubes or apparatus into the United States. After a careful appraisal of the situation, the members skillfully skirted the issue by concluding that they lacked jurisdiction to deal with the patent structure. As a consequence, on 3 March White introduced another almost identical bill (House Resolution 9971) eliminating the offending provision. It was reported out of the committee on 15 March, and on the same day passed the House of Representatives by a vote of 218 to 124.[16]

Despite these several transformations, all three remarkably similar proposals drew heavily upon the Department of Commerce's experience as well as the recommendations of the national radio conferences. Secretary Hoover noted that the bills contained eight distinctive features. They firmly established the federal government's jurisdiction over all phases of radio. They created an administrative organization which exercised control by requiring that a license be issued as a prerequisite to the operation of a transmitting station. The bills retained complete supervision of channels within the Commerce Department and declared that there should be no ownership or vested rights allowed in wavelengths. They recognized the public interest as paramount in all forms of radio activity. They granted authority to issue or refuse a license to the secretary of commerce while establishing an appeals provision as a check upon arbitrary power. Both attempts at legislation also provided for the formation of a national commission. They required applicants to obtain a construction permit in advance. Finally, the propositions authorized revocation of licenses for failure to operate or for violation of the law. In effect, the measures granted wide discretionary power to the secretary of commerce and firmly established radio supervision as a province of the Department of Commerce.[17]

As in the past, the White bill in its final form received widespread support from numerous government departments, the National Association of Broadcasters, and listener associations. Here, however, the similarities stopped. Whereas previously the Commerce Department's prominent position had gone unchallenged, now, primarily as an outgrowth of the McDonald assault, many used the hearings as a forum from which to attack the department. It scarcely needs to be added that most were promoting their own interests at the same time. Radio control was becoming an important question, and in the United States this meant it was becoming a political issue.

Manifestations of the opposition confronting the bill were both subtle and far-reaching. Representative Sol Bloom, Democrat from New York, demurred, stating that so vast a responsibility as broadcast regulation should not be bestowed upon an already "overburdened" secretary of commerce. Edwin L. Davis, Democratic representative from Tennessee, challenged both the monopoly and commission provisions contained in the White bill. While conceding the urgent need for a law to supervise the medium, Davis nonetheless insisted that the restraint of trade and illegal combination section should be more stringent. He observed that the measure that had been considered in the previous session had allowed the secretary of commerce the right to refuse a license to any person or corporation who in his opinion was attempting to monopolize radio. Davis contended that House Resolution 9971, unlike its predecessor, had been weakened because the department could act only after a federal court had ruled a violation existed.[18]

In addition to this criticism, Representative Davis also argued that the White bill gave too much power to an administrative official. Leaning heavily upon the McDonald proposal, Davis suggested that an independent agency modeled after the Interstate Commerce Commission be established to oversee all forms of communications. The Davis amendment received much support and tremendous publicity.[19]

Secretary Hoover fought to contain the assault on the Commerce Department's position. He argued that the creation of a separate panel was unjustified because such a body would merely duplicate the work of the ICC and the FTC. He added that regulation was, in most respects, a purely administrative affair best performed by a cabinet official. While Hoover managed to defeat Davis' amendments in the House of Representatives, thereby effectively containing the threat until the passage of House Resolution 9971, other attacks continued.[20]

At exactly the same time that Davis was advancing his proposals, numerous groups began to maneuver for position. The bloc formed by universities and colleges operating stations, which was allied with the Agriculture Department and the land grant colleges, wasted no time in seeking to enhance their place in the electromagnetic spectrum. Working quietly and behind the scenes, the educators attempted to secure increased power and more channels, while demanding preferential treatment over those private companies engaging in broadcasting. Dean Harry J. C. Umberger, director of extension at Kansas State Agricultural College, lamented that while "radio had demonstrated its utility as a means of disseminating educational information," the field had been completely dominated by commercial concerns.[21]

On the other hand, independent owners voiced their own frustrations. Norman Baker, manager of KTNT (Muscatine, Iowa) and head of the organization the American Broadcaster, claimed that the legislation had been designed to eliminate the smaller broadcasters. He charged that the "radio trust" was out to get the "little fellow." Baker, claiming to represent over twenty small stations, opposed the creation of a commission (whose members, he charged, would surely be trust-appointed), argued against the licensing of transmitters, and demanded a full-scale investigation of the industry. White reported that the Baker attack negatively influenced the voting of several House members from the Midwest.[22]

In addition to the Baker assault and the backstage maneuvering of the educational broadcasters, the legislation faced the formidable hurdle of mounting labor opposition. The Chicago Federation of Labor had been planning to create an outlet but was refused an operating channel and a license by the Department of Commerce. The latter, following the recommendations of the Fourth National Radio Conference had declined to act on the CFL request in light of the thirty existing stations and backlog of twenty additional applications for permits in the Chicago area. The CFL retaliated by claiming that the White bill presented a "menace to the people." They warned that "the Secretary of Commerce would become more powerful than the President" if such a measure passed. They were joined in their criticism by the Trade Association of Schenectady, which also voiced labor opposition to certain aspects of the radio bill. H. M. Merrill, chairman of the association, contended that a "Secretary of Commerce, allied with the enemies of labor," could make it impossible for labor ideas and programs to be broadcast. Merrill cautioned White that since so much opposition had developed, the matter should not be rushed through Congress.[23]

While White disregarded Merrill's advice, the Senate, for all practical purposes, did not. The majority of the senators, according to the New York *Times*, expressed little interest in radio law. Low attendance at the hearings conducted by the Committee on Interstate Commerce (five members out of fifteen) reflected considerable sentiment to defer the whole affair until the next session. Many concluded the senators' negligible activity stemmed from their lack of expertise in technical matters. However, congressional knowledge had rarely been a prerequisite to voting. More importantly and more to the point, most senators had little reason to show concern; they lacked a political need to act. Moreover, in an election year with a third of the Senate up for reelection, many desired to become reacquainted with their constituents. Thus, one can easily understand the dearth of agitation for the immediate passage of the White bill felt by the majority of senators. By March, Senate inactivity had ceased to matter because the industry took the situation into its own hands.[24]

The manager of the Los Angeles *Times'* broadcasting station, KHJ, John D. Daggett—affectionately known to thousands of West Coast listeners as "Uncle John"—erroneously observed in the summer of

1925 that Secretary Hoover held "the future of radio in the palm of his hand." Unbeknownst to Uncle John, as well as to countless others, negotiations were being conducted between the telephone and radio groups to mold their own future by establishing the perimeters of broadcasting. As Harry P. Davis had indicated previously, a clear definition of the situation remained a prerequisite to the enactment of intelligent legislation. In effect, the "tendency toward consolidation," which had been so much a part of American life since the Civil War, had come to broadcasting.[25]

The industrial maneuvering pivoted on interpretation of agreement B, a section of the cross-licensing accords drawn up fully two years before the medium expanded. Like many diplomatic and legislative pronouncements, it contained ambiguous language, so much so that the participants could not agree on an interpretation to delineate "fields of interest" in broadcasting. The telephone company accepted that agreement B allowed it exclusive rights in transmitting programs for tolls or advertising as well as the franchise for sale of receivers to tenants of apartments or hotels. The radio group, according to this interpretation, was denied any use of the telephone company long-lines system. While AT&T did not contest the right of its rivals to manufacture and sell sets, it did claim that loudspeakers, head phones, and amplifiers of vacuum tubes constituted essentially nonradio devices and could be produced and sold by AT&T alone even if such accessories were to be used for broadcasting. The radio group, on the other hand, claimed exclusive rights in wireless telegraphy and defined its other privileges to include the manufacture of parts and receivers for broadcasting, the acquisition of advertising, and use of the AT&T wire system.[26]

In 1923, AT&T launched its offensive by claiming that the agreements even allowed its subsidiary, Western Electric, to assemble receiving sets. This constituted a direct affront to its adversaries, which considered manufacturing their own special province. Furthermore, AT&T challenged its opponents by building facilities and connecting these and other existing stations to its lines in many areas where RCA affiliates were already operating or under construction. In Washington, D.C., for example, RCA had already begun a station when AT&T announced plans to establish a new outlet to cover the capital area. With the naval transmitter, NAA, located in Arlington, Virginia, this meant that there would be three facilities in the area. RCA interpreted AT&T's challenge as clearly intended to limit the effectiveness of its outlet by forcing the radio group to share the available operating time and by compelling it to compete for available talent for programming.[27]

The radio group's first inclination was to stand and fight the telephone company on its own ground. Leaning heavily upon the recommendations of the First National Radio Conference to prohibit advertising over the air, RCA sought unsuccessfully to have the Commerce Department intervene against WEAF for implementing "toll" broadcasting. When it became obvious that this strategy had failed, the alliance reexamined its priorities and changed its *modus operandi*. Since RCA was so firmly entrenched in the lucrative business of selling receivers, Young and Sarnoff cautioned that there was little need to respond overtly to the AT&T attacks. Instead, they both urged their associates to follow a "wait and see" policy. As a part of its holding strategy, they sought arbitration to resolve the dispute over agreement B. Through this process they hoped to define the issues more clearly and thereby delineate the boundaries of each faction's rights.[28]

After much maneuvering in the summer and fall of 1923, the fear of public censure drove the competing groups to seek some realistic approach to the conflict by turning to arbitration. The cross-licensing agreements provided the machinery. On 20 May 1924, after much delay, hearings began before a single referee, Roland W. Boyden of the Boston law firm of Ropes, Gray, Boyden, and Perkins. The parties bound themselves to the referee's findings.[29]

The "Draft Decision" of Boyden's report, which appeared on 13 November 1924, represented a substantial victory for RCA, General Electric, and Westinghouse. Its scope encompassed a wide range of topics, including the manufacture and sale of vacuum tubes, receiving sets, and loudspeakers; the distribution of hotel and apartment house systems; and the implementation of broadcasting. While Boyden emphasized the inadequacy of agreement B to cover the uses and practices developed since 1920, he nonetheless upheld the radio group position almost *in toto*. AT&T, however, quickly recovered from the unfavorable verdict. The firm contended that the cross-licensing agreements were an illegal conspiracy in restraint of trade; hence, AT&T could not be held to a ruling that condoned illegal action.[30]

The Boyden decision forced both organizations to enter into substantive negotiations. Moreover, both sides, like the navy and the Commerce Department before them, wished to avoid the open confrontation necessary to gain a victory sweeping enough to cripple their adversary. In 1925, after innumerable conferences and explorations, the outline of a settlement upon which broadcasting would be organized began to take shape. Gradually, the prevailing animosity subsided and a spirit of compromise slowly invaded the bargaining.

It was symptomatic of all radio developments that the events shaping the final denouement had been at work for some time. From the moment that AT&T entered broadcasting, there had been substantial internal dissension over the propriety of such exploitation. Many executives considered such an activity a heretical departure from the real mission of the company—the telephone. Events in 1924 reinforced this view and created ample support in the firm for a scheme advanced by David Sarnoff.[31]

The first predicament cited by the antibroadcasting faction to symbolize the problems evoked when the company deviated from its fundamental mission was the "Kaltenborn incident." In 1924, Hans von Kaltenborn, associate editor of the Brooklyn *Daily Eagle*, examined U.S.-Soviet relations over WEAF. In this program, Kaltenborn criticized Secretary of State Charles Evans Hughes for his handling of Soviet overtures to the Department of State. An angry Hughes called up AT&T and "laid down the law." The telephone company, having originally created its "toll" facilities with little idea of taking responsibility for what went out over the air, now began to have second thoughts.[32]

Another and equally frustrating matter was the Federal Trade Commission's investigation of the industry. The inquiry produced uneasiness and generated a great deal of adverse commentary about the telephone company, criticism that grated against the psychological grain of the more traditional element in the firm which opposed conducting business in this fashion.[33]

Finally, the apparent AT&T victory over WHN (Ridgewood, New York) posed additional significance. The telephone company threatened a court action against this station for violation of patents and failure to pay a license fee. The move produced an outcry in the press charging that the "radio trust" was attempting to bring WHN into line. In effect, the broadcasting activities of AT&T were threatening to produce a new villain for Americans in the 1920s, the telephone company.[34]

Against such a background, the pivotal figure in the negotiations with AT&T, David Sarnoff, continued the struggle to organize broadcasting. After adroitly exploiting the unpleasantries bombarding the telephone company, Sarnoff implemented a two-pronged plan to resolve the conflict. First, he suggested that AT&T disengage itself from broadcasting. Next, he proposed the creation of a national company to distribute programs over the telephone company wire system. To make his scheme more attractive to AT&T, he even conceded it the right to manufacture receiving sets. His skill in bargaining, coupled with the growing uneasiness held by some factions inside AT&T, seemed to have brought a resolution of the conflict in sight.[35]

In the summer and fall of 1925, however, the radio group experienced its own setback when Westinghouse attempted to create its own network. After a capital outlay of more than $3.5 million on broadcasting in the preceding five years, the firm was understandably anxious to maintain a secure position in any settlement with AT&T. Harry P. Davis, Westinghouse vice-president proposed that the company establish a "Mid-Continent Chain" composed of six newspaper affiliates in the Midwest. Using a combination of short-wave transmission and interconnection, he envisioned joining WMAQ (Chicago *Daily News*), WWJ (Detroit *News*), WEAP (Fort Worth *Dispatch*), WDAF (Kansas City *Star*), WHAS (Louisville *Courier-Journal*), and KSD (Saint Louis *Post Dispatch*).[36]

Because he saw Westinghouse increasingly overshadowed by RCA in the negotiations, Davis insisted upon an independent role for his organization, owner of the premier station KDKA. His argument had considerable persuasive power. He emphasized that while the chain could generate substantial revenue from advertising because of the newspapers' expertise in exploiting this resource, the news media, of all the factions, would be least inclined to misuse the sale of air time. Their experience in the field had taught them valuable and lasting lessons. In addition, Davis cited their considerable influence with the federal government and politicians as the factor most likely to ensure the success of this undertaking.[37]

Even though it was never implemented, the Davis proposition served its purpose well by giving Westinghouse considerable leverage with GE and RCA. First, it brought Westinghouse more fully into the negotiations, which up to then had been a Sarnoff effort. Secondly it protected the Westinghouse outlets in Pittsburgh, Chicago, and Springfield-Boston, while preserving their identity.[38]

With unity assured, a settlement of the dispute became possible. In January 1926, the board of directors of RCA agreed to the formation of a new firm to be jointly owned by the three radio group associates with RCA controlling 50 percent; General Electric, 30 percent; and Westinghouse, 20 percent. The company would broadcast for revenues while maintaining studios and producing fare to be nationally distributed over the AT&T wire system. Due to the activities of Harry P. Davis, the partners agreed that while a chain was to be created, no station of that network would lose its identity. Despite the projection that the undertaking would operate for the first three years at a deficit of almost $1.5 million, it was expected that the creation of such an organization would increase the prestige of the participants, provide complete entertainment and continuous operations, increase public interest in broadcasting, reduce competition, increase sales of receivers, promote radio as a key factor in merchandizing and publicity, and reduce the operating costs of individual companies.[39]

Late spring brought news of the final accord, as the former combatants issued a revised license agreement establishing a clear demarcation line between radio communications on the one hand and public service telephony on the other. In May the "Service Agreement," detailing ways the radio group could use AT&T's wire system, and the "Option Agreement," deeding WEAF to RCA, virtually had reached their final form.[40]

AT&T agreed to this arrangement because it would be able to disengage itself from operating broadcasting stations and hence exit from public scrutiny. The firm received $1 million for selling WEAF: in addition, it discontinued its Washington, D.C., affiliate, WCAP. More importantly, AT&T promised to provide the wire services for chain hook-ups. This last concession was not totally altruistic, however; it was estimated that the telephone bill for the new establishment's first year of operation alone would be over $800,000.

When the National Broadcasting Company finally achieved incorporation on 9 September 1926, it became the telephone company's largest customer.[41]

The organization of broadcasting in 1926 heightened the necessity for federal control to establish order in the ether. But, whereas the formation of NBC had been primarily a New York solution to the problem of organization, the resolution of the legislative impasse was to be accomplished by the Chicago approach to government-industry relations.[42]

The Crazy Man from Chicago

In April, while negotiators for the radio and telephone groups were striving to adjust their respective "spheres of interest," the U.S. District Court of northern Illinois stripped away the meticulously constructed facade of power that the secretary of commerce had created. The decision was rendered in a case brought by the Justice Department against the Zenith Corporation of Chicago. WJAZ, owned and operated by Zenith, precipitated charges of "pirating" a wavelength and operating for longer periods of time than specified in its license.[1]

The firm had been authorized to transmit Thursday evenings on 930 kHz, but in December 1925 it jumped to an unoccupied Canadian frequency of 910 kHz, after failing to obtain a clear channel or secure permission for more time from the Commerce Department. The department could ill-afford the internationally embarrassing incident, the first "air piracy" case in its history, and it therefore charged Zenith with criminal violation of the Radio Act of 1912. Judge James H. Wilkerson, however, ruled the provisions of that law "too general, indefinite, and ambiguous" to justify criminal prosecution. Moreover, he added that the Commerce Department lacked discretionary authority and could not allocate channels, assign hours of operation, refuse licenses, or limit the power of outlets. His decision destroyed the entire extralegal structure that Secretary Hoover had so painstakingly fashioned.[2]

Eugene McDonald, president of Zenith, had challenged the department in order to force judicial clarification of the broadcasting situation and thus to hasten definitive legislative action. McDonald had gained a reputation as a "crazy man" among his Chicago business associates through his varied, seemingly illogical reactions to industrial problems. In reality, he always followed a well-thought-out game plan designed to confuse his opposition and achieve his own ends. The Zenith case, then, was not an isolated occurrence prompted solely by one company's frustration with the Department of Commerce; rather, McDonald followed the lead of other boldly defiant Chicago-based firms which had chosen to force federal intervention. Swift, Armour, and other meat packers, as well as the Chicago utilities magnate Samuel Insull, each had previously rebelled in order to bring about government regulation for their corporations. Sol Bloom, Democratic representative from New York, summed up the Chicago approach to government-industry relations in his observation that the radio trade was trying to create chaos in the air so that the authorities would intervene and supervise broadcasting. James C. Harboard, president of RCA, foresaw the same result. He remarked that while the Zenith decision "was unfortunate in one sense . . . it might serve to impress Congress with the great need of sound radio legislation."[3]

McDonald was not blindly calling for just any type of regulation, however; he wanted to displace the secretary of commerce from his dominant position. Reiterating the opinion he had advanced in the winter of 1924–25, McDonald argued that "one-man control of radio with the Secretary of Commerce as supreme czar" could not be tolerated. He predicted that "if the White bill becomes a law, Mr. Hoover will absolutely control broadcasting in the United States." In place of one-man rule, the Chicago businessman urged the creation of an independent commission to oversee radio. He advised the lawmakers that "almost without exception" broadcasters supported this approach.[4]

Secretary Hoover understood the critical nature of the Zenith case. He, like McDonald, utilized the ruling to pressure Congress for action. In contrast to the McDonald proposal, however, he championed the White bill to assure implementation of his own legislative plan. Stressing the urgent need for an immediate decision, the Department of Commerce indicated that other businessmen were ready to follow WJAZ's lead by changing to more desirable wavelengths. Hoover warned that if all owners randomly selected their own frequencies the immediate result would be a loss of effective control and the ultimate result would be total chaos, constant disruption for listeners, amateurs, commercial concerns, and the military services. To avoid this impending disaster, Hoover urged Congress to pass the White bill providing the Commerce Department with the discretionary authority necessary to combat the congestion. Without such a measure, he said, the secretary of commerce would lose command of broadcasting, and anarchy would surely follow.[5]

By the time the Zenith decision neared its final denouement in the courts, Hoover's previous virtual invulnerability on broadcasting matters had been shattered. In May 1926, Senate inactivity gave way to a challenge to the secretary of commerce which threatened to displace his department from its domination of radio. On 3 May, the first frontal assault came from the Senate Committee on Interstate Commerce, when Senator Clarence C. Dill of Washington introduced a revision of a previous bill calling for the creation of an independent commission.[6]

The Senate committee deemed radio a service of great consequence and interest to most segments of the public, and though it recognized many substantial objections to the creation of additional federal agencies, it stated that Congress was impelled to establish an independent panel to supervise broadcasting. Echoing the sentiments of Eugene McDonald, the senators furthermore observed that the power of radio control "is fraught with such great possibilities that it should not be entrusted to any one man nor to any administrative department of government."[7]

Relying heavily upon McDonald's ideas, Senator Dill argued that Congress "must steer the legislative ship between the Scylla of too much regulation and the Charybdis of the grasping selfishness of private monopoly." The commission would issue licenses when "public convenience, interest, or necessity" dictated and would be given complete jurisdiction:

1. To classify apparatus and operators
2. To prescribe the nature of service to be rendered
3. To determine the location of stations
4. To regulate the purity and sharpness of emissions and the equipment
5. To establish areas to be served

6.   To make inspections of stations and apparatus
7.   To impose regulations consistent with law to prevent interference between facilities
8.   To regulate stations on railroad trains
9.   To control chain broadcasting
10. To administer outlets where a charge was made to listeners

In effect, each passage in the House bill containing the phrase "secretary of commerce" was replaced in the Senate version by the words "independent radio commission." The Zenith decision had removed most of the secretary of commerce's assumed authority; the Dill revision sought to deny such power to the Department of Commerce once and for all. This legislative challenge to Department of Commerce jurisdiction, the first since the interdepartmental struggle during the early days of the Harding administration, appeared more ominous with each passing hour.[8]

What underlay the Senate proposal was presidential politics. As the 1928 election approached, internal divisions within both major parties intensified, and the prospect of a "radio campaign" thrust the bill into the congressional arena. A strange alliance was formed and played havoc with the proposal. Many Democrats could support a commission because they felt one-man domination of broadcasting meant closing the airwaves to the party out of power. Senator Joseph T. Robinson, Democratic minority leader from Arkansas, took up the cry and charged President Coolidge with attempting to maintain authority over the medium through the secretary of commerce. Robinson declared that administrative control of radio would mean "full publicity for Coolidge's speeches, while political opposition would be deprived of the right to speak through the ether waves."[9]

The other part of the alliance consisted of Republicans who had always opposed Hoover and certain other presidential aspirants. Several Republican members of the Committee on Interstate Commerce envisioned themselves as prospective nominees and, viewing Secretary Hoover as the frontrunner to head the Republican ticket, regarded him as the man to beat. One such aspirant was James E. Watson, chairman of the Committee on Interstate Commerce and majority leader in the Senate, who strongly opposed the nomination of the secretary of commerce for president and "sat down" to defeat him as Republican standard-bearer. Watson pushed the commission through his committee in order to deprive Hoover of the advantage of "advertising himself" over the airwaves.[10]

Among Republicans, the traditional, small, but vocal anti-Hoover faction composed of older Progressives and representatives from the farm bloc increased in power and membership in direct proportion to Coolidge's disinclination to head the ticket in 1928. The result was strong Senate support for an independent panel to remove the Commerce Department from its main role in governing radio. Two days after the introduction of the Dill bill, the National Association of Broadcasters, demonstrating its grasp of the legislative scene, reported that the upper chamber would pass a measure creating a separate body. The NAB reminded its members that the House of Representatives had committed itself to placing authority in the hands of the secretary of commerce—and the result, the organization predicted, would be deadlock.[11]

Secretary Hoover did not lack support in the struggle with the Senate. There was great sentiment against giving supervision to a commission. The "Darling of the Gods," Calvin Coolidge, after numerous difficulties with the Shipping Board, the Tariff Board, and the Federal Trade Commission, opposed establishing more federal bureaus and thereby increasing government expenditures. He threatened to veto the Senate bill if it passed both houses of Congress.[12]

Numerous politicians, broadcasters, amateurs, and scientists joined the president in his dislike for a commission. One of their number, Senator Edward I. Edwards, New Jersey Democrat, flatly stated that he would not support any "measure which sets up an independent bureau of control." Senator Hiram Bingham, Connecticut Republican, also opposed the creation of another agency on the ground that such regulation was more inefficient than one-man supervision. W. G. Cowles, vice-president of the Travelers Insurance Company, owner and operator of the largest outlet in Connecticut, observed that the "word commission strikes terror in the hearts of those who are interested in the development of broadcasting." Henry B. Joy, an industrialist and amateur from Detroit, opposed "government by commission" because there was no one to "shoot at." At the annual

RCA dinner in 1926, Michael I. Pupin, inventor, engineer, and the Horatio Alger of the scientific community, heatedly declared, "The Senate is wrong . . . when it proposed to solve a complicated scientific problem in its own way without any knowledge of the science . . . my message to the Senate is—Hands Off!"[13]

Secretary Hoover adroitly capitalized on these feelings. He noted that any government department seeking to regulate broadcasting would perform three functions. The first two, minimizing interference among operators and advancing the radio art, were duties best administrated by a cabinet official. The third, determining who might transmit, should be placed in the hands of a commission which, during its periodic meetings, could also ensure that the secretary of commerce was handling the situation properly. The panel's infrequent meetings would drastically curtail its projected expense. Hoover never tired of pointing out that he had always supported a commission to check the power of the secretary of commerce. He stoutly maintained, however, that the Department of Commerce could best administer any radio law.[14]

To curry sentiment in his favor, Secretary Hoover had created a vast constituency supporting his plan. The White bill had evolved from four national conferences, representing deliberations by all segments of the industry. Besides, the Department of Commerce had stood the test of time; it represented a known commodity, while the commission was an untried experiment. In addition, many corporate executives publicly supported the secretary of commerce out of fear of retaliation should the White bill be enacted. Thus for differing reasons businessmen, bureaucrats, and listener associations backed the approach taken in the House of Representatives. Outside of the upper chamber it was difficult to find many who disagreed with the *Pennsylvania Farmer*, a Philadelphia newspaper, which urged Congress to "Let Hoover Do It." The American Radio Relay League even suggested that, in the event of further Senate procrastination, Secretary Hoover should continue to govern by forming new extralegal agreements at yet another national meeting. Because of the combination of these sentiments, Hoover was able to hold the House of Representatives in line and, with the support of the president, contain the Senate assault.[15]

The Department of Commerce's policy of "containment" of the Dill bill, however, resulted in consequences unforeseen by Hoover and his aides. Many special interests, including the NAB, the military services, and the educational broadcasters, took the congressional impasse as an opportunity to advance their own positions. They were in some ways encouraged in their covetousness because many congressmen willingly incorporated suggestions into the bills in the hope of undermining Hoover's constituency. For example, the NAB desired legal protection of established interests. In support of this argument, Dr. Alfred N. Goldsmith affirmed that the pioneers in broadcasting should be considered first when the time came to real-locate wavelengths among competing groups. Paul B. Klugh, executive secretary of the NAB, noted that too much attention had been focused upon the question of determining a regulatory power for radio; he cautioned that the real question, that of priority, had been overlooked in the debate. He continued, "The man who has been in the business, who has spent his money," could not be ignored. Representative White, who was totally opposed to including a priority clause in the House bill, nonetheless shifted his position somewhat as a result of the congressional stalemate. In November, he noted that any licensing authority would have to consider priority and length of service when administering the new law.[16]

Like the NAB, the military services protected their sphere by obtaining a special section in the bill. Both the navy and the army were anxious to include a provision protecting the Interdepartmental Radio Advisory Committee. After some deliberation, White and Dill agreed to this plan and altered their measures to include sections giving the president the power to select wavelengths for the military services. In effect, the proposal provided the first legal sanction for the IRAC.[17]

Another group, the educational establishment working through the Association of College and University Broadcasting Stations and allied with the Department of Agriculture, also tried to profit from the deadlock. They continued to seek preferential treatment in the assignment of wavelengths and division of time. Previously, the collegiate broadcasters had encountered stiff opposition to their proposals in the House of Representatives. Wallace White had argued that, if they were given special treatment, "it would be only a short while before Congress would be the arena in which labor organizations, amateurs, religious bodies and all manner of groups and interests would be fighting for the same special privilege." Furthermore, he opposed appointing academicians to the commission created by the House bill.[18]

In the Senate, however, the educators found much more success. Because Clyde W. Warburton, director of extension for the Department of Agriculture, recognized the increased maneuverability that the Dill bill offered the colleges and universities, he advised them to abandon their strategy of behind-the-scenes politics and to strike a more agressive posture. He contended that Dill, unlike White, desired "the providing of opportunities" for educational outlets. In addition, he intimated that the Committee on Interstate Commerce would be very responsive to their overtures. By working through E. O. Holland, president of the State College of Washington and an old friend of Senator Watson, the Agriculture Department and the educational broadcasters secured a paragraph in the Dill bill recognizing both their special contribution to the medium and the need to protect their service from competition with commercial interests.[19]

On 2 July 1926, the Dill bill, creating an independent commission, passed the Senate. Immediately after its passage, the House and Senate formed a joint committee for the purpose of reaching a compromise between the two proposals. Since the legislative session would end on 3 July, the committee decided to let a decision on radio control run over into the next session. Wallace White indicated that the great differences among the members, as well as the session's approaching adjournment, made immediate agreement impossible. He also observed that opponents of the Senate action had "a real job on their hands" if they were to defeat the scheme advanced in the upper chamber.[20]

Secretary Hoover assumed an offensive posture when confronted with the congressional challenge and subsequent stalemate. To some degree, Congress actually aided him in his move; its failure to enact the most urgent, if not the most important, bill before the First Session of the Sixty-ninth Congress aroused widespread antagonism. The criticism that had been aimed at the Department of

Commerce dissipated; now lawmakers became targets for numerous newspaper editorials and objects of public censure for their inability to act on the radio issue.[21]

By capitalizing on this shift in blame for the sad state in which broadcasting found itself, Hoover managed to produce another advantage in promoting the Department of Commerce stance. In June, the secretary of commerce had asked the attorney general for an opinion on the Radio Act of 1912. The department maintained that the Intercity Radio case, which stated that the secretary of commerce did have some discretionary authority, and the Zenith case, which stated that he had none, were in conflict. On 2 June, the Justice Department unofficially informed Secretary Hoover that it agreed with the Zenith case; under the Radio Act of 1912, the Department of Commerce had no discretionary power. With the White and Dill measures before Congress, the Justice Department decided against publicizing its decision. William J. Donovan, assistant to the attorney general and a personal friend of Secretary Hoover, contended that if legislation were enacted, "there will be no occasion to send out the opinion. . . . Should the bill fail, it would be of assistance to the Department of Commerce to have the opinion."[22]

Five days after the session adjourned, the Department of Commerce urged the attorney general to publish the opinion. On 10 July, the complete text of the ruling, stripping the secretary of commerce of discretionary power in supervising the medium, was published in the New York *Times.* On 13 July, David B. Carson, director of the Bureau of Navigation, instructed all personnel that the Department of Commerce, guided by the opinion of the attorney general, would cease to prescribe the hours of operation for broadcasters and would issue licenses to all applicants who wished to establish transmitters. As Hoover indicated, "with a little encouragement" the whole matter could be settled.[23]

From July, when Secretary Hoover abandoned all efforts to guide broadcasting, until December, when Congress reconvened, the "lid blew off," fulfilling most of Hoover's dire predictions. As a result, the electromagnetic spectrum became a "Hertzian bedlam." Not since the "take-off" in broadcasting during the Harding administration had the number of outlets increased so rapidly. By

31 December 1926, there were 719 stations operating in the United States, as compared to 528 at the end of 1925. In addition to this great proliferation, the radio inspectors from the nation's nine districts reported that sixty-three facilities had increased power and another sixty-two had changed wavelengths.[24]

Facing the prospect of chaos engulfing broadcasting and having no hope for remedial legislation until Congress convened in December, the National Association of Broadcasters expostulated that "broadcasters must regulate themselves." The NAB warned that owners who changed their frequencies or hours of operation were committing a grave mistake and jeopardizing the entire industry. The organization urged its members to sign a "certificate of promise" to ensure that they would operate only on their designated channels until Congress could devise some solution. In the first week of implementing this policy, over 150 businessmen signed the certificate.[25]

In a similar effort, representatives of the Radio Manufacturing Association, the NAB, the American Radio Relay League, and the Associated Manufacturers of Electrical Supplies formed a Radio Protective Committee "to war against anarchy in the ether." Orrin E. Dunlap, Jr., radio editor of the New York *Times*, suggested that the president intervene to bolster industry cooperation by urging firms to maintain their assigned wavelengths until Congress enacted a radio bill. Secretary Hoover, the ever-vigilant monitor of policies of the industry and a vociferous supporter of the "certificate of promise" and the Protective Committee, quickly eliminated this suggestion. He contended that "it might even dull the activites of the agencies that are at work" if the president were to become involved.[26]

The established interests were saved, however, from relying on only the industry's efforts and the threat of presidential intervention. A decision in the Circuit Court of Cook County Illinois, provided additional protection for those plagued by interference and wave piracy. The case resulted when WGES, operated by the Coyne Electrical School, jumped to the wavelength of WGN, The Chicago *Tribune* outlet. On 17 November, Judge Francis S. Wilson held that, in the absence of a congressional mandate, WGN had acquired rights by reason of the "outlay and expenditure of money" and that "priority of time creates a superiority of right." The court ruled the WGES could not interfere with WGN within a radius of 100 miles. Stephen B. Davis, of the Department of Commerce, contended that a ruling following up this decision in a higher court would protect businessmen against wavelength piracy.[27]

When the legislators assembled for the short session of the Sixty-ninth Congress, they faced a debate on broadcasting that had been intensified by the prospect of continued chaos and confusion. In the interim since July, congressmen had been besieged by letters and petitions from constituents and listener associations. Many lawmakers also announced that their mail was being inflated daily by the demands for prompt action on radio legislation. Senator David I. Walsh, Massachusetts Democrat, declared that further delay in action would force many members to ask for additional appropriations for clerical help to process the incoming mail concerning the issue. Congressmen could readily accept the San Francisco *Chronicle's* assessment that millions of Americans expressed interest in these bills. In Vermont, radio fans forced the State Senate to adopt a resolution instructing their congressional delegation to obtain "prompt passage of a measure to protect owners and users of radio apparatus."[28]

Among broadcasters the prospect of a new law so aggravated internal divisions as to destroy the little harmony that had previously existed. Henry A. Bellows, director of the Washburn-Crosley outlet in Minneapolis, observed that there existed a sharp division among businessmen: many of the small owners who operated solely for advertising feared government regulation, while many of the large organized segments actively courted such intervention. The Radio League of America, under the direction of Norman Baker, reflected the small operators' apprehension and flatly opposed both bills, charging that both were sponsored by "AT&T and five big trusts as well as the NAB." Indeed, Baker claimed that Secretary Hoover always had discriminated systematically against independent owners. However, even among the broadcasters and segments of the industry that supported federal regulation, the question of Department of Commerce control versus supervision by an independent commission occasioned deep divisions. Thus, senators and representatives were besieged by a host of interests clamoring for special consideration on a topic about which the lawmakers knew very little. Naturally enough, their instincts took control, and they sought to compromise, offend as few as possible, and give the problem to someone else.[29]

On 7 December 1926, Secretary Hoover made his last major effort to secure the passage of the White bill. Hoover's interest in regulation was decreasing in inverse proportion to his quest for the Republican presidential nomination. Utilizing his strategic position as secretary of commerce, Hoover poised, ready to launch a campaign to secure his long-sought goal. On the seventh, President Coolidge delivered a message to the Sixty-ninth Congress. The chief executive, relying entirely upon a memorandum prepared by the secretary of commerce, indicated his oppostion to the creation of a commission and emhasized his desire that supervision remain in the Department of Commerce. On the next day, the House and Senate conferees (House—Frank D. Scott of Michigan, Wallace White of Maine, Frederick P. Lahback of New Jersey, and Ladislas Lazaro of Louisiana; Senate—James E. Watson of Indiana, Clarence C. Dill of Washington, and Frank R. Gooding of Idaho) assembled to try to work out an agreement. Their task was made considerably easier because many of the sections in both the White and Dill proposals were the same. Allocation of authority posed the one important exception; they were given the responsibility of deciding whether to favor the Commerce Department or a new, independent agency.[30]

On 21 December a compromise measure emerged; the conferees agreed to a provision that for the period of one year would place supervision in the Federal Radio Commission established by the Senate bill. Although under its terms control of broadcasting would revert from the FRC to the secretary of commerce at the end of that period, the proposal granted the agency wide-ranging powers to stabilize the medium. The lawmakers intended for the panel to classify all stations, assign bands of wavelengths, determine an equitable geographic distribution, regulate interference between transmitters, and develop guidelines for chain operations. In a startling contrast to the Radio Act of 1912, which had provided no provisions for administrative discretion, the conference committee gave the FRC complete authority to establish order in the airwaves.[31]

Equally important, the forty-one provisions of the bill considerably expanded federal power. With tactics designed to remove all existing impediments, the law repealed several prior statutes and congressional resolutions, including the Radio Act of 1912—the earliest practical basis of national control. Because the government's authority had never been precisely delineated, the proposal stipulated that all forms of communications fell under federal juridisdiction. In order to guarantee industry-wide acquiescence, the bill forbade any unit to operate without a permit granted under the terms of the act. Hence, sixty days after its passage, every prior license automatically terminated. All amateurs, business concerns, and broadcasters —roughly 18,000 in all—were compelled to seek new authorization or face criminal prosecution. As a part of each new request, the applicant had to waive any claim to use or own any channel against restraint by the United States. Congress decreed that the existing chaos justified such drastic action.[32]

In other provisions, the conferees developed a comprehensive regulatory standard. The lawmakers correctly assumed that continued routine licensing would contribute to the prevailing chaos. Thus, they rejected the basic standard of the 1912 act that any individual with ample desire and motive should be sanctioned to operate a transmitter. Instead, they substituted a more qualified and conditional permission. Congress ruled that the electromagnetic spectrum represented a valuable natural resource to be conserved as carefully as mineral wealth, water power, farm land, and forest preserves. Consequently, constructing and operating an outlet constituted a privilege rather than a right. According to this interpretation, only licenses serving public interest, convenience, and necessity should be issued; moreover, under no circumstances should applicants secure a vested interest or property right in the ether. While the standard of public interest, convenience, and necessity lacked direct precedent in any federal law, its interpretation constituted the fundamental requirement for securing a permit for many years to come.[33]

The measure also filled many breaches in previous legislation. It limited the term for a commercial license to three years, protected free speech, prohibited the governing body from exercising censorship, restricted monopoly, and provided for the equitable geographic distribution of facilities. Another significant section stipulated equal treatment for all politicians. Thus, if a station provided one candidate a forum, it had to afford a similar opportunity to other office seekers. Finally, the measure continued the crucial sections of the Radio Act of 1912 allowing the president "in times of war or public peril or disaster" to control all stations. The bill, however, applied to private holdings only. Government facilities were exempt from the requirements of the act; the president himself assigned their frequencies and established their classes. In effect, this part permanently ensconced the Interdepartmental Radio Advisory Committee.[34]

The act did protect businessmen against arbitrary administrative actions. Section 16, the appeals provision, provided for complete judicial review of all FRC decisions. In fact, cases were directed to the District of Columbia Court of Appeals, which was authorized to reach an independent judgment regarding the soundness of the agency's rulings. The law also allowed the court to secure additional evidence and to alter or revise the commission's findings. As a result, the court evaluated FRC conclusions and also functioned as an administrative unit.[35]

On 27 January, the members of the conference committee submitted their revised plan to the House and Senate. They warned their colleagues that rejection of their efforts would eliminate the only chance of obtaining legislation during that session of Congress, which would adjourn on 4 March. Secretary Hoover, completely immersed in presidential politics and making preparations for the Republican primaries, offered no objections to the arrangement. Wallace White, while noting that he was far from satisfied, nonetheless indicated that "most of the people in the radio game felt that we worked out a pretty satisfactory result." Accordingly, on 30 January, the House of Representatives accepted the report. It was not until 19 February, however, that the Senate, confronted with bank and farm bills, voted favorably on the measure. Four days later President Coolidge signed what the Washington *Post* labeled the "most important legislation of the session" into law. Broadcasting, at long last, had turned the corner.[36]

7

Turning the Corner

Alfred N. Goldsmith once noted, "There are some years in the development of radio which mark the end of one era and the beginning of another." The year 1927 occasioned just such a turning point in the maturation of the American broadcasting system. Business and government decisions all coalesced in a cycle of mutual influence which initiated wave after wave of intricate action and reaction. The passage of the Radio Act of 1927 provided the means for federal control of the medium at the same time that technological advances ensured the growth and expansion of network radio. The ultimate synchronization of these public and private elements assured that broadcasting could continue its prosperous, almost triumphant expansion.[1]

Seven years after KDKA's first transmission, Congress finally agreed on a comprehensive regulatory scheme. Despite its enthusiastic reception, the 1927 act had several administrative deficiencies. In their zeal to embarrass Secretary Hoover, the lawmakers had purposefully weakened the Federal Radio Commission by dividing its authority, limiting its tenure, curtailing its funds, and failing to confirm its members. Above all, several legislators aimed to strip Hoover of his power over communications and defeat his bid for the presidency. In addition to the lack of congressional support for the FRC, several flukish turns of events, notably various deaths and delays in setting up the agency, created an organizational nightmare for the commissioners. Primarily because of these problems, the FRC's early history represented one of the strangest chapters in American government.

Developments in the private sector directly affected the intricacies of regulation. Regardless of the intentions of Congress, many broadcasting issues progressed toward a resolution determined solely by technical and economic changes. Scientific advances improved transmission and reception to such a point that radios became household necessities, thereby ushering in the age of the mass audience. The medium's vast popularity, in turn, attracted national advertisers to use it as a vehicle for promoting mass consumption and profit. As a direct result of these developments, network operations achieved immediate and long-lasting significance. In fact, Merlin Aylesworth observed, the year 1927 saw broadcasting emerge "squarely on its own feet."[2]

As internal developments solidified, stature of American radio received international recognition. Later in 1927, the first worldwide radio meeting since 1912 convened in Washington, D.C. Under the secretary of commerce's direction, the United States shaped and led the proceedings, thereby ending three decades of British domination of the airwaves. Once order had been imposed within the national industry and in the international sphere, it became imperative to enforce effective federal supervision.

In the crucial year of 1927, the radio act established a sound legal basis for government jurisdiction. In addition, regulation by a commission replaced unilateral control by a cabinet official when the FRC appeared on the federal roster. Following the administrative procedures created by the new law, the bureaucracy began to unravel the tedious frustrations of national officials, businessmen, and listeners alike. As a part of this process, the FRC developed a pattern for supervision of the medium, while the Washington Conference of 1927 definitively proved the United States' domination of international communications. As nebulous conceptualizations and chaotic discord gave way to solid ideas and profit-oriented corporate decisions, the mass audiences, national advertisers, and competitive organizations characteristic of network radio in its heyday began to develop. After the search for order had made way for a period of more stable, if less flamboyant, evolution, the American broadcasting system assumed a recognizable form.[3]

The success of the Radio Act of 1927 depended neither upon its platitudes and ringing declarations nor even upon the intentions of Congress; rather, the Federal Radio Commission constituted its main advantage. From the very beginning, however, the panel encountered an overwhelming series of obstacles which almost ruined it in its infancy. Indeed, so great were the hindrances during its first year that one might marvel that the beleaguered unit accomplished anything at all.

After its inception, the new bureau operated under restraints imposed by a jealous Congress sensitive to every political current and trend. With caution typical of the legislative branch prior to a presidential election year, the lawmakers divided authority between the Commerce Department and the FRC to forestall any possible misuse of power. To limit the president's potential for unduly biasing the commission through purely partisan appointments, Congress required Senate consent for all of his selections. Moreover, the chief executive was required to choose one representative from each of five designated geographic zones. According to other limitations, not more than three members could belong to the same political party. Other provisions forbade the president to choose any individual with an interest in companies operating telegraph, telephone, or broadcasting stations or those manufacturing or selling any radio equipment. By creating six-year, staggered terms and by stipulating the other geographic, political, and financial controls, the lawmakers hoped to defuse the possibility of a partisan body using its rulings unfairly in order to influence business or politics.[4]

Although the FRC maintained all licensing authority for one year, the Department of Commerce retained important duties during that time. The department received all applications for licenses, even though it could not act upon them. Moreover, it kept other significant technical and supervisory functions, including authority to inspect stations, examine operators, and investigate violations of the act. In the election year, Congress missed few opportunities to undermine Secretary Hoover's power by resolutely scrutinizing communications.[5]

Given the difficulties created by these limitations, any future success hinged on the men who would be appointed to the FRC. Many observers declared that the members of the panel must "know their stuff." Rear Admiral Stanford C. Hooper suggested that one or two lawyers, a couple of experienced technicians, and one knowledgeable businessman would make an ideal contingent. But many others wondered aloud if talented individuals might even consider serving in governmental positions that would lose all power after only one year. President Coolidge once again consulted Herbert Hoover for assistance in finding them.[6]

The secretary of commerce recommended a remarkable group to the president. In every case the appointees remained deeply committed to the broadcasting system Hoover had fashioned over the course of the preceding seven years. By handpicking the members of the FRC, Hoover not only maintained control of the situation but also ensured that the new law would be properly administered. The designated chairman, Rear Admiral William H. G. Bullard, had enjoyed a long and distinguished career in communications. He had organized the Department of Electrical Engineering at the Naval Academy and had served as superintendent of the Naval Radio Service from 1912 to 1916, and as director of naval communications first in 1919 and then again in 1921. He had also helped create the Radio Corporation of America. Colonel John F. Dillon, an 1894 alumnus of the Army Signal School, had continued his military career until 1912. Afterwards, he joined the Department of Commerce, where he held the post of federal inspector in the Bureau of Navigation from 1919 to 1927. At the time of his nomination, he was supervising the Sixth Radio District in San Francisco. Orestes H. Caldwell, an editor for the McGraw-Hill Publishing Company of New York, had been an engineer and technical writer. In the early years of his career, Dr. Henry A. Bellows a Harvard Ph.D. in English, edited and taught. From 1925 to 1927, he had managed WCCO, a Minneapolis station. The fifth member, Eugene O. Sykes practiced law in Aberdeen, Mississippi, and from 1916 to 1924 had served on the Mississippi Supreme Court. Thus, Hoover nominated a naval radio expert, a Commerce Department inspector, a broadcaster, an engineer and editor, and a state supreme court judge to the newly created unit. Only in the case of Judge Sykes could critics later protest that the president appointed a politician to the FRC.[7]

As eminently qualified and remarkably suited as the five appointees were, they faced a tense, complex, and frustrating situation which tested them mightily. In the first place, their bureau had been ordered to sort out and resolve the tangled problems that had developed during seven years of near chaos. To do this, they were given one year. Almost immediately, Congress began to cloud their already dubious chances for success further by procrastinating over appointments, withholding funds, and vociferously protesting any help offered the commission by the Department of Commerce. Its critics expected the panel to perform a miracle without money, offices, secretarial and clerical aides, even without a duly confirmed membership.[8]

Most experts joined Elisha Hanson, attorney for the Newspaper Broadcasters' Association, in urging quick Senate confirmation of the president's nominees. Such was not to be the case. The Radio Act of 1927 received approval only nine days before the Sixty-ninth Congress expired. In the melee of the session's closing days, the Interstate Commerce Commission failed to muster a quorum to approve the nominations. In addition to the time limitation, opposition to Hoover continued to influence the legislative process. Many senators immediately recognized that Hoover had outmaneuvered the congressional desire to separate the new bureau from Commerce Department influence by selecting a group which reflected his own philosophy and policies. Consequently, Henry Bellows, John Dillon, and Orestes Caldwell encountered adamant opposition because they were too closely identified with the secretary of commerce. In fact, Clarence C. Dill stated that the committee "wanted to make it impossible to pick men who were with the Department of Commerce." Yet, in spite of their opposition to Hoover, the majority of the lawmakers concurred that the FRC could solve many of the problems at hand. Finally, after a poll on the Senate floor, they consented to confirm three commissioners. Subsequently, President Coolidge gave recess appointments to Caldwell and Bellows, enabling the new agency to gain full membership.[9]

The interim between the passage of the radio act and adjournment engendered other problems. In the rush to finish last minute business, Congress failed to pass the deficiency bill appropriating funds for the FRC. Consequently, no money supported its work. Because the Radio Act of 1927 provided that unexpected payments made to the Department of Commerce under the item "wireless communications laws" could be given to the new agency, Secretary Hoover tranferred $28,313.86 to it for the remainder of the 1927 fiscal year. His largesse sparked immediate controversy. Representative Sol Bloom, Democrat from New York, labeled Hoover's actions illegal; the congressman insisted that without a specific appropriation the FRC legally could not conduct business. His argument proved so persuasive that, one year later, even the bureau's own general counsel endorsed it. But both Hoover and Coolidge disregarded the assertion, and the president directed the secretary of commerce to disburse the funds.[10]

Even with the limited money from the Commerce Department, the FRC's position remained tenuous. Only a month after its organization, death complicated the other staffing problems; Commissioner Dillon expired first, and Chairman Bullard followed him less than a month later. Since the Senate had failed to confirm two of the five original members, these two received no salaries. By the end of 1927, the financial strain forced Dr. Bellows to resign. This left Judge Sykes as the only duly confirmed commissioner, aided by Orestes Caldwell, who could remain in the position solely because McGraw-Hill continued to pay his salary.[11]

The FRC's lack of offices, equipment, and staff further disrupted its operations. Once again the secretary of commerce intervened in the new agency's behalf. Hoover loaned the FRC a suite formerly occupied by the Bureau of Navigation and provided equipment and clerical assistance. He placed the Radio Division and the Bureau of Standards at the commission's disposal for its engineering and research staff. Also, at his urging, the Justice Department detailed Bethuel M. Webster, Jr., special assistant to the attorney general, to assist the FRC in handling hearings and court cases. As a direct result of Congress's refusal to fund the FRC it fast became an extension of the Commerce Department, in spite of the Senate's expressed desire to circumvent the secretary of commerce.[12]

As the commissioners gamely tried to sort out their resources, industrial and technical developments further compounded the complexities of their already confusing domain. Mechanical advances dreamed of for almost a decade suddenly materialized. High-powered transmitters introduced in the mid-1920s by the corporate giants began to replace 100, 500, and 1,000-watt stations. They used 5,000 to

50,000 watts to generate a powerful carrier-wave frequency which built up weak electromagnetic waves into extremely powerful ones. Engineers immediately undertook extensive field studies of coverage and signal intensity to complement this development. As they learned how far transmissions carried in urban settings and what areas they served, broadcasters could adjust their apparatus more effectively to overcome absorption, interference, and distortion. In fact, by the end of 1927, the more powerful and reliable transmitters emerged from attics, shacks, and laboratories and took what would become their accustomed place towering above rural landscapes and big city skyscrapers. By the next year, forty high-power facilities blanketed the entire nation.[13]

Better radio receivers complemented the improved stations. Translating electromagnetic signals into sound simply reversed the transmission process, which changed music and speech produced in the studio into radio waves. The transmitter modulated and amplified the impulses, while the receiver intercepted them and converted them back to sound. Originally, sets were exceedingly difficult to operate. In 1923 and 1924 engineers decidedly improved upon crystal outfits by introducing the three-element vacuum tube into radio circuits. This change necessitated additional sources of electrical power to operate the mechanisms. Consequently, all receivers relied on three separate batteries: A heated the filament, B placed a charge on the plate, and C placed a charge on the grid. But messy spills occurred regularly with the commonly used "dry" batteries. To further complicate matters, the tricky maneuvers necessary to line up two and sometimes three separate condensers made tuning an exacting, exasperating art. On most radios, frequency shifts had to be performed by changing three plug-in coils. The listener had to adjust several knobs to bring in distant stations. If he erred in the necessary twistings and turnings his set would burst into nerve-shattering whistles and squeals. While one did not have to be a skilled engineer to operate the equipment, a solid background in electronics certainly helped.[14]

Time brought advances, however. In 1927, the superheterodyne receiver came into widespread use. This system was adapted for radio reception after its creation by Edwin H. Armstrong for anti-aircraft detection during World War I. Through this method, the incoming signal combined with an unmodulated one produced in the set by a circuit called the local oscillator. Heterodyning, or beating together these two frequencies, produced a third frequency equal to the difference between the other two. The receiver could then readily amplify this new impulse and subsequently transform it into an audible tone. At first, these models lacked commercial feasibility since the operator had to coordinate five dials carefully to hear a particular program. This complicated tuning adjustment seemed beyond the ability of most laymen. Consequently, several major research laboratories undertook considerable developmental work in the hope of adapting these outfits for mass consumption. By 1927, their efforts had paid off in a product with simplified one-knob tuning and excellent selectivity, amplification, and detection which far surpassed its predecessors in sensitivity.[15]

In turn, other technical advances produced further simplified products of high quality and reliability. Scientists and engineers tinkered with component parts for receivers throughout the 1920s. In the process, they extensively researched acoustics and loudspeakers. Western Electric manufactured the first cone speakers in 1922–23. These early devices used horns for amplification, but as a side effect they produced reverberations which gave a "tinny" quality to music and speech. In 1925, General Electric's electrodynamic loudspeaker overcame this drawback and by 1927 was encouraging high-fidelity reproduction in most units. Because it eliminated headphones by transmitting sound directly into the room, whole families could now enjoy programs without interrupting other activities.[16]

Fascination with the constantly improving sets grew rapidly. Next, A-C tubes enabled radios to operate on household electricity. Such a system had an inherent difficulty in that alternating current produced a loud distracting hum in the mechanism. The Westinghouse laboratories succeeded in eliminating this distortion by developing a special method of operating the plate and filament. They devised the A-C tube which maintained the outer surface of the cathode at a constant potential regardless of the supply of alternating or direct current for power. This invention encouraged householders to buy sets that operated from an electrical outlet rather than cumbersome dry cells. Production of new table units and consoles that fit

***Figure 8. Superheterodyne
Receiver, 1922.***

The superheterodyne circuit, de-
veloped during World War I by Signal
Corps Major Edwin H. Armstrong,
improved frequency reception.
*Courtesy of Smithsonian Institution,
Photo No. 43, 984.*

***Figure 9. Armstrong Receiver,
1923.***

The experimental Armstrong receiver,
produced in 1923, by superheterodyne
developer Edwin H. Armstrong.
*Courtesy of Smithsonian Institution,
Photo No. 60,143-A.*

comfortably into living rooms further improved their appearance and sales. As service progressed from a hit-or-miss, now you hear it, now you don't proposition to a reliable and highly intelligible signal, more and more families joined the ranks of the mass audience.[17]

With the increase in listeners, network radio began to emerge as a well-defined component of American business. The National Broadcasting Company, the first corporation established solely to conduct chain operations, began 1927 with the first coast-to-coast transmission. Millions of Americans tuned in to hear Stanford tie Alabama (seven to seven) in the Rose Bowl. Also in January, NBC expanded the dual concept originally developed in New York City by RCA's WJZ and WJY during the 1920s. In this earlier instance WJZ had supplied serious entertainment while WJY provided lighter fare. NBC adopted this principle and formed two semi-independent groups. The Red Network and its base station WEAF offered popular features, while the Blue Network transmitted more refined, sophisticated programs through its cornerstone WJZ.[18]

With the flexibility offered by two divisions, NBC undertook an aggressive campaign to extend its corporate activities. Branches and studios were constructed in Chicago, Washington, D.C., and San Francisco. At the same time, the company sought outlets in all major urban areas. Since most independent businessmen lacked enough quality programs and talent to fill their broadcast day, they eagerly accepted access to the chain. Equally important, many of them desperately needed outside capital. Network hook-ups brought in revenues and allowed station managers to charge higher rates to local sponsors. Moreover, since General Electric, Westinghouse, and RCA owned NBC, they willingly committed their facilities to it. Thus, by the end of the first full year of operations, NBC had grown from nineteen to forty-eight units. Indeed, the firm quickly outranked potential rivals competitively simply because it had secured the most powerful and prestigious stations in cities across the United States.[19]

NBC based its relations with its local affiliates on the business practices established by AT&T. When NBC assumed responsibility for the telephone company's chain, it found a history of sporadic service. Informal arrangements called for the parent organization to furnish entertainment only a few evenings each week. While NBC continued the informality, it expanded the daily offerings to cover a sixteen-hour broadcasting schedule. The corporation transmitted two broad classifications of programs, depending upon who sold the advertising time, the network itself or the local station. "Sponsored" programs were those for which national advertisers bought time directly from the chain; NBC paid its outlets $50 an hour to broadcast all such features that were carried over the airwaves from six to twelve o'clock at night, and $30 an hour for daytime fare. "Sustaining" shows, produced and developed by NBC at its own expense, were sold to the local affiliates at the rate of $45 per evening hour and $15 per daytime hour; the individual stations then sold time to local businessmen at whatever rates they could.[20]

For its sponsored programs, NBC solicited advertising on the basis of expanded metropolitan outlets and increased coverage. It offered retailers organized opportunities to sell their goods by sponsoring entertainment for a national audience. Following AT&T's example, NBC presented access to a minimum number of facilities referred to as the basic network. In this arrangement, the Red and Blue organizations overlapped with respect to programs and stations. The basic format consisted of units located in major urban areas, including New York, Boston, Washington, D.C., Chicago, Cleveland, Detroit, and Cincinnati. NBC executives knew most advertisers desired to reach the large concentrations of substantial buying power within these population centers. NBC also offered geographical groups available in the Southeast, Southwest, Northwest, Mountain, and Pacific Coast regions to augment its basic system. The chain also had a number of low-powered facilities called "bonus" stations, which it included without charge. Thus, advertisers could address certain sections or the entire nation by securing the basic group and adding regional blocs.[21]

After organizing its affiliates, company officials devised a complicated formula for assessing rates within a maze of costs and discounts. They figured the charges for sponsored programs using an hour as the fundamental period. On this basis, a quarter-hour segment cost the advertiser 40 percent of an hour period and a half-hour cost 60 percent. The number of days, weeks, or months a show ran, as well as the time of day it was broadcast, also affected the tariff. Night rates were double daytime transmissions because of the larger audiences during the evening. To further complicate matters, NBC offered discounts and rebates for consecutive weeks of use to encourage businessmen to employ its facilities.[22]

In September 1927, the firm presented its first formal rate card. Between seven and eleven in the evening New York time, the Red Network charged $3,770 per hour for coverage in fifteen localities. For the same period, the Blue offered nine cities for $2,880. (Over the next few years these charges dramatically increased.) Those who wanted to sponsor shows before seven or after eleven could get similar service for half price. Of course, this format varied according to the number of blocs involved and the length of the contract. Thus, for example, Remington Rand bought a half-hour on Thursday evening from 9:00 to 9:30 P.M. for twenty-six weeks at a total cost of $58,199.44. This figure included a 5 percent discount and coast-to-coast coverage. On the other hand, the National Lumber Manufacturers Association sponsored a daytime feature dramatizing the history of their industry for six weeks. The cost, which included service to nine cities, came to $12,900. Before long Maxwell House Coffee, General Motors, Goodrich Tires, and Atwater Kent had made hesitant moves by lending their names to concerts and musical variety shows.[23]

By October, NBC's success had enabled it to move from lower Broadway in downtown Manhattan to Fifth Avenue in uptown New York City. The new streamlined, acoustically engineered and air-conditioned studios provided ideal conditions for producing carefully coordinated sound effects and music. But these improvements occasioned a need for orchestras, actors, announcers, and writers. Company directors perceived the obvious advantage of securing leading entertainers, under exclusive contract; to further that aim, they organized an Artists Bureau and Concert Service. Although NBC had been established primarily to promote the sale of RCA receivers, by the end of its first year network business ventures had grossed nearly $4 million. In much the same way that broadcasting's popularity forced private companies and government departments to reevaluate their role in communications, NBC's success forced RCA to reexamine the importance of interconnecton.[24]

The early lead NBC amassed after initiating chain hook-ups provided enough momentum to keep the firm well ahead of the United Independent Broadcasters, the forerunner of the Columbia

Broadcasting System, for some years. In most major urban areas, NBC had attracted the most important stations (and sometimes their closest competitor). In addition, its Artists Bureau and Concert Service had virtually monopolized many advertisers by contracting many of the leading entertainers. Because of difficulty in attracting affiliates and securing sponsors, CBS's early history sometimes resembled a fly-by-night bookmaking operation. The venture was often forced to rely on secret trips, money secured from mysterious individuals, and the fear that at any moment the "sheriff" would appear and close down the organization. However exciting the vision of such corporate intrigue might appear, reality showed a business teetering on the verge of ruin.[25]

Ironically enough, David Sarnoff himself sparked the formation of CBS. Surmising that there was money to be made in chain operations, Arthur Judson, a manager for symphonic orchestras and conductors, and George Arthur Coats, a promoter, decided to profit from the possibility of establishing a network and artists' bureau to rival NBC's. They approached Sarnoff and offered to trade their plans for launching a competitor for a contract for Judson's Radio Program Corporation to supply entertainers for NBC. In effect, the Judson-Coats scheme resembled the spite franchise, a familiar practice in the public utilities business. Under the spite franchise, an entrepreneur would buy a small utility company in an area that was being unified by a larger concern and hold on, forcing his larger counterpart to buy him out at an inflated rate. Judson and Coats intended to use virtually the same tactics, except that instead of a one-time payoff they wanted to supply talent for the network. Perhaps if they had approached Merlin Aylesworth, NBC's president, instead of Sarnoff, they might have achieved their goal. Aylesworth's former job as managing director of the National Electric Light Association had well acquainted him with the spite franchise. In any event, because Sarnoff knew nothing of the practice, the pair's audacity thoroughly offended him. His consequent brusque refusal to buy them out might well rank with the most significant misjudgments in radio history.[26]

As a result, on 27 January 1927, Judson and Coats joined Francis Marsh, a New York song broker, and Edwin Ervin, assistant manager of the New York Philharmonic Symphony Society, to establish the United Independent Broadcasters. They carefully chose this particular name to protest RCA's so-called monopoly of the airwaves. Because the UIB associates lacked any direct experience in their new endeavor, they retained Major J. Andrew White, a radio pioneer, editor, and announcer, to head the new company. In White they gained an invaluable asset; his expertise dated from 2 July 1921, when his blow-by-blow description of the Jack Dempsey-Georges Carpentier fight inaugurated all network transmissions.[27]

The organizational task at hand fiercely challenged the skills of all involved. In order to survive, the new partners needed money, outlets, long-distance telephone lines, and talent. Contacts in Philadelphia helped them sign WCAU, owned and operated by Leon and Issac Levy. The Levys in turn put them in touch with others anxious to secure affiliation. By proposing to match NBC's rate of $50 per hour for ten hours of program time per week, UIB hoped to attract independent operators. Eventually, sixteen stations, including facilities in Boston, Baltimore, Pittsburgh, Cincinnati, Detroit, Chicago, and St. Louis, joined the chain. After some deliberations, WOR, a Newark, New Jersey, outlet owned by Bamberger's Department Stores, agreed to serve as head station.[28]

But since UIB had only tentative financing, it desperately needed a solid economic basis. To meet their immediate requirements, Judson borrowed funds from Mrs. Christian Holmes, a patron of the New York Philharmonic. He then unsuccessfully approached Atwater Kent, Adolph Zukor of Paramount, and the Victor Talking Machine Company. Victor broke off negotiations because RCA purchased it, but Columbia Phonograph Record Company, Victor's arch rival, saw an opportunity for head-on competition and joined UIB.[29]

Several aspects of the contractual agreement proved significant. The record company provided $136,000 to form a new organization. In light of its substantial investment and in order to advertise itself, it insisted that the new firm change its name from UIB to the Columbia Phonograph Broadcasting System. In addition, both parties agreed that Columbia could leave the association and cancel the contract after presenting one month's prior notice. After three months of losses amounting to $100,000 each, the phonograph company exercised its option and withdrew from the arrangement, leaving only the name Columbia Broadcasting System (CBS) in its wake.[30]

Despite the gloomy financial picture, Arthur Judson was convinced that success waited just around the corner. Happily, AT&T finally allowed Columbia access to its long-distance lines for chain operations. In an attempt to salvage this opportunity, Judson approached the owners of WCAU, the most solvent affiliate. Leon Levy, a dentist, and his brother Issac D. "Ike" Levy had owned WCAU since 1924. Because they shared Judson's optimism, they introduced him to another friend, Jerome H. Louchheim, a bridge and subway builder and avid sportsman. After agreeing to join the Levys in financing the venture, the contractor became chairman of the board. Ike Levy, vice-president, Leon Levy, secretary treasurer, and Major White, president, completed the firm's slate of officers.[31]

Citing the economic difficulties caused by losing the Columbia Phonograph Record Company's support, they negotiated new, more favorable contracts with their outlets. Finally, on the evening of 8 September 1927, sixteen members carried Major J. Andrew White intoning, "This is the voice of Columbia," to introduce "The King's Henchman," an opera composed especially for the occasion by Deems Taylor and Edna St. Vincent Millay. Worry about getting to the first transmission changed to concern over staying in business.[32]

In 1927, American business and technical achievements were dramatically recognized by other nations as the United States hosted the Washington Radio Conference. Here, in striking contrast to the confused political and regulatory scene, the American stance on international affairs articulated a well-organized, well-planned program. Indeed, through careful preparation and skillfull maneuvering, the secretary of commerce's ideas filtered into the treaty signed by the delegates. In the months preceding the meeting, amateurs, businessmen, and bureaucrats discussed frequency allocation, technical standards, and general strategy under the supervision of the Commerce Department. By the end of the summer, a unified policy had emerged. It stated that American business must continue at the forefront of world development. In addition, it insisted that all participants acknowledge the fundamental differences separating the privately controlled American industry from the governmentally run European systems. Moreover, it argued that the spectrum should be allocated according to services rather than to nations. Finally, it emphasized that any international accord should protect amateurs.[33]

The very location of the 1927 conference in Washington, D.C., rather than in some other capital underscored the United States' growing importance in communications. The 1912 talks had been held in London, the center of radio power at that time. Holding the 1927 meeting in Washington symbolized an assumption of prestige and influence by the United States. Representatives from eighty countries participated in the event opened by President Coolidge, chaired by Secretary Hoover, staffed by committees filled with Americans, and conducted in both English and French rather than in French alone. The international delegation met to revise the Radio Convention of 1912, which had been rendered obsolete by phenomenal growth.[34]

Throughout October and November, the representatives studied several particularly troublesome and controversial issues. During that time, differences in management between Europe and the United States provoked considerable disagreement. Since broadcasting and other radio activities in America belonged almost exclusively to private enterprise, the nation's delegates were barred from signing documents binding to these companies. The Europeans, on the other hand, firmly desired such constraint. To satisfy both parties, the secretary of commerce proposed that regulatory matters be divided into a two-part agreement. The first manifesto would include matters in the domain of sovereign governments: protecting public interest, avoiding interference, and protecting human life. The second section would deal with economic and technical principles and methods of operation, or the province of private management. The United States could then sign and consider itself bound only by the first section. By insisting that the offending issues be grouped together in the "Supplementary Regulations," Secretary Hoover and the U.S. delegation followed a strategy planned months before the conference.[35]

After some discussion, the other participants accepted Hoover's proposal. Accordingly, the final treaty contained three parts. The "Convention" and "General Regulations" amended the London Conference of 1912 and as such were signed by the United States. The nation refused, however, to accept the "Supplementary Regulations" section because it contained provisions relating directly to the management of private firms. Since each nation could sign any part of the document it wished and since signatories were obligated only by the specific provisions they had signed, subdividing the treaty resolved the dilemma.[36]

The assemblage favored American communications in other ways. For example, the frequency allocation scheme, which the gathering adopted, closely paralleled the policy developed at the Second National Radio Conference. Under this plan, space in the electromagnetic spectrum pertained to services, not nations. This arrangement created three major bands: low-frequency (10 to 550 kHz), broadcasting (550 to 1,500 kHz), and high-frequency (1,500 to 60,000 kHz). This division allocated channels to mobile, fixed, broadcast, and special services (radio beacons, amateurs, and radio compass) as follows: 10 to 100 kHz for long-distance transoceanic users; 100 to 550 kHz for ship-to-ship, ship-to-shore, and ground-to-air traffic; 550 to 1,500 kHz for broadcasters; and 1,500 to 60,000 kHz to be apportioned among forty groups, including mobile, fixed, and amateur users.[37]

Many delegates acceded to American policies because they recognized U.S. domination over communications. Just as in 1912, when Britain influenced the field since it controlled ship-to-ship and ship-to-shore traffic, the United States' overwhelming preponderance in 1927 guaranteed it the leadership.[38]

As stability was imposed within the industry by network radio and in the international arena by the Washington Conference, it became imperative that the Federal Radio Commission establish order domestically. In the short time before death and financial problems reduced the committee's ranks, its members had tried determinedly to accomplish this task. Fortunately, the secretary of commerce had already successfully arranged amateurs, commercial operators, and experimenters, so their licenses were free from dispute. Had these groups been awaiting action, the commission might well have floundered endlessly with no idea where to begin. As it was, its first ruling confirmed all coastal, point-to-point, technical, and experimental licenses previously granted by the Department of Commerce.[39]

Next, the agency turned its attention to the worsening broadcasting situation. Indeed, the prime purpose of the Radio Act of 1927 had been to ensure orderly development of this enterprise. When the FRC assumed authority, 733 stations, operating with little regard for proper power, designated hours, or frequency assignment, occupied ninety-six channels. One hundred twenty-nine licensees ignored the ten-kilohertz division established by the Department of Commerce to prevent interference. Forty-one others transmitted programs on the six wavelengths that had been reserved for Canadian use. To further complicate matters, many observed only twenty, ten, five, or even two-kilohertz separations in the metropolitan areas, where a fifty-kilohertz standard had been created by the Department of Commerce Finally, portable stations continued to multiply, adding to the cross talk, overlapping, and electrical mumble-jumble that threatened to destroy the industry. As the FRC began looking for solutions, Secretary Hoover exhorted all parties to exercise patience.[40]

The new commissioners relied heavily upon the policies and practices Secretary Hoover had developed in trying to distribute a limited number of channels among an unlimited number of outlets. In addition to their pragmatic appeal, the secretary of commerce's decisions represented precedent through which the agency could defend its own actions. In effect, the FRC used the extralegal program established by Hoover as its foundation. Of course, skeptics might argue that with William D. Terrell, head of the Radio Division, secretly monitoring the FRC meetings and the Bureau of Standards assisting it such a result could hardly be avoided. As the Buffalo *News* observed, in attempting to strip the secretary of commerce of his power, Congress had "been licked at its own game."[41]

In its very first days, the FRC began incorporating Hoover's approach into its own plans. From 29 March to 1 April 1927, it staged public consultations to elicit ideas on projected changes. Based upon these hearings, it decided to maintain the broadcast band established at the Second National Radio Conference. Consequently, the authorities ordered all rural stations back to a ten-kilohertz separation and reestablished the fifty-kilohertz division in urban areas. This action opened ninety-six channels; however, the government immediately closed six of these frequencies to Americans by designating them for the exclusive use of Canadians. Again following the Department of Commerce policy, the FRC at first issued only sixty-day licenses to facilitate changes in frequencies and power after the short-term permits expired.[42]

While the FRC's preliminary administrative work concentrated on clearing the Canadian wavelengths and instituting proper separation by insisting that broadcasters return to their assignments, the commissioners also hoped to develop a reallocation scheme to resolve the issues of overlapping and interference. Operating upon a premise developed by Secretary Hoover and confirmed by the Fourth National Radio Conference, the commissioners declared that the sheer number of transmitters necessitated a dramatic reduction. In fact, they estimated any plan "which does not at the very outset eliminate at least 400 broadcasting stations cannot possibly put an end to interference."[43]

Death and circumstances interrupted the allocation program. Commissioner Dillon died on 8 October 1927. Bellows resigned on 31 October, and Chairman Bullard died on 24 November. The president promptly nominated three newcomers to ease the strain on the remaining members. Two of the appointees took office in 1927. Since Sam Pickard, a former educator and chief of the Radio Division in the Agricultural Department, was serving as the secretary of the FRC, he enjoyed an easy transition to commissioner. The other, Harold A. Lafount, a civil engineer, had manufactured receivers before his nomination. In early 1928, Coolidge suggested Judge Ira E. Robinson, a former chief justice of the West Virginia Supreme Court for the third vacancy. But even with its full complement of members, the group lacked confidence in its own authority because one member only, Eugène Sykes, had received Senate confirmation.[44]

In the time allotted it in 1927, the FRC barely managed to hold its own. Even though the Radio Act of 1927 had embodied a comprehensive regulatory plan, other more pressing matters dulled its long-awaited prospects. Politics, distrust of Hoover, limited funds, curtailed staff, and lack of office space had combined to hinder the bureau's effectiveness. Moreover, the loss of three qualified members created further difficulties and necessitated time-consuming adjustments. Equally telling, the position of network radio in the broadcasting system depended upon resolving the problems facing the FRC. Until these were settled and a definite regulatory program established, advertisers and broadcasters faced a degree of uncertainty hardly conducive to business expansion or corporate relationships. Moreover, interference marred reception and disrupted programs. Without order, commercialization could not continue to develop and expand. Thus, as 1927 drew to a close, attention shifted back to Washington, D.C., where the lawmakers once again would take up the problem of government regulation.[45]

8

The Federal Radio Commission

When Congress reconvened in the winter of 1928, radio control still confused a good many of the lawmakers. Although the Federal Radio Commission had been designed for a one-year term, many felt it deserved a longer tenure. Moreover, its vast undertaking seemed to merit more time, while the complexities at hand encouraged continuation of regulation by a commission. So, even after bitterly attacking almost every phase of its operations, Congress extended its authority through 1928. The next year, President Hoover successfully lent his support to encourage Capitol Hill to continue the body "until otherwise provided by law." Imperfect as it was, perhaps because its imperfections blended so artfully into the scheme of all things bureaucratic, the FRC outlasted many of those same politicians who voted it into existence.

Even though the legislators granted the panel more power, they refused to relinquish complete control to it. Beginning in 1928, safeguards stipulated by Congress dictated regulatory policies. First and foremost, an equal quota provision known as the Davis Amendment appeared in the 1928 extension. This section required a survey of the five geographic zones created in the original act and an equal redistribution of broadcasting facilities within them. In a corollary, Congress also directed the agency to eliminate stations.

Circumstances have a way of altering even the best laid plans, and so they did in the case of the FRC. Early successes culminating with its extension in 1928 endowed its members with a streak of independent confidence. Since they not only administered the

law but also interpreted it, their aggressive campaign to free themselves from congressional meddling took on an ironic twist in that
the entity designed to end Department of Commerce domination
of radio adopted the very practices that department had developed
over the preceding seven years. Using these activities as its precedents,
the FRC instituted a general allocation plan, technical and engineering
standards, and program requirements. These actions served to
curtail signal interference by forcing several hundred duly licensed
operators off the air. Although many authorities have concluded that
the commissioners followed no specific pattern, their efforts to restore
order by eliminating stations and curtailing congestion stemmed
directly from Department of Commerce policies.

In the ensuing rush to secure places in the electromagnetic spectrum,
those broadcasters with abundant financial resources, expensive
modern equipment, effective management, diversified programming,
and first-rate legal counsel fared best. The FRC's rulings, following
Hoover's example, ensured commercial domination of the medium.
The failure of smaller religious, educational, municipal, and private
outlets to cope with technical changes, market conditions, and internal
weaknesses relegated them to near oblivion in the national system
established by the bureau.

Many station owners immediately recognized the menace to their
facilities and began to fight it. In the ensuing court cases, individual
broadcasters tried to counteract unfavorable administrative rulings
by challenging every aspect of the Radio Act of 1927. To their dismay,
the federal judiciary unequivocally confirmed both the constitutionality of the statute and the legality of the vast majority of the
FRC's decisions. In fact, by the early 1930s, the commission was
enforcing its allocation policies, technical and engineering standards,
and program requirements without outside interference.

The FRC had begun as a temporary overseer for broadcasting.
Originally, it was to preside over the medium until one year after its
first meeting, at which time control would revert to the secretary of
commerce. The projected transfer on 15 March 1928, would return
authority to the Department of Commerce and reduce the commission
to an advisory and appellate body. As the end of the statutory period
approached, an increasing number of lawmakers sought to halt

the shift. Accordingly, in January 1928 three bills were introduced in Congress amending the Radio Act of 1927 and extending the status quo for an additional year.[1]

The resulting continuance did not indicate unconditional congressional sympathy for the FRC, however. On the contrary, the proposal's most ardent proponents bitterly attacked the agency's inaction and delay in resolving broadcasting difficulties. While foes and supporters alike recognized that the general aura of uncertainty pervading its operations had curtailed the body's effectiveness, they still believed that it should have accomplished more than it did. In effect, enormous public interest in radio prompted congressmen, who anticipated widespread hostility directed at themselves, carefully to place the blame for inaction elsewhere.[2]

Even the two men most responsible for the 1927 act dealt the FRC a devastating blow. While Senator Clarence C. Dill recognized that criticism might undo all his previous work, he nonetheless chided the "cowards and dullards" of the FRC for their inability to develop a consistent reductive policy for broadcasting stations. Moreover, he rebuked them for their susceptibility to influence from the secretary of commerce and the Radio Corporation of America, General Electric, and Westinghouse. Meanwhile, the bill's other sponsor, Representative Wallace White, groused that the FRC's policies had complicated the situation to an extent that only the commissioners could untangle the mess. White and Dill echoed both the House and the Senate in their insistence that eliminating licenses constituted the only feasible means for reducing congestion. Congress subsequently ordered the FRC to close transmitters.[3]

Southern and Western members of Congress added to attacks against the agency with their protest that it had failed to distribute facilities equally among the states, as specified in section 9 of the Radio Act of 1927. These critics charged that the South and West had suffered discrimination at a time when the North and East were served by many broadcasters. For the most part, however, these lawmakers were protesting a shortcoming which in no way reflected government policy. The outlets in the North and East actually had been constructed before the passage of the 1927 act because of economic and demographic factors beyond federal control. Thus, while the industry had, indeed, developed less in the South and West than in other sections of the nation, the authorities would have been hard pressed to change that situation.[4]

Nonetheless, to correct the geographical imbalances, Representative Edwin L. Davis, Democrat from Tennessee, introduced yet another amendment to the Radio Act of 1927. It declared that since all U.S. residents were entitled to equal service, the FRC should distribute licenses, frequencies, and power according to the population and area of the states within the five districts established by the legislation. This proposal sparked a rancorous debate. Critics of the measure claimed that it involved a matter best left to the FRC. Moreover, they argued that its provisions had been grafted onto a system designed to serve administrative purposes. They also asserted that it disregarded certain engineering and technical problems and focused on economic factors completely outside the agency's authority. *Electrical World* protested that the regional proposal was as absurd for communications as for other public services. It proclaimed, "No one would think of demanding that there be an equal mileage of railroads in every zone, or an equal production of electric power, or an equal number of telephones."[5]

While the debate over the Davis Amendment raged among politicians, businessmen, engineers, and journalists, the FRC's statutory mandate ended. Some legislators chafed against the embarrassment of having failed to agree before the time ran out, some stood aghast at the prospect of returning control of the industry to Secretary Hoover, and others didn't even care. Presidential candidate Hoover entreated the panel to continue its work until Congress could extend its tenure, and the lawmakers speedily responded eight days later with "An Act Continuing for One Year the Powers and Authority of the Federal Radio Commission Under the Radio Act of 1927."[6]

The new measure duplicated the original bill with the addition of the Davis Amendment. This provision stipulating an equitable distribution of broadcasting service had been included in the final version in order to appease Southerners who threatened to delay the legislation further. Despite the extension, however, Congress had only postponed making any final decision for a year.[7]

After completing the 1928 bill, the Senate began to consider approving the commissioners. Of the five members, Judge Sykes alone had previously been confirmed. As proceedings began, Orestes H. Caldwell drew fire as the "stormy petrel" of the agency. Throughout March, Representative Davis and Senator Dill criticized his alleged favoritism to RCA, General Electric, and Westinghouse. Ignoring Congress's refusal to pay the man a living wage, Senator Dill attacked Caldwell for accepting a salary from McGraw-Hill while in government service.[8]

Yet, while Caldwell seemed too preoccupied with special interests, Ira E. Robinson garnered criticism for his lack of familiarity with communications. The Navy Department protested his nomination to the vacancy created by Admiral Bullard's death on the pretext that the position should have been filled by another naval officer. Furthermore, Admiral Stanford C. Hooper observed that the Naval Communications Service strongly felt it deserved representation on the panel. In all fairness, however, Hooper also recognized that few career officers would take the post "considering the status of the FRC." Other industry leaders and engineers attacked Robinson, claiming that inexperience in technical matters disqualified him. Many worried that his appointment would begin a trend toward delegating radio issues to influential lawyers rather than technocrats.[9]

Despite widespread opposition to Caldwell and Robinson, most lawmakers realized that a prolonged battle over appointments would further reduce the bureau's effectiveness. On 31 March, the Senate completed the membership of the FRC for the first time since its organization by confirming both disputed candidates as well as Sam Pickard and Harold A. Lafount.[10]

With the commission empaneled and the act extended, public sentiment began to favor permanently continuing the FRC. After Congress finally ratified the panel's membership, it increased the organization's appropriations. In the process, the unit began to grow as more money allowed an enlarged staff. Beginning with several clerks on loan from the Commerce Department, it expanded to fifty-seven employees in 1928. The next year, it increased to ninety members. More funds and personnel allowed the body to establish engineering and legal divisions. With time, the commissioners abandoned the concept that they individually represented the five zones from which they had been appointed. As early as 7 April 1928, they began to facilitate their work by specializing in separate provinces: Robinson studied legal problems, Sykes answered procedural questions, Caldwell examined technical developments, Pickard handled press relations, and Lafount coordinated activities with other government bureaus. Specialization refined the FRC and added to its self-sufficiency. As the scope and complexity of its work expanded, the members gradually acquired a reputation for vast expertise on communications. In effect, they formed an impartial body that Congress consulted extensively. Moreover, as the group gained stature and power, it acquired a constituency among industry leaders who lobbied actively for its continuation. These efforts succeeded so well that on 4 March 1929, Congress granted an additional year's extension without a whimper.[11]

Following the 1929 legislation, the movement to establish permanent powers for the FRC gained irreversible momentum. In his annual message, President Hoover called for "the reorganization of the Radio Commission into a permanent body from its temporary status." Keeping in mind a proposal for a communications commission advanced by Eugene McDonald, president of Zenith, Senators James Watson of Indiana and James Couzens of Michigan supported the president, albeit to advance their own aims. By promoting a single overseer for radio, telephone, telegraph, and cables, the two lawmakers hoped to consolidate control of communications which at the time was scattered among several government bureaus. Since they realized that the broadcasting industry had to be stabilized before legislation could group wire and wireless services under one bureau, they supported the FRC as an inevitable step toward that end.[12]

Early in December 1929, Congress began legislation to perpetuate the FRC. After this measure passed without debate on 16 December, the president signed the law. The three years it took to transform the FRC from a temporary body into a permanent regulatory authority convinced many groups that the agency might even achieve the goals many had considered impossible only a short time before.[13]

Suspense, skulduggery, and intrigue might titillate listeners and sell plenty of advertising, but broadcasters far preferred other less sensational characterizations for their industry. Equally damaging signal interference threatened to prejudice the fickle public against its new diversion as well as the bureau empowered to police that enterprise. In a drive inspired as much by a desire for self-preservation as any other motive, the FRC began to develop a national regulatory policy to encourage a more orderly approach to radio. During the secretary of commerce's primacy, commercial licensees had come to dominate the airwaves. In continuing this general pattern, the FRC insulated this class from challenge by other operators and protected itself from attack by the most powerful group of broadcasters. In the matter of preferential treatment, FRC supervision meant maintaining the status quo.[14]

Since Congress had described the regulatory standard the bureaucrats should use in terms of public interest, convenience, and necessity, the FRC's first step toward establishing a national system involved defining these terms. Four radio conferences and seven years of control by the Department of Commerce had already begun the process. The commissioners agreed that the prevailing scarcity of channels required that those available be used economically, effectively, and as fully as possible. In practical terms, this meant that they favored the applicants with superior technical equipment, adequate financial resources, skilled personnel, and the ability to provide continuous service. According to this interpretation, established broadcasters with demonstrated ability best fulfilled the public interest standard. In most instances, priority and financial success guided the FRC in favoring one operator over another.[15]

Furthermore, the commission ruled that licenses should be granted to serve the general population rather than any private or selfish interest. Using this logic, it labeled facilities operated by colleges and universities, religious institutions, and city and state governments "propaganda stations." Consequently, these smaller entities lost out in the competition for favorable wavelengths, increased power, and full-time operations. In contrast, the FRC ruled that businessmen who sold air time truly served the public because their programming aimed to reach all of the people rather than a specific clique or small community. The agency also excepted advertising from the sanctions against special interest groups because its revenue constituted the only financial support received by broadcasters. Following this reasoning, commercial advertising stations served the nation because they used their financial and technical ability to provide continuous entertainment for the general populace. By such special interpretation of already ambiguous guidelines, the FRC favored the corporate giants.[16]

The commissioners felt that Congress had explicitly directed them to reduce interference and congestion by eliminating broadcasters. Under this pretext, they began forcing stations to close down. The easiest and quickest method would have been simply to abolish several hundred operators. However, the Radio Act of 1927 blocked this approach because it protected owners from arbitrary administrative action. Moreover, such a policy would have deluged the FRC with hundreds of temporary injunctions and court cases. In order to avoid such legal entanglements, the agency decided to develop a comprehensive allocation scheme instead. By interpreting the Davis Amendment to require an immediate rearrangement of transmitters to secure geographical equality, the FRC established its legal foundation. According to Orestes H. Caldwell, the panel "intended to get rid of stations," and reallocation constituted the means to achieve this goal. Using the geographical justificaton, the bureau assigned applicants "outside the public interest" less desirable frequencies or forced them to operate part time. By relegating noncommercial facilities to obscure channels and condemning them to sporadic hours, the FRC hoped to convince their owners to cease operations quietly. In such a way, it planned to carry out the congressional mandate while avoiding legal difficulties.[17]

To begin instituting their plan the bureaucrats borrowed some of Secretary Hoover's techniques. Throughout the spring and summer of 1928, the staff of the FRC consulted government radio experts, engineers, and industry representatives on a general allocation policy. National trade associations such as the Broadcasting Committee of the Institute of Radio Engineers, the National Association of Broadcasters, the Federal Trade Association, and the Radio Manufacturers Association suggested innumerable ideas. Among other things, the engineers urged that categories be instituted to reflect power and service areas. They also proposed fifty clear channels to serve rural listeners as a partial solution to the existing geographical inequities. While the primary motive for these consultations had been to create an aura of receptiveness, the agency did adopt several propositions in line with its general scheme including those advanced by the engineers.[18]

While it was polling its constituency for suggestions, the FRC began to pressure small operators to surrender their licenses voluntarily. Immediately after passage of the 1928 radio control bill, the bureau closed thirteen portable stations with the argument that the Davis Amendment authorized fixed facilities only. On 25 May 1928, the FRC promulgated General Order Number 32, which required 164 small broadcasters to justify their continued operation. While comparatively few owners suffered under this edict, it nonetheless warned of more changes to come.[19]

The next formal step occurred on 30 August 1928, when the FRC implemented General Order Number 40, the allocation project. While the plan combined several independent proposals, it also closely followed recommendations advanced at the Second and Fourth National Radio Conferences. Through its provisions, 690, 730, 840, 910, 960, and 1,030 kHz were reserved for Canadian use. Local, regional, and clear channel outlets divided the remaining ninety United States frequencies.[20]

As suggested by the engineers, transmitters were categorized according to power and geographic area. The order also bequeathed forty powerful stations a separate or "clear" channel for each to use with 5,000 to 50,000 watts for night programs. To equalize geographic distribution, eight were assigned to each district. In contrast to those forty unimpeded wavelengths, the order allocated thirty-four others to regional operators also distributed equally among the five divisions. These transmitters, 1,000 to 1,500 miles apart, used less than 1,000 watts; their distance and low output thus enabled them to operate simultaneously during the entire day. Geographic separation and a restricted field also kept broadcasters using the remaining fifteen wavelengths from interfering. Of these, each zone was allowed six to be used by facilitaties with 100 watts or more and five for stations under 1,000; the final four were created for outlets using five kilowatts, but these last were allowed to encompass two or more districts.[21]

Anticipating possible adverse reaction to the redistributions, the FRC launched an educational and public relations campaign to counteract this threat. Its press releases explained that the familiar broadcasting band originally established by Secretary Hoover had been retained in order to reduce inconvenience to listeners. The campaign then outlined the unfamiliar aspects of the plan. Under the proposal to reach all geographic regions, service for small communities, well-populated areas, and metropolitan sections would emanate from low-powered, local facilities. Clear channel, high-powered operators would send programs to "rural and remote" listeners. In addition, the FRC restated its contention that public interest could be served only by creating "the best possible reception conditions throughout the United States." Accordingly, it justified the proposed reductions by declaring that listeners' rights surpassed those of owners. In pursuing this line of reasoning, it asserted that it would be "better that there should be a few less broadcasters than that the listening public should suffer." Above all, the FRC affirmed its desire to "introduce order into the broadcast chaos" by providing all-encompassing service and reducing signal interference.[22]

In reality, however, the allocation plan represented Machiavellian manipulation. The commissioners maintained their belief that high-powered transmitters used the spectrum most efficiently. Furthermore, by improving reception they hoped to enlarge the audience further. They expected that clear channel stations would limit the market for expensive receivers. Obviously programs transmitted on high power could be picked up on the inexpensive sets more easily afforded by most listeners. Using the strategy of packing small operators closely together, while limiting their range and operations, the FRC aimed to eliminate roughly two hundred of them. It hoped to reclaim these wavelengths "rendering minimal public service" after their holders failed within a year or two.[23]

On 8 September 1928, the panel began assigning licenses to the categories created General Order Number 40. In the ensuing contest for favorable assignments, over 700 broadcasters struggled to survive. Relying on their considerable resources, commercial owners snapped up all of the clear channels, as well as the vast majority of regional wavelengths. These frequencies offered more than immediate profits; over the course of the following years their value might increase by millions of dollars. Unlike this preferred class, small broadcasters, educational stations, and religious organizations were packed closely together on mainly local channels. Even exceptional facilities like WHA, the pioneer educational outlet of the University of Wisconsin, faced restricted hours, shared time, and several shifts of frequency assignment. Clearly revenues for the less-favored could in no way equal those of their larger competitors. By selectively defining public interest and by manipulating frequency allocation, the FRC rewarded commercial broadcasters far in excess of other radio users.[24]

With the new allocation plan well underway the commission began to formulate extensive regulations governing technical operations. Uniform rules and requirements constituted one of the major priorities to ensure success of the allocation scheme. Other motives directed this activity as well. As a signatory at the Washington Radio Conference, the United States had agreed to implement a high level of electronic excellence. To fulfill that agreement partially, the FRC had already incorporated the "Standard of Good Engineering Practice" developed at the international meeting into its own rules and regulations. Also, the Radio Act of 1927 specifically directed the regulators to curb interference by enforcing rigid qualifications. Furthermore, creating scientific norms fitted comfortably in the agency's total plan since modernization required amounts of time and money excessive for many owners and would reduce numbers further.[25]

To determine appropriate criteria and practices, the FRC resorted to the conference technique used to such advantage by the secretary of commerce. In cooperation with the Radio Division of the Commerce Department, the FRC's Engineering Division consulted RCA, AT&T, Westinghouse, the Bureau of Standards, the Naval Communications Service, and the Institute of Radio Engineers. By early 1929, the numerous meetings and conferences produced an agreement calling for more stringent enforcement of engineering requirements. To continue the benefits of its new allocation arrangement, the FRC was charged to maintain frequency assignments by revoking the license of any who failed to comply. The conferees also agreed that the agency should outline technical principles and incorporate them into its rules and regulations covering carrier waves, ratio of day power to night power, harmonics, modulation, transmission fidelity, mechanical reproductions, and the location of high-powered stations. By promulgating these procedures, among others, and by mandating modern equipment, the consultants hoped to eradicate interference and disorder. Stations were directed to modernize their equipment and maintain high performance. The FRC forced those falling short of its requirements to remodel their transmitters and studios. Failure to comply precipitated revocation of licenses or nonrenewal.[26]

Since the success of the allocation scheme depended upon maintaining assigned channels, the bureau first ordered licensees to adopt crystal quartz control apparatus. This mechanism, vibrating at a fixed frequency in the operating circuit, enabled engineers to measure assigned wavelengths accurately. When the FRC assumed its duties, only twenty-five broadcasters owned this equipment. Over 200 had added it to their apparatus by the end of 1929.[27]

As the FRC implemented technical and engineering requirements, it also sought to expand its jurisdiction into the controversial area of program regulation. Utilizing the wide-ranging discretionary powers given it by the Radio Act of 1927, the commission resolutely scrutinized entertainment. While recognizing that it had been specifically prohibited from exercising censorship, the FRC interpreted the term to mean no prior interference or restraint over radio shows. In accord with this interpretation, its *Second Annual Report* argued,

> "Since there are only a limited number of channels and since an excessive number of stations desired to broadcast over these channels, the commission believes it is entitled to consider the program service rendered by the various applicants to compare them, and to favor those which render the best service."

After the report, the agency examined the character and diversity of features generated by applicants for licenses and renewals. Selective awards of frequencies according to the characteristic standard of public interest, convenience, and necessity, established a broad form of censorship.[28]

Although the FRC set the policy, the Department of Commerce actually collected the information. At the same time that William D. Terrell, head of its Radio Division, was assuring Congress that his agency did not "pass on the quality of broadcast programs," he directed his subordinates across the United States to submit detailed reports on the character of entertainment transmitted in their area. Accordingly, radio inspectors provided detailed comments and actual transcripts. In the course of gathering information, local authorities revealed aspects of their own personalities. In one report on WEAF, the inspector noted that when the Happiness Boys sang the ditty "All Nuts Do Not Grow on Trees," several mortified young women rushed from the room—a direct contradiction to the image of the bold flappers of the "Roaring Twenties." His counterpart in California reporting on KTM in Santa Monica noted that one Saturday night it played "I'm Good for Nothing But Love." While the righteous bureaucrat admitted that this "song might have its place as a sociological study," he personally believed that it bordered on the indecent.[29]

From across the United States similar reports and commentaries swelled the FRC's already substantial dossiers on broadcasters. After consulting these compilations, the agency established guidelines for acceptable programming. In the process, the commissioners perfected the method of "regulation by raised eyebrow" announcing standards in statements, public addresses, and reports prior to their clarification in actual cases. This retaliation often followed public objection, engendered by specific offerings. The bureaucrats first turned their wrath on "fortunetelling" shows, those with astrologists and "mental scientists" advising listeners on marital problems, employment, and investments. An FRC ruling that these features violated the public interest began a successful campaign to eliminate them. Next, the agency went after medical lectures which offered advice or advertised cures; once again, these offerings gradually disappeared. After two successes, it was a small step to begin denying licenses to those broadcasters who abused their privilege by transmitting "defamatory or false information." As in the case of allocation and technical standards, programming requirements allowed the FRC to continue its crusade to reduce signal interference by eliminating outlets.[30]

Through these actions the FRC made great inroads against both the amount of interference and the number of facilities. In the process, it continued to favor commercial advertising stations. Commissioner Caldwell fondly pointed to them as models of excellence that "have been the best in the maintenance of radio's rules of the road." He also observed that these enterprises sported the best service records, the most popular shows, and the most efficient equipment, and had faithfully adhered to the government's regulations.[31]

On the other hand, the commissioners voiced scant praise for small businessmen, educational and religious institutions, or public service groups. One representative case involved WMBO, a small Auburn, New York, station owned by the Radio Service Laboratory. Because its precarious financial condition forced its owners to purchase the least expensive equipment, it failed to maintain its frequency. In turn, its intermittent, unreliable transmissions caught the attention of the New York radio inspector. After evaluating WMBO's transmitter and programs, the official reported that he could find no justification to continue its license. Inability to finance expensive modern apparatus doomed WMBO and countless others either to extinction or to an inferior wavelength. From 1927 to 1932, broadcasters declined from over 700 to 604. The number allowed on the air at night withered to 389 facilities. Moreover, educational stations continued to decline dramatically. Of the 202 licensed between 1921 and 1936, 164 lost their licenses through government action, internal weaknesses, or transfer of their frequencies to commercial owners. The congressional mandate directing the FRC to eliminate broadcasters allowed commercial advertising facilities to dominate the airwaves.[32]

Beginning in 1929, the industry felt the full thrust of the FRC's reductive policies. Accordingly, as broadcasters were forced to curtail their programming, move to unfavorable wavelengths, or, in extreme cases, cease operations, they indignantly challenged the government's right to order such measures. Even though most station owners had lobbied for passage of the Radio Act of 1927 and many had strongly supported the commission, those aggrieved by the panel's decisions protested every aspect of its control. First and foremost, they questioned the constitutionality of the legislation. By arguing that their enterprise did not qualify as interstate commerce, they tried to negate any congressional prerogative to pass laws about radio. Next, they claimed that the act allowed the FRC to take property without compensation or due process. Finally, they contended that the regulatory standard of public interest was overly vague and involved the unlawful delegation of legislative authority. In effect, the plaintiffs asked the courts to rule the 1927 act an invalid exercise of the federal government's power. The ensuing court battles produced several landmark cases which confirmed the legal foundation of the American radio system.[33]

The judiciary responded enthusiastically and almost unanimously by approving the Radio Act of 1927 and the vast majority of the FRC's decisions. Countering the charge that broadcasting failed to qualify as interstate commerce, a lower court established in the case of *White-hurst* v. *Grimes* that "radio communications are all interstate." In the first federal rulings on the commerce clause powers of the FRC, the Court of Appeals of the District of Columbia in a series of decisions begun in 1929 with *General Electric* v. *FRC* and the *City of New York* v. *FRC* held to the position without exception. The decision read in part, "In our opinion radio is a species of interstate commerce and as such is subject to federal regulation." By this means the judiciary unanimously accepted congressional power to control the medium. In 1931, in *American Bond and Mortgage Company* v. *United States*, the Supreme Court declared that since electromagnetic transmission and reception were interstate commerce, Congress could indeed set limits for broadcasting. In short, federal regulators uniformly received vindication in their appearances before the bar.[34]

Other cases unequivocally confirmed the wide discretionary powers bestowed on the FRC by the Radio Act of 1927. In 1933, the Supreme Court declared in *Nelson Brothers Bond and Mortgage Company* v. *FRC* that the regulatory standard of public interest, convenience, and necessity was not vague and did not involve the unlawful delegation of legislative authority. It ruled that the context of the nature of radio transmission and reception, the scope and quality of service, and the equitable geographical distribution of facilities defined public interest. Moreover, in the same case the justices upheld the FRC's right to define what constituted good public service. In fact, they affirmed the agency's right to eliminate stations that failed to adhere to this definition and decreed that Congress could grant the FRC the power of deletion. They said, "That the Congress had the power to give authority to delete stations, in view of the limited radio facilities available and the confusion that would result from interference, is not open to question." Equally important, the tribunal also stated that terminating a license did not violate the due process clause of the Constitution because businessmen had no rights superior to the exercise of regulatory power. According to this interpretation, the bureau could legally determine the number, location, and activities of all stations. This decision definitively sanctioned the panel's technical, engineering, and financial guidelines and affirmed its regulatory status.[35]

The apparent intrusion on the hallowed ground of the First Amendment stemming from the FRC's decision governing programming generated the greatest controversy. Indeed, broadcasters consistently charged that unfavorable administrative decisions censored their right to free speech. In the first case concerning this issue (*General Electric* v. *FRC*, 1929) the Court of Appeals of the District of Columbia recognized the FRC's right to consider past offerings as a part of the station's record of public service. In the famous and exceedingly significant Brinkley case (*KFKB Broadcasting Association, Inc.* v. *FRC*, 1931) the same body squarely confronted the censorship issue. It declared, "Appellant contends that the attitude of commission amounts to censorship of station. . . . This contention is without merit . . . since the commission has merely exercised its undoubted right to take note of appellant's past conduct, which is not censorship." Citing the Biblical reference "by their fruits ye shall know them," the opinion established a maxim which to this day guides the regulators.[36]

Ironically, on several highly publicized occasions when the FRC was reversed, it benefited from the ruling and further increased its power. In one instance, in 1928, the panel had ordered WGY, owned by General Electric in Schenectady, New York, to leave the air at sunset in order that KGO, another GE holding in Oakland, California, might dominate the wavelength shared by the two during the daytime. When the firm objected to the arrangement, the Court of Appeals of the District of Columbia upheld the company's claim. Citing WGY's substantial investment in the station and equipment, GE's status as a radio pioneer, and an adverse effect to more than 2 million listeners, the judges reversed the bureau and ordered it to allow WGY to continue its operations during the same hours as KGO.[37]

The following year, the Supreme Court refused to hear the case because the Radio Act of 1927 had made the lower court an administrative agency. As such, its rulings could not be reviewed by the justices within the Judiciary Act of 1789. Under this law, courts established by the Constitution can rule only on matters of law, not on matters of administrative discretion.[38]

The interference generated by the two stations seemed minute in comparison with the consternation felt by government officials.

Several senators had predicted just such an eventuality during the previous debate on broadcasting. With their worst fears confirmed, the legislators returned to Congress and altered the Radio Act of 1927 with remarkable celerity. On 1 July 1930, the president signed a law limiting the jurisdiction of the Court of Appeals of the District of Columbia to purely legal questions. Through this amendment the FRC received conclusive fact-finding powers. Its judgments henceforth were subject to additional consideration for legal error only. In point of fact, the amendment equated the commission with other federal regulatory bodies, fulfilling the fondest hopes of all supporters of the FRC.[39]

The necessity of defending its rulings forced the FRC to modify its image and procedures. Prior to the challenges, committees heard applications informally; in fact, in most instances its members did not even keep a written record of their decisions. When court appearances followed these judgments, the old policy was changed immediately. With the FRC under attack, the commissioners modified their practices to provide a specific formula for each applicant to follow. To screen petitions and discard incomplete or obviously frivolous requests, the panel directed all solicitations to examiners who conducted hearings, summoned witnesses, and collected information. If the examiners approved, the documents were then routed to the license, engineering, and legal divisions for comment. These departments, in turn, sent their recommendations to the full panel for final adjudication. Each step of this process paralleled that of a courtroom in that all parties were represented by counsel and allowed to submit evidence. Such procedural changes increased the FRC's ability to withstand legal challenges.[40]

As the commission's policies suffered more frequent questioning, the need for some reference manual for general use became increasingly apparent. In answer to this need, the FRC codified and systematized all of the unwieldy general orders by which it issued its decisions into "Rules and Regulations." This handbook offered all parties easy access to the FRC's allocation, technical, and programming requirements. Its availability forestalled many problems stemming from simple ignorance of the body's specifications.[41]

Finally, the bureau's membership itself reflected a judicial bent. As legal issues increasingly dominated members' time, lawyers and politicians, replaced radio experts. During Hoover's presidency, William D. L. Starbuck, a patent attorney, James H. Hanley, a Nebraska lawyer and politician, and Thad Brown, an Ohio politician and general counsel to both the Federal Power and Radio Commissions, joined the FRC. These changes achieved the desired result; after procedural reforms, organizational modifications, and staff replacements, the FRC successfully combated the challenges and court tests of its authority.[42]

The culminative effect of the federal judicial rulings and the agency's reorganization established the FRC's supremacy in radio regulation. The courts unequivocally upheld the constitutionality of the Radio Act of 1927, its broad and wide-ranging powers, and the standard of public interest. In other rulings, the vague language contained in the 1927 act had been defined in the FRC's favor. Moreover, these initial rulings established precedent to govern all future legal interpretations (unless specifically overruled). The process also unanimously affirmed the administrative decisions implemented by the panel. As a direct result of these rulings, the commercial advertising stations became even more firmly entrenched. It was no coincidence, then, that their ascendency remained in direct proportion to the administrative and judicial power enjoyed by the FRC.[43]

9

Network Radio

Commercial broadcasting flourished under the comprehensive system engendered by the Federal Radio Commission. The solitary stature once enjoyed by NBC broadened to include another contender. After a deceptively poor start, William S. Paley's fresh leadership dramatically altered CBS's accepted business practices. By introducing long-term contracts with a clause ensuring him exclusive access to the affiliates and an option guaranteeing him use of the station's best time, Paley stabilized coverage by binding his outlets securely to the network. Accordingly, CBS could deliver sponsors a national market during peak listening hours. Because NBC failed to offer comparable concessions, the gap between the two rivals lessened.

While CBS profited, NBC's slow response to Paley's innovations rendered it at a decided disadvantage. Yet other preoccupations ruled out any immediate reaction. Since NBC remained an RCA subsidiary, a federal anti-trust suit brought against the radio group entangled the broadcasting enterprise as well. After the suit materialized, David Sarnoff moved to take advantage of the Justice Department's case. For some time he had tried to dissassociate RCA from General Electric and Westinghouse. In light of the impending legal proceedings the two corporations agreed to divest themselves of RCA. The resulting realignment completely freed RCA from its parent firms. Drawing on vitality generated by the separation, NBC then revised its policies to more closely parallel those of CBS.

During the months consumed by the ensuing readjustment, network operations gradually dominated American broadcasting. At its completion, NBC and CBS controlled program production, distribution, and talent. In addition, both owned several stations outright, managed others, and exerted a pervasive influence which directly affected the economic stability of independents. Those fortunate enough to become outlets gained revenues from sponsored and sustaining features in exchange for granting NBC or CBS free air time. They, in turn, collected and redistributed earnings from national advertisers according to the market value of the affiliate's location and coverage. These sums totaled about one-fourth of both networks' income by the mid-1930s. Besides increasing available cash receipts, interconnection allowed local managers to increase their rates to local businessmen. Understandably, the chains attracted nearly three-fourths of the unlimited time stations, all but two of the clear channel transmitters, and all the higher power regional facilities.

Although local merchandising benefited radio finance, the economic well-being of NBC and CBS depended on attracting national sponsors. They therefore dedicated Herculean efforts to selling broadcasting. Their promotional campaigns and scientific studies emphasized the medium's efficacy as a retailing tool. In fact, these tactics proceeded so vigorously that advertising eventually supported all of commercial radio.

The developing pattern for sales and consumption highlighted the means by which huge profits could be extracted from broadcasting. After retailers accepted radio, network and station time sales clearly garnered the greatest income. Following NBC's president Merlin Aylesworth's candid observation in 1932, that "Radio has taken its place in promotion and exploitation," Americans rejected the European recourse of using a sales tax on receiving sets to finance broadcasting. Instead, they substituted an advertising oligarchy which in effect allowed businessmen to determine entertainment programs and policies for government overseers.

The rosy actuality of subsequent events received little foreshadowing in CBS's lean years. By the fall of 1928, the firm's financial resources had dwindled to a pittance. Beginning in 1927, Jerome H. Louchheim, a Philadelphia millionaire, had tried to help the network. In 1928, he supplied $15,000 on 5 January, $75,000 on 13 January,

$100,000 on 14 June, and $10,000 on 11 September. Louchheim finally balked when a survey projected continuing economic difficulties. His subsequent refusal to pour additional funds into the venture, rather than prompting direct action from the other partners, reduced them to quarreling and faultfinding.[1]

Desperately hoping to salvage some of his investment, Louchheim urged his close friend Samuel Paley to join his organization. Paley, founder and president of the Congress Cigar Company, had ample reason to support CBS. After his Philadelphia-based corporation had sponsored the "La Palina Smoker" over the air, its cigar sales had skyrocketed from 400,000 to over a million a day. In addition, broadcasting especially intrigued Samuel's son William, who managed all of Congress' advertising. William's brother-in-law, Dr. Leon Levy, enthusiastically seconded Louchheim's proposal and encouraged the younger Paley to pursue his interest in radio in general and CBS in particular. After consulting his father at some length, the youth purchased a controlling interest in CBS, where he was elected president two days before his twenty-seventh birthday. Under Paley's banner, the firm acquired an enthusiastic leader, and the older radio pioneers gained a formidable competitor.[2]

William Paley's background contrasted sharply with that of David Sarnoff, his chief rival. Indeed, their East Central European Jewish ancestry constituted their only feature in common. After the older Paley had parlayed his knowledge of cigar making into a million dollar business, William attended the best schools secure in the knowledge that a job with the family firm awaited him after graduation. On the other hand, David Sarnoff lived the Horatio Alger myth: at ten he delivered papers; at twelve he sang in a synagogue and at weddings for thirty cents a performance; then, after his father's illness, he single-handedly supported his family. Finally, years later, he worked his way up to the office of corporate president. At the time William Paley entered radio, Sarnoff already had twenty years of experience in the industry. Of course, Paley lacked radio background, but the wealthy Philadelphian had found a territory where his considerable talents could fully develop.[3]

Almost immediately after his takeover, the youthful executive tried to begin the drastic changes CBS needed to survive. For almost a year he forestalled impending economic crisis with family support and various loans from the Chemical Bank and Trust Company. In the fall of 1929, after negotiating for several months with Adolph Zukor, chief of the Paramount-Famous-Lasky Corporation, Paley finally obtained financial standing to supply his capital needs. Zukor wished to protect his motion picture empire and at the same time "cover all his bets." He therefore established an elaborate process to buy a half interest in CBS. Under the terms of the agreement, Paley divided the corporation's stock into Class A and B. He exchanged 50 percent of the Class A held by his family and friends for 58,823 shares of Paramount with market value of $65 per share. In turn, Zukor promised to buy back this $3.8 million worth of securities for $5 million by 1 March 1932, provided that CBS earned $2 million profit in the ensuing two years. Although the proposition seemed a gamble in 1929, CBS actually earned $3 million by 1932. Despite Zukor's obligation to buy back his stock for almost $70 a share, Paramount could not meet the terms of the original contract because the Depression had forced its stock to a paltry $9 per share. To salvage part of the investment, Paley modified their arrangement. Under the new terms, he offered to buy back Zukor's CBS holdings for $5.2 million. With this capital Zukor could then repurchase Paramount's certificates from CBS for $4 million. Paley thereby regained complete control of the network, while letting Zukor off the hook, thus beginning a series of successful ventures for the fledgling broadcaster.[4]

The financial stability gained by the CBS-Paramount exchange allowed Paley to escalate competition with NBC, which was already underway. In 1928, he purchased WABC in New York City from the Grebe Radio Manufacturing Company for $400,000. Immediately he sought other connections to carry CBS shows with his new flagship. Therein he encountered his first major obstacle, because NBC had secured most of the more powerful, pretigious facilities.[5]

In order to overcome this disadvantage, CBS revised its business practices. As originally developed, NBC's contract had allowed individual broadcasters to preempt the chain. Even though NBC might want to deliver a national hook-up, it had to yield if the outlet wanted to transmit its own local features. Consequently, NBC could never guarantee advertisers nationwide service. In addition, it had charged its associates for sustaining fare. In place of this, Paley offered members free unsponsored programs if they agreed to carry CBS's entire commercial schedule during peak listening hours (the time when sponsors desired to reach a large audience). By August 1929, Paley had standardized network policy. An option clause in the contract granted CBS access to all the time of the outlet in return for free chain-produced features, and an exclusivity proviso prohibited the affiliate from allowing any outsider to use its transmitter. CBS could extend the two-year covenant twice for additional one-year terms. Barely twelve months after Paley assumed control, he had devised the contemporary framework which, despite some government-imposed modifications, still serves as the basis for industry-wide relations.[6]

The revised pacts served their purpose and secured new membership. By 1929, CBS divided forty-nine stations between a basic chain of six groups and twenty-two facilities with four supplementaries. The units encompassed a diversified geographic representation: South Atlantic (3); East South Central (5); West South Central (6); West North Central (2); Mountain (2); and Pacific or "Don Lee" Coast Unit (5). By the end of 1929, CBS had added eleven more for a total of sixty; by 1931 it had swelled to seventy-six, and by 1933 to ninety-one. As it expanded, CBS ownership entered important markets in Charlotte, Chicago, Cincinnati, Minneapolis, New York, St. Louis, and Atlantic City in order to help subsidize costly network operations. By 1933, CBS had grown to the world's largest chain.[7]

A mere preponderance of stations could not guarantee a superior percentage of the radio audience. To compensate for unfavorable wavelengths, low power, and unfamiliar call letters, Paley established superior programming as CBS's priority. Since NBC had contracted most well-known talent and since the remaining established entertainers commanded salaries well beyond CBS's ability to pay, the company decided to develop fresh personalities. In 1929, as a first step in this policy, Paley organized the Columbia Artists Bureau. The new subsidiary sought out and trained young performers that it then passed on to the network.   Under ideal conditions obscure talent signed on for a guaranteed $100 a week, appeared on a sustaining feature, developed a following, and moved on to secure sponsorship. While many failed dismally, the success of others, including Morton Downey, Bing Crosby, and the Mills Brothers, fanned the imaginations of starstruck aspirants across the nation.[8]

Paley next took up concert management, after merging several companies into the Columbia Concert Corporation. Under Arthur Judson's direction, this new CBS agency provided artists and orchestras for its parent organization and also booked musicians for theaters and concert halls. In the course of confronting its problems with expansion, affiliate contracts, and programming, CBS evolved into a truly diversified broadcasting corporation.[9]

By the end of 1929, Paley's business innovations had forced NBC to reevaluate its own practices and procedures. After some soul searching, its executives agreed to try to make NBC self-sustaining. Of course, longevity and powerful affiliates endowed NBC with an appearance of strength. Beneath this facade, however, little noticed industrial and corporate weaknesses gradually had deteriorated its capacity for effective competition. A decade's worth of events largely beyond the chain's control eventually coalesced to alter its destiny.[10]

During the emergence of broadcasting in 1921–22, manufacturers and electrical companies had entered the industry simply to increase receiver sales by stimulating listener interest. Their short-lived ascendancy dwindled, and by 1929, they owned an insignificant number of stations. In turn, the broadcasting corporation, a new breed devoted exclusively to transmitting programs, replaced them.[11]

As a result of their withdrawal from station operations, emergent enterprises, including Philco, Zenith, and Emerson, directed their energies to challenging the RCA-GE-Westinghouse axis. Sales-minded capitalists who stressed promotion over scientific research and engineering dominated these newer, more aggressive firms. Since the major technical objectives already had been achieved, those who best reduced costs and prices reaped the industry's financial rewards. The ensuing struggle between established businessmen and their fledgling rivals weakened the radio giants. Although the larger concerns stressed research, quality, and the avoidance of price competition, the newcomers challenged them with innovation, slick packaging, and hard hitting rivalry. General Electric, Westinghouse, and their sales agent RCA suffered further because the complex relationship between the three hindered any unified effort. Since General Electric and Westinghouse pursued separate policies and objectives, control procedures became almost impossible to co-ordinate. Consequently, their disparities weakened RCA. Moreover, the stock market crash and the ensuing Depression intensified economic pressures brought on by the challengers.[12]

David Sarnoff exploited the changing industrial conditions to separate RCA from General Electric and Westinghouse. He requested that his company be granted increased facilities and responsibilities in answer to outside threats to the radio group. To allow RCA to compete effectively with Zenith, Philco, and Emerson by unifying retailing and production, he insisted that it should change from sales agent to radio manufacturer. Accordingly, using General Electric and Westinghouse funds, RCA purchased the Victor Talking Machine Company in February 1929, acquiring as a result Victor's factory in Camden, New Jersey. In the autumn, General Electric and Westinghouse finally agreed for RCA to assume total self-sufficiency by developing its own research, engineering, manufacturing, and marketing divisions. To expedite this process, General Electric turned over its Harrison Tube Plant to RCA while Westinghouse similarly transferrred its Lamp Works in Indianapolis. To further protect the newly independent offspring while ensuring it additional revenue, the parent companies also ceded Sarnoff all their NBC stock, making the network RCA's wholly owned subsidiary. He reimbursed them for their plant facilities, funds, and NBC securities with additional blocks of RCA stock. Since they would be repaid by larger revenues from RCA only if the firm remained solvent, both corporations developed an even deeper commitment to its success.[13]

In May 1930, Sarnoff's drive for autonomy received unexpected support. In that month, the Justice Department filed an anti-trust suit against General Electric, Westinghouse, American Telephone and Telegraph, and the Radio Corporation of America. Because the cross-licensing arrangements developed shortly after World War I seemed unduly favorable to the four enterprises, the federal government acceded to criticism from monopoly-conscious congressmen and other RCA critics. Its subsequent demand that those industrial accords be dissolved further served Sarnoff's purpose.[14]

Since AT&T had already relinquished membership on the RCA board of directors and all stock in the company, it compromised with the Justice Department. In return for cancelling the AT&T cross-licensing agreements, the attorney general dropped the telephone company from its case. Throughout 1931, the GE-Westinghouse-RCA axis searched for a policy to protect their diverse interests while successfully countering the Justice Department charges. Andrew W.

Robertson, chairman of the board of Westinghouse, Gerald W. Swope, president of General Electric, and David Sarnoff of RCA met to explore endless options proposed by hundreds of specialists. Owen D. Young, General Electric chairman of the board, hovered in the background to soothe bruised feelings and arrange compromises to keep the group on the right track. After months of debate, the businessmen narrowed their choices to proceeding with a judicial determination of the issues or settling out of court following the government's suggested guidelines. While all denied violating federal law, they nonetheless recognized the toll that delay, uncertainty, and possible adverse publicity could exact. Finally, they opted to settle out of court. All concurred, however, that the settlement should guarantee RCA's survival.[15]

The Justice Department also agreed to an out-of-court arrangement. It strongly urged completion of this adjustment by the trial date (15 November 1932) and further stipulated that the companies enter into a consent decree rather than a simple dismissal of the case. Also, it declared that General Electric and Westinghouse must completely divest from their RCA stock and withdraw their officials from the RCA board of directors. Most importantly, the department completely accepted the decision to protect RCA.[16]

A final agreement among General Electric, Westinghouse, and RCA required almost three months more of round-the-clock negotiations. On 21 November 1932, the Department of Justice officially approved a twelve-document consent decree. As a result of its many stipulations, the newly independent RCA was free to pursue radio manufacturing, maritime communications, and broadcasting. For yielding their ownership rights and facilities to RCA, General Electric and Westinghouse received RCA debentures and property. Thanks to the anti-trust suit and his own determination, David Sarnoff attained an independent, financially sound corporation.[17]

The consent decree's sweeping policy changes profoundly affected NBC as well. As a part of the benefits which RCA gained, the network obtained program rights for all of the General Electric and Westinghouse broadcasting facilities. Moreover, NBC assumed operations of some Westinghouse and General Electric stations, including KDKA in Pittsburgh, KYW in Chicago, WBZ in Springfield, Massachusetts, and WBZA in Boston. Excepting WBZA, all held clear channel, 50,000-watt licenses. As a part of its management, NBC furnished all entertainment, sold the time to advertisers, and collected and retained all revenues. With the ten other stations it already controlled, the chain secured outlets for its transmissions in all major markets. Ownership of these subsidiaries profited NBC more than did its entire network operations.[18]

While NBC established policy for its own stations, the company also revised its relationship with its independent affiliates. Originally, it had paid them for receiving commercial broadcasts and had charged them for sustaining fare. Despite the rapid increase in its business, NBC informally continued these transactions through 1931. Then, as competition intensified, it adopted formal arrangements closely resembling those written by CBS. Under the new terms, NBC offered each participant an annual contract with a renewal option. A time clause required the outlet to accept specific programs upon twenty-eight days' notice. By revising its business practices, NBC gained access to a national audience for crucial time slots.[19]

To reinforce these adjustments, NBC modified its programming practices. It abolished hourly charges for sustaining features; in their place, the chain substituted an invariable monthly charge of $1,500. To enhance its image, it introduced political and current event discussions, opera and music appreciation transmissions, and a farm and home forum which it sent to members without charge. Upon RCA's independence, NBC, its most important subsidiary, revised many of its own business practices in order to compete more effectively with CBS. In 1933, after a successful transition, NBC moved into the vast Rockefeller Radio City complex. In many ways, this sixty-story structure, which cost $250 million and covered three square blocks, symbolized the industry's new era.[20]

While the corporations and the federal government negotiatied RCA's future, broadcasting settled into a recognizable routine. Its format resembled that of the newspaper business in the sense that individual listeners represented little direct income. Their true value lay in the advertising revenues an outlet could attract based on the size of its audience. However, as with any new medium, many businessmen hesitated to invest much capital for unknown returns. Moreover, during the severe economic depression, many commercial establishments reduced their advertising budgets. To overcome hesitation by their largest potential revenue source, both NBC and CBS tried to demonstrate radio's promotional value. To reinforce these efforts, they adapted their programming to boost circulation by attracting the largest possible audience. As these modifications succeeded and more merchandizers patronized the medium, the network, in turn, fell more and more under the supreme power of the ad men.[21]

NBC and CBS relied on marketing and public relations, testimonials from businessmen already committed to the airwaves, impartial studies, and scientific research to promote broadcasting. The salesmen concentrated their efforts on firms that produced articles for mass consumption, contending that broadcasting ideally suited inexpensive convenience goods, such as food and drugs, soft drinks, cigars, cigarettes, and petroleum derivatives, as well as higher-priced radios, refrigerators, and autos. Since such products enjoyed widespread distribution, offered high repeat sales, and generally constituted small units, broadcasting could substantially increase their demand.[22]

After identifying the concerns and commodities best suited to the airwaves, NBC and CBS devoted themselves to the serious business of selling air time. They surmised that their efforts could succeed only by generating direct or indirect purchases. In countless testimonials, articles and books, both chains repeatedly ballyhooed the "fourth dimension of advertising." As a classic example, NBC elaborately compared A&P newspaper and radio budgets. Needless to say, its scrutiny of cost and circulation detailed the numerous benefits broadcasting publicity brought the food industry.[23]

Following the premise that satisfied patrons could best sell radio to their skeptical peers, the networks encouraged testimonials supporting their public relations program. H. F. Jones, Campbell Soup Company's manager, reported that CBS advertising had increased the sale of their three most popular flavors by 30, 35, and 100 percent. In the same vein, George Washington Hill, the American Tobacco Company president, credited sponsoring an NBC show with increasing his corporation's profits by over $3 million during 1930 and 1931.[24]

In parallel efforts, NBC and CBS used scientific, demographic, and engineering studies to emphasize broadcasting's saturation and popularity. NBC boasted that 86.7 percent of all families tuned into the Red Network, while 84.8 percent listened to the Blue. Not to be outdone, CBS confidently claimed that 90.2 percent of the nation followed its programs. In a supposedly impartial analysis, the National Association of Broadcasters found 83.7 percent of all urban households glued to their receivers for five hours and four minutes a day, while 88.5 percent of all rural units averaged five hours and eighteen minutes daily. The NAB gloated that only sleeping and working occupied more time than listening to the radio.[25]

CBS refined the selling process to an art. Paul Kesten, head of the promotional department, and his assistant Victor Ratner continually cited surveys and statistics proving strong public preference for CBS. To put "solid statistical meat" on their assertions, they cited evidence gathered by the accounting firm of Price, Waterhouse and Company and the Massachusetts Institute of Technology. Not surprisingly, these research studies extolled CBS triumphs: WABC first in New York City, KMOX leading in St. Louis, and CBS out in front in Boston. Since the two executives theorized that appearances outweighed mere facts, they occasionally fabricated statistics, manipulated research results, and inflated listener surveys. Undeniably, however, their hucksterism did attract important sponsors to the chain.[26]

Equally telling, network programming policies conformed to the public relations campaigns. In fact, advertisers started selecting material for the time periods they purchased and determining the success or failure of local features and even sustaining fare produced by NBC and CBS. To increase their identification factor, businessmen paid for designated themes such as the Eveready Hour (batteries), Clicquot Club Eskimos (soda), A&P Gypsies (groceries), Cities Service Hour (gasoline), and Ipana Troubadors (toothpaste). In time, programming ensured patrons the most profitable listening audience by adapting to a household's cycle of social activity. Thus, daytime serial dramas, spun out day after day in quarter-hour episodes, promoted products geared to the housewife. Goods consumed by the entire family sponsored half-hour and hour nighttime series.[27]

The case of the American Tobacco Company demonstrated the sponsors' growing power. In the first six months of 1932 alone, the company disbursed $954,398 to NBC, thereby outspending all of its competition. Its controversial, dynamic president, George Washington Hill, personally adopted NBC and radio. Because the chain valued American Tobacco Company support, it specifically warned all comedians and entertainers against "burlesquing" NBC's most important client. The scrupulous care taken with his account proved to be in vain, however, when in 1931 Hill ended his exclusive relationship with NBC and began to transmit over CBS as well. The change took place ostensibly because NBC prohibited mentioning prices over the air. At Columbia, Hill could hear announcers praise American Tobacco's "nickel" cigars. Probably a more significant factor was that Lord, Thomas, and Logan, Hill's advertising agency, had allied itself with Paramount, half-owner of CBS. In any event, after the switch, NBC's president Merlin Aylesworth plaintively informed Hill, "You will always find me knocking at the door," thereby voicing the sentiment of all his fellow broadcasters toward their sponsors.[28]

As advertisers utilized commercial programs, the offerings changed substantially. At first, radio had merely imitated other mass media. Later, after recognizing its unique potentialities and limitations, broadcasters and advertisers adapted material specifically for the airwaves. While the enterprise yielded few true innovations, it converted other forms of entertainment to its own use by synthesizing and assimilating them.[29]

Until late 1929, NBC and CBS primarily transmitted music during national hook-ups. Vocal and instrumental solos, operas, and the increasingly popular dance tunes and jazz constituted the nucleus of commercial fare. By the end of 1929, however, drama began attracting listeners' attention. After successfully bringing off several stage performances, network executives realized that they could create plays more effectively in their own studios. In addition, businessmen approved of their relatively low development and production costs in comparison with their widespread drawing power. When eighteen NBC outlets transmitted "The Rise of the Goldbergs," it garnered enthusiastic public approval. NBC's study of its appeal and popularity observed that a large following existed "for good programming of a Jewish type," and although the feature "concerned a Jewish family, a vast majority of requests to keep it on the air came from Gentiles." All told, NBC estimated that 900,000 families wrote its sponsor, the Pepsodent Company, thanking them for the Goldbergs.[30]

The success of the Goldbergs prompted NBC to exploit many facets of the audience. In fact, executives subordinated prejudices to monetary considerations in exploring other possible segments of the market. Thus, John Royal., vice-president of NBC programs, suggested that General Electric sponsor Paul Robeson for thirteen broadcasts. Royal observed that the popular black entertainer "would make a great hit with the niggers . . . and it is true that darkies buy General Electric articles as well as anyone else."[31]

While network executives tried to develop other entertainment to appeal to ethnic and racial groups, serials saturated the airwaves. "Sam 'n Henry" was originally transmitted over WGN (the Chicago *Tribune* station), but a bitter salary dispute forced it off the air. Accordingly, Freeman Fisher Gosden and Charles J. Correll switched their program over to the rival Chicago *Daily News* station WMAQ under the new title of "Amos 'n Andy." With the name "Sam 'n Henry" copyrighted, WGN confidently predicted that the show could never succeed under another title. The claim proved false after "Amos 'n Andy" became the biggest hit on radio. In addition to its peculiar brand of humor, which to a degree reflected Gosden's boyhood, it introduced several long-used gimmicks, including the musical signature, the daily serial format, and the opening and closing commercial in one package.[32]

In the summer of 1929, NBC delivered "Amos 'n Andy" to a national audience. Once again the Pepsodent Company sponsored a show which dominated all listening. But in contrast to the approbation gained by the Goldbergs, several critics severely attacked the series. The most important of all, Roy Wilkins of the National Association for the Advancement of Colored People, blasted "Amos 'n Andy" for exploiting blacks. He argued that it misled Americans, with the result that, "The white people of the nation have the most fantastic ideas of their twelve million negro citizens and we have found that we can never trust their intellect or discretion." Despite the criticism, NBC cavalierly ignored what Royal called "figments of Wilkins' imagination." The chain retained "Amos 'n Andy" because its wide circulation attracted avid sponsors.[33]

During 1931 and 1932, vaudeville-style comedy hours and variety fare began to rival series in popularity. With the collapse of vaudeville and a theater slump, many well-known entertainers switched over to broadcasting. Soon, NBC's line-up included Eddie Cantor (sponsored by Chase and Sanborn), Jack Pearl (Lucky Strike), Ed Wynn (Texaco), Al Jolson (Chevrolet), and Rudy Vallee (Fleischmann's Yeast). Not to be outdone, CBS acquired Burns and Allen (Robert

Burns' cigars), Jack Benny (Canada Dry), Stoopnagle and Budd Pontiac), and Howard and Shelton (Chesterfield). By 1933, comedy and variety had become so popular that Cantor's show evicted "Amos 'n Andy" from its lead in the Crosley ratings.[34]

As series, comedy, and variety hours held sway over the nation's airwaves, a little noticed change altered the nature of programs. During radio's early years, NBC and CBS created all their own offerings. But beginning in 1929, advertising agencies entered the business. By 1931, they controlled virtually all the network commercial fare. Pure profit motive accounted for this change. In 1931, a single hour over NBC cost $10,000. The publicists received a 15 percent commission from the chain to negotiate between it and the sponsor. Developing and producing material extracted an additional 15 percent from their clients. Since this shift benefited NBC and CBS by increasing their business and profits, they readily acquiesced. Under the new arrangement, public relations firms furnished entertainment for the time periods they had brought for their patrons, which the networks then distributed to their outlets.[35]

As NBC and CBS relinquished their control over this sphere, they redirected their attention to sustaining features. Both utilized these to increase circulation and to meet Federal Radio Commission guidelines. Many businessmen, more accustomed to newspapers and periodicals, expected the chains to develop unsponsored services comparable to commercial programming in order to "compose a well-rounded magazine of the air." By attracting goodwill and larger audiences, their transmissions gained additional sponsors while allowing NBC and CBS to raise their hourly rates.[36]

Moreover, by providing a balanced and diversified format, NBC and CBS complied with FRC requirements. Special reports and educational and religious programs offset commercial entertainment. In fact, the two began to compete through their public service transmissions. NBC continually emphasized that sponsored features constituted only a portion of its broadcast day. It praised the wide variety of operas, lectures, government reports, social welfare material, and news that rounded out its scheduling. In like fashion, CBS extolled its American School of the Air, its Schelling Symphony Concert for children, its National Student Federation, and other shows on national life, religion, education, science, and current affairs.[37]

To complement the noncommercial offerings, NBC and CBS developed public service standards. In 1927, seven years before Franklin D. Roosevelt instituted industry self-government as a part of the New Deal, NBC created an advisory council to ensure "the best programs available for broadcast in the U.S." In 1930, CBS established requirements to which shows had to conform before the chain would transmit them. From that time on, both organizations issued an almost yearly list of manifestos, orders, codes, and pronouncements dealing with entertainment and advertising criteria. Of course, skeptics might well argue that network approval of commercial programs supplied by advertising agencies constituted a mere formality. Be that as it may, the FRC pictured NBC and CBS as models of industrial self-regulation.[38]

By 1933, when Eddie Cantor's variety hour replaced "Amos 'n Andy" as the nation's most popular amusement, broadcasting's economic and financial structure had been firmly established. "Right or wrong," as Owen D. Young observed, "advertising dominated radio." The sale of time produced substantial profits, making the airwaves an adjunct to mass consumption. Indeed, payments to NBC for just the first six months of 1932 demonstrated the immense sums involved:

American Tobacco Company	$954,398
Standard Brands	863,648
Pepsodent Company	843,173
General Motors	648,598
Swift and Company	542,877
Great A&P Tea Company	534,537
General Foods Corporation	456,783
General Oats Company	440,206
General Mills	370,497
General Electric	357,486

As a result of the aggressive sales campaign, the medium generated the fastest growing source of advertising dollars in America. In fact, as the Commerce Department reported, "In no other country of the world is radio advertising used directly and indirectly, as extensively as in the United States."[39]

Of course, not everyone approved of that structure. Indeed, criticism abounded, eventually growing into an outright revolt against the American system of broadcasting. While the dissenters pursued diverse courses of action, their fundamental desire to alter radio in the United States united them. However, their success depended neither on the force of their arguments nor even the justice of their cause; rather, political power determined the resolution of their protest.

10

The Abortive Revolt

Intensified dissatisfaction with the broadcasting industry culminated in an outright revolt against commercial advertising, programming, and the Federal Radio Commission. While the flurry of charges and countercharges contained some rightful complaint, most of the rhetoric abounded in inconsistencies and outright falsehood. In many instances, protests of favoritism, vested interests, and monopoly had begun in the early years of radio telephony and telegraphy and continued for decades afterward. In fact, the same challenges formulated during the Hoover and early Roosevelt administrations form the basic criticisms voiced today against broadcasting.

Commercial advertising stations and the networks easily blunted the attack against the industry simply because of their challengers' self-defeating reactions. The reformers, led by university and college officials, claimed special treatment for themselves, yet attacked favoritism and special privileges for their adversaries. In addition to other contradictory requests, their demands for the United States to adopt the British system of broadcasting doomed their proposals.

Furthermore, the radicalization of the dissidents' charges prompted diverse coalitions in defense of the American system. To diffuse complaints directed at the industry, politicians, network executives, commercial broadcasters, and government bureaucrats rallied to the concept of a unified communications commission.

Centralized authority over radio, telephone, telegraph, and cables could appear to reform without structurally altering established economic relationships . Since these factions desperately wanted to maintain the existing order, good business turned out to be good politics.

Consequently, the Communications Act of 1934, which created the Federal Communications Commission, became law after the desire for a unified agency won support from the new Democratic administration. In the end, it proved difficult to compromise the effectiveness of profits, popular programs, technololgical developments, and success. The reformers failed to reverse fourteen years of history.

After the Radio Act of 1929 resolved the status of the Federal Radio Commission, Congress instituted hearings on wire and wireless services. Because the lawmakers had studied broadcast regulation for almost a decade, they took up the issue confidently. Many agreed with government officials and businessmen who hoped to develop a uniform supervisory policy for all interstate communications. At the time, the president, through his Interdepartmental Radio Advisory Committee, shared authority with the Department of State, the Post Office Department, the Commerce Department, the Interstate Commerce Commission, and the FRC. Consolidating control in one bureau would streamline that piecemeal arrangement. Although such a plan had been introduced in the 1920s, and in due course had been rejected, many felt that its time had come.[1]

During 1929 and 1930, the Senate Committee on Interstate Commerce, directed by Michigan Democrat James Couzens, examined a bill establishing an independent regulatory agency for radio, telephone, telegraph, and cables. The majority of broadcasters, bureaucrats, and industry leaders recognized the advantage of unification and supported the Couzens bill, but many cautioned the committee against undue haste. Louis G. Caldwell, the FRC's general counsel, pointed out that the newly instituted FRC had had insufficient time to stabilize broadcasting. He argued that another organization should be created only after the commission had imposed regulatory standards to supervise all radio users. Accordingly, he suggested that the agency should expand and consolidate power by assuming those varied radio duties performed by the Department of Commerce. After enlarging its organization, securing more authority, and establishing regulatory requirements, the panel could then easily cede to an all-encompassing commission. Caldwell's evolutionary recommendation won acceptance among the committee members. Obviously, the lawmakers hoped to avoid further industrial disruption in the midst of the nation's most severe depression.[2]

By focusing attention on communications, the Senate hearings served opponents of the American system as a forum and rallying point. Politicians, small businessmen, educators, scientists, and engineers voiced substantial dismay at the way in which the 1927 act and subsequent FRC rulings had affected noncommercial broadcasters. New York Democratic representative Emanuel Cellers argued that the FRC had always intended to crowd smaller independent operators off the air. The National Radio Club of Washington, D.C., charged that the panel overtly discriminated against the less powerful. Moreover, the club adamantly contradicted the government's view that order could be imposed only by eliminating minor stations; it argued that the FRC used this policy to justify sanctions against the politically weak.[3]

During the hearings, critics claiming to be "fighting the cause of every independent broadcasting station, of every independent communications company" vociferously charged the networks with monopoly. In one resolute outburst, the Radio Protective Association of Chicago demanded that the FRC revoke all the station licenses granted General Electric, Westinghouse, and RCA for violation of the antimonopoly provisions of the Radio Act of 1927. The association vigorously complained that lessened competition and restrained commerce resulted from the fact that the National Broadcasting Company and the Columbia Broadcasting System either owned or controlled the nation's most powerful and important transmitters[4]

Mounting charges of monopoly and favoritism against the FRC's allocation program reinforced other allegations. Many reformers claimed that smaller facilities languished in inferior positions while larger ones increased their power and snapped up all the clear channels. In fact, many contended that network association constituted a prerequisite for obtaining favorable wavelengths. Perennial critic Congressman Edwin Davis charged that there "has not been anything like an equitable distribution of licenses, wavelengths, power, and station time." Senator Clarence C. Dill demanded to know why network outlets dominated all of the clear channels. Indeed,

Dill asserted that the FRC's policies had endangered the national security by having "every important station in the United States owned by some chain." [5]

University and college broadcasters, too, lamented FRC favoritism toward profit-oriented facilities. A scathing report issued jointly by the National Advisory Council on Radio in Education and the American Political Science Association concluded, "Educational broadcasting has become the poor relation of commercial broadcasting, and the pauperization of the former has increased in direct proportion to the growing affluence of the latter." Scholars also fiercely deplored the existing level of programming. Robert M. Hutchins, president of the University of Chicago, charged that broadcasters ignored the needs of the universities' minority patrons because of the "delusion that a mass audience is the only audience."[6]

Advertising agencies garnered their share of the blame. The well-known scientist and inventor Dr. Lee De Forest decried the debasement. He declared, "I have lost no opportunity to cry out in earnest protest against the crass commercialism, the etheric vandalism of the vulgar hucksters, agencies, advertisers." Others deplored the lack of choice in programming during the peak listening hours when commercial stations relied on ad men to produce and develop shows. Admiral Stanford C. Hooper lamented that the majority of New York City's thirty stations (more than even existed in all of England and Germany combined) depended on commercial entertainment and promotional messages. He mainly complained that the uniformity of their product, even though offered by a large variety of outlets, denied listeners any range of selection. Representative Charles L. Abernethy, Republican from North Carolina, summed up the dissidents' frustrations, concluding that Congress' sole accomplishment "has been to serve the purposes of a group of advertisers."[7]

The furor over programming reverberated to Capitol Hill and beyond. A Lucky Strike advertising controversy admirably demonstrated the growing concern. On Saturday evenings the American Tobacco Company sponsored an orchestra on NBC. In the course of the program the firm used paid testimonials from athletes and actors to underscore the Lord, Thomas, and Logan agency's slogan, "Reach for a Lucky instead of a sweet." This strategy evoked such intense hostility that the National Food Products Protective Committee mobilized the American Medical Association, the National Child Welfare Association, the Boy Rangers of America, the American Physical Educational Association, and the Congregational, Reformed, and Methodist churches to petition the FRC to revoke the licenses of all NBC stations carrying the show. The enraged petitioners denounced the public threat from the athletes' testimonials. The committee insisted that false and dangerous claims for Lucky Strike unfairly attacked the nation's food industry in order to create a vast children's market for cigarettes. In response, NBC and the American Tobacco Company deleted the testimonials from the commercial announcements to placate the angry protesters. Their partial capitulation satisfied the FRC, which then ignored the other charges and refused to press the case further.[8]

In face of the growing rancor, the FRC decided to respond to the more vehement attacks against its policies. Before the congressional committee, the commissioners denied favoring network outlets with frequency assignments. They explained that powerful stations naturally gravitated toward NBC and CBS because such a relationship helped increase their revenues and circulation. The regulators also contended that they treated stations as independent units; under law each had a right to enter into contracts with networks. Furthermore, commission policy emphasized that broadcasters deserved the same discretion in advertising as newspapers and magazines. The members continually assured the lawmakers that since the livelihood of all three depended upon maintaining listener or consumer approval, self-interest dictated wise use of promotions.[9]

Charges of FRC favoritism toward chain outlets and the networks threatened the commission most. In 1931, the agency warned its supposed favorites that advertising abuses engendered the principle objections to the American system. The next year, the Senate responded to tremendous pressure from educators, newspapers, magazines, and religious institutions by requiring the FRC to investigate its own alleged discrimination as well as the advertising imbroglio.[10]

The inquiry proceeded quickly to produce an impressive-looking, if commonplace document, for which NBC and CBS answered most of the questions concerning their affiliates. While the FRC never seriously questioned the crucial role of public relation firms and sponsors, the study did detail more complexities than most critics had been willing to recognize. Although it agreed that the FRC's policies worked a severe hardship upon small, noncommercial outlets, it stressed that internal weaknesses among the less-favored more directly undermined their survival. In its first defense, the bureau charged that scholastic and nonprofit organizations failed to help themselves. The FRC reported that since the beginning of 1932 it had licensed ninety-five institutions of higher learning, yet only forty-four transmitted shows. In addition, the semester system used by many schools prevented most from developing continuous programming. Thus, even when the government had granted them full-time, year-round licenses, many had to discontinue operations during the summer months. A perennial money shortage prevented their managers from buying new equipment or maintaining full schedules by hiring efficient full-time personnel. Internal problems already hindered this group and FRC policies only reinforced them.[11]

The report also highlighted the deteriorating relationship between schools and commercial broadcasters. Although this rift boded little good for either side, it endangered the scholars most. Historically, university and college officials had hoped to develop and produce shows for commercial advertising stations and networks. In 1930, they organized the National Advisory Council on Radio in Education to further this goal. The council opted to promote cooperation using funds donated by John D. Rockefeller, Jr., and the Carnegie Corporation. In spite of its activities the hours set aside for instructional programs dwindled in direct proportion to the increased value of network air time.[12]

Longstanding relationships suffered. During 1928 and 1929, New York University alone had developed eighty features for WOR. In 1930, the station informed school officials that it could offer their productions on only two evenings per week because advertising agencies and their clients had purchased the time formerly allotted to the educators. In another instance, WMAQ in Chicago had maintained traditionally cordial relations with the University of Chicago. Unfortunately, it too eventually ceased cooperating. Judith Waller, the university liaison in WMAQ's highest councils, valiantly used her influence as educational director of the outlet and a member of the University of Chicago Radio Committee to combat the change. In spite of her finest efforts, despite WMAQ's earnest desire to transmit instructional features, it abandoned the programs for lucrative commercial ones. After the station joined NBC, University of Chicago offerings were either entirely eliminated or shifted to the very poorest hours.[13]

The pressure to sell air time, reinforced by advertising agencies' preeminence in programming, discouraged academicians from cooperative ventures. Indeed, many concluded that profit making automatically excluded educational broadcasting, and some further argued that commercial outlets and networks exploited the schools to demonstrate public spirit or to fill up gaps in their schedules in the absence of sponsored entertainment.[14]

The FRC's investigation provided critics with ammunition against American broadcasting even though the agency tried to minimize the negative aspects. Shortly after the panel released its report, reams of published attacks scored the system. The most vocal of these aroused considerable public wrath. In 1932, the president of the *Ventura Free Press* published *The Empire of the Air*, a condemnation of the radio trust. In this volume, H. O. Davis characterized the monopoly control of General Electric, Westinghouse, and the Radio Corporation of America as a nefarious stifling of the free enterprise system perpetrated by Owen D. Young and David Sarnoff. Davis charged "Advertising is King of the Air" because a weak and ineffective FRC had allowed the commercial advertising stations to dominate the airwaves. Among his gratuitous panacea Davis recommended limiting advertising, prescribing stringent new regulation for networks, granting nonprofit facilities 25 percent of all channels, and enlarging the FRC to represent the public more effectively.[15]

James Rorty, a former advertising writer, produced *Our Master's Voice: Advertising* and *Order on the Air!* In both books he criticized the "business-owned, business-administrated, and business-censored" system, which used radio as a sales medium. He emphasized, however, that the industry's growth and development reflected the nation's cultural and social milieu rather than the trend toward hucksterism. He concluded that the American setting made it inevitable. He predicted that those who would try to reorganize broadcasting faced serious opposition from the public and business alike.[16]

Finally, Jerome G. Kerwin, an assistant professor of political science, presented *The Control of Radio*. His more scholarly survey began by critically comparing communications in other nations. His survey enumerated the unique aspects of the American system and its domination by business. He emphasized that outside the United States, radio had become a government monopoly which more or less excluded advertising. After discussing the various alternatives, Kerwin condemned promotional excesses fostered by private, FRC-approved monopolies. He concurred with critics attacking the American structure; in fact, he declared that programs geared to a thirteen-year-old's standards debased tastes and pandered to the most banal fashion and trends. He continued, "The privately controlled commercial broadcasting system needs a corrective which because of its nature the system cannot apply to itself." He then suggested that the federal government intervene by nationalizing five to ten channels, erecting its own network, establishing its own long-distance wire service, and developing and producing high-quality programs without advertising. These and other pronouncements focused attention on Congress, the FRC, programming, and advertising. What had begun as a logical step to coordinate wire and wireless services through one government agency turned into an outright challenge to commercialism. During the evolution, the dissidents radicalized their position and sought change through political action.[17]

Oddly enough, the supposed ivory tower of education supplied the true revolutionaries. Many FRC actions fanned the flames of resentment of the thinning ranks of college and university broadcasters to a dangerous level. For example, the FRC had ordered frequency shifts for the Rennselaer Polytechnic Institute's station, WHAZ, on three separate occasions during one month. Palmer C. Ricketts, president of Rennselaer, futilely protested that the government decisions interfered with WHAZ's programs by estranging the listening audience through continuous disruptions. Nor was RPI's plight unique. Connecticut State College's transmitter received orders to shift on nine separate occasions, while six other institutions of higher learning moved six times each. J. C. Futrall, president of the University of Arkansas (station KUOA), claimed the academicians "had been shoved off by the FRC into unfavorable channels so that they do not get out as extensively or as well as they did." When their situation worsened, educators stepped up their conferences and corollary activities.[18]

The schools tried to safeguard their remaining facilities from profit-oriented encroachment through political alliance. Originally, the Agriculture Department seemed a sure benefactor for their interests. But soon the chains began to compete by actively disseminating agricultural information. In 1929 NBC sent thirty-two stations the National Farm and Home Hour. Shortly thereafter, CBS increased its commitment by appointing former Agriculture Department Radio Division chief and FRC commissioner Sam Pickard vice-president in charge of affiliate relations. Consequently, CBS also began to develop and produce features geared to the nation's farm population. As the networks continued to transmit Department of Agriculture features, many of the educators' strongest government supporters insisted, "It would be wiser to attempt to resolve the problems by cooperating with commercial stations and appeals to the FRC." Once more, the scholars found their influence diminishing in the face of gains by the networks and their affiliates.[19]

After the defection of the Agriculture Department, the angry collegians turned to the secretary of the interior for support. The secretary, in turn, directed Commissioner of Education William John Cooper to meet with the clamoring pedagogues. His interviews in late 1929 and early 1930 with representatives of the Association of Land Grant Colleges, the National Educational Association, and the American Council on Education proved Cooper to be a strong and resourceful leader. He oriented the groups to political action; under his tutelage they formed the National Committee on Education by Radio, financed by the J. C. Penney Foundation, the Payne Foundation, and the Carnegie Corporation. The committee drew heavily upon recommendations previously advanced at the Fourth National Radio Conference and the legislative hearings on the 1927 act to demand dedication of 15 percent of all broadcasting channels for scholarly and government agencies, representation on the FRC, and a guarantee of permanent schedules for instructional programs during the peak evening hours.[20]

Throughout 1930 and 1931, the National Committee on Education by Radio conducted an investigation with the aim of rallying educators to their own defense. Its conclusions dramatized the plight of nonprofit organizations. In the course of its campaign, it championed educators at FRC hearings and sought congressional allies. In these forums the committee rejected cooperative ventures between pedagogical programs and business enterprise because linking the two would impair independent thought and teaching.[21]

From 1931 to 1934, the university and college officials, following the traditional pattern of special interest groups, demanded changes including a band of frequencies set aside for their exclusive use. Accordingly, in 1931, Senator Simon D. Fess, Republican from Ohio, introduced a bill calling for the allocation of 15 percent of all broadcast channels to educational facilities. His action unleashed a barrage of measures supporting additional benefits for noncommercial radio users. All proposed to limit network control of air time sharply and to guarantee nonprofit institutions a place in the electromagnetic spectrum. In 1933–34, the Wagner-Hatfield bill consolidated these divergent efforts. This measure would have nullified all licenses within ninety days after its passage. During that period the new Federal Communications Commission would allocate one-fourth of all channels "to educational, religious, agricultural, labor, cooperative and similar nonprofit making associations."[22]

Many critics surpassed mere attempts at modification by supporting complete nationalization of the medium. In the early days of broadcasting, the Navy Department and the Post Office had written separate plans to establish a federal monopoly of radio. In the heat of the legislative battle, many wished to reexamine that possibility; these reformers looked to Britain for inspiration. Dr. Robert A. Millikan, an eminent physicist, rhapsodized, "The programs that are on the air in England are incomparably superior to anything to be heard here, for the English government has taken over completely the control of radio." In 1933, Representative Edwin Davis rallied opponents of advertising in support of his Radio Omnibus bill, which proposed to underwrite station costs by substituting a licensing charge for the revenue extracted from sponsors. Backers of the measure argued that government ownership and operation following the British example posed the only real alternative to commercial domination of the airwaves. Because of the clamorous, multifaceted reform attempts, a full-scale revolt shook even the most fundamental premises of the American broadcasting system.[23]

The continuing confrontation between the reformers and traditionalists generated serious rifts that carried over into Washington politics. Indeed, the furor thoroughly disrupted legislative momentum for a communications commission. Initially, supporters of unification had envisioned beginning with a smooth transfer of the Commerce Department's Radio Division to the Federal Radio Commission. In 1930, Senator Clarence C. Dill had introduced Senate Resolution 176 supporting this shift. But the heated debate on broadcasting delayed his proposal as well as the Couzens bill. Finally, the legislative process ground to a halt as a determined group of reformers deadlocked Congress.[24]

In the ensuing impasse President Hoover forcefully intervened to bypass the congressional stalemate. By drawing upon the extensive domestic prerogatives of the presidency, he aimed to unite bureaucrats, businessmen, and legislators behind a national radio policy based upon unified control. In pursuing this objective, he hoped not only to eliminate waste and inefficiency, enhance coordination, and secure economical administration but, more importantly, to preserve and protect the radio system he had worked to create as secretary of commerce. Accordingly, he launched a multifaceted campaign drawing upon government committees and executive orders to forge a coalition supporting passage of the Couzens bill.[25]

In 1931, the president organized several federal committees to study coordination and unification. For almost a year a host of panels examined almost every aspect of communications, including aviation, navigation, commercial affairs, and national defense. The most important of these organizations—the Committee to Investigate the Duplication of Government Communications Facilities—reported that the lack of unified federal radio policy hindered both the private and public sectors, endangered the nation's security, and represented a wasteful use of that precious national resource—the electromagnetic spectrum. Echoing the sentiments expressed by the other panels, the group urged the president to support consolidation and unified control.[26]

The next year, President Hoover quickly implemented the panel's recommendation. On 20 July 1932, he issued an executive order transferring the Radio Division of the Commerce Department to the FRC. Renamed the Division of Field Operations, the new section inspected all stations and apparatus, measured frequencies, monitored all traffic, conducted examinations for licenses, and investigated violations of the Radio Act of 1927. The new division not only enlarged the staff and responsibilities of the FRC but also brought the concept of a unified communications commission closer to reality. By circumventing the legislative deadlock, Hoover had begun consolidation and aligned his administration squarely behind unification.[27]

During the last months of his term of office, the president sought to forge a coalition of network executives, commercial broadcasters, and government bureaucrats. At Hoover's urging, these powerful factions abandoned their strategy of waiting quietly for passage of the Couzens bill. As the reformer's demands intensified and the possibility of abrupt change of the existing order increased, these groups finally intervened to assure that Congress would leave business and governmental practices unaltered. Those that stood to lose the most were forced into collective action at the request of the nation's chief executive.[28]

To prevent Congress from striking out alone to develop some new policy, supporters of a communications commission mobilized the government and private enterprise. The recently unified partisans converted several authoritative figures to their cause. One, Admiral Stanford C. Hooper, had previously supported eliminating the commission form of control because he felt that those members inexperienced in radio affairs had bowed to political considerations. In 1929 and 1930, he had advocated transferring supervision back to the Department of Commerce, but the president's support of unification and the bitter attack on radio altered his position. By the end of 1931, after consulting extensively with David Sarnoff, Admiral

Hooper maintained that navigation and transportation safety depended on commercial radio. Moreover, he also argued that commercial stability and national defense were intimately related to the maintenance of the American system. He continually stressed that if such firms as the Radio Corporation of America were adversely affected by congressional legislation, the nation's security would be endangered. He never tired of pointing out the navy's traditional hostility to foreign radio interests, the value of ship-to-ship and ship-to-shore communications to the fleet, and the pivotal role his department played in aiding American business. Under his careful and reasoned arguments before government panels and congressional committees, the aura of national security extended to cover commercial radio. On a more practical level, when confronted with the possibility that Congress might innovate, he responded, "My purpose is to forestall such a calamity." He further exclaimed, "It is up to all of us who know this game" to work for a new communications commission. Above all, Admiral Hooper indicated that any legislation would have to conform to the general outline established by the Radio Act of 1927. If that were maintained as a guide, the reformers would be easily outmaneuvered. Following the admiral's lead, the Naval Communications Service joined with other government agencies and business firms to work for passage of the Couzen's bill.[29]

The business community also feared that Congress, pressured by the reformers, might unleash some totally unknown scheme in their midst. Like Admiral Hooper, General James G. Harbord, president of RCA, enumerated the inherent dangers of bringing the rampant conflicts among radio users before Congress. He cautioned that self-interest dictated support for a unified commission. Owen D. Young seconded this assessment and insisted that the lawmakers maintain their original goal of eliminating confusion and duplication by combining all services under one body. David Sarnoff observed that through a single panel Congress could promote commercial stability and defend the nation. By the end of President Hoover's administration, several other industrial leaders indicated that considerable pressure could be brought on Congress. Merlin H. Aylesworth, president of NBC, asserted that General Motors, Pontiac, Chevrolet, and Buick, four of the leading network sponsors in

Michigan Senator James Couzen's home state, could be depended upon to support the chain against those who sought to revamp the American broadcasting system.[30]

In 1933, proponents of unification gained additional support from the Roosevelt administration. As the new president increased his broadcasting addresses to the nation, he felt pressed to create a sympathetic regulatory agency to ensure his ready access to the airways. Initially, he was willing to rely on the existing FRC if he could secure the voluntary resignations of Hoover's appointees on the panel. When it became apparent that those resignations would not be forthcoming, the president considered two alternatives. He could follow the advice of some of his most ardent supporters and create a Bureau of Propaganda which would supervise radio. This new organization would "guide and control the mind of the masses on the policies of the administration." In fact, Senator Clarence C. Dill even went so far as to suggest that "it would be a good thing to follow the system in Germany." Or, the president could follow the example of his predecessor by advocating the establishment of a new agency and appointing his own supporters, thereby ridding the government of Republican holdovers. In this, as in many other programs, Roosevelt chose to follow Hoover's lead. Continuity not change characterized the new administration's communications policy.[31]

In the fall of 1933, the president directed Secretary of Commerce Daniel C. Roper to assemble an interdepartmental committee to investigate the entire question of communication. Billed as a part of the New Deal's governmental reorganization program, the president primarily charged the committee to recommend a national policy to supervise radio, telephone, telegraph, and cables. Above all, the new panel had to establish a scheme to increase efficiency and cooperation, enhance coordination and consolidation, and aid economic recovery.[32]

The "little group" of eleven members that assembled under the leadership of the secretary of commerce began work in late September. Composed entirely of government representatives, it contained some of the most distinguished names in radio, including Admiral Stanford C. Hooper (Naval Communications Service), J. H. Dellinger (Bureau of Standards), and the former chairman of the FRC, Charles

Saltzman. In a master stroke, Roper also appointed as ad hoc members Clarence C. Dill, chairman of the Senate Interstate Commerce Committee, and Sam Rayburn, chairman of the House Commerce Committee. Any radio legislation would be directed to these two congressional committees, therefore, involving their chairmen in the formulation of an administrative proposal gained both their support and their stamp of approval.[33]

Almost immediately, special interest groups who recognized the critical nature of the panel's deliberations deluged the Roper Committee. Once again, university and college officials led the fight to reform the commercial structure. Joy Elmer Morgan, chairman of the National Committee on Education by Radio, reported to the panel that a unique opportunity existed to undertake a thorough and impartial reorganization of broadcasting. Above all, he insisted that new legislation should protect and promote educational broadcasting as well as limit the control advertisers had over private stations and programming. Furthermore, George Carter Cameron, a writer and authority on radio affairs, suggested that the medium had reached a stagnation point because the FRC had allowed the commercial interests to gain control over all the important broadcasting facilities. He insisted that the Roper Committee must not allow this domination to continue. Privately, however, the reformers feared that the board would further entrench the existing system. The viewpoint was best expressed by Drew Pearson in his "Washington Merry-Go-Round" column. He indicated that the Roosevelt administration had undertaken a secret move under the guise of the Roper Committee to continue the old deal in radio.[34]

Actually, the most telling threat to commercial domination of the airwaves went almost unnoticed by the general public. Josephus Daniels, the ambassador to Mexico, entered the debate urging the Roper Committee to support a federal monopoly of radio. He recommended that the United States Government acquire and operate every station in the nation. In this scheme of remarkable similarity to the British Broadcasting Corporation, funds would be accrued by collecting a licensing fee on each receiving set. Daniels forcefully argued that if only Congress had accepted his advice during World War I, the present difficulties could have been easily avoided. Even though Daniels' proposals went almost unnoticed in the press, FDR directed the secretary of commerce to give serious consideration to the plan.[35]

The Daniels' suggestion galvanized the Roper Committee into action. Faced with an entirely unacceptable solution, the committee moved to defeat it; but, because of the close personal relationship between the president and his former mentor, they moved very carefully. First, the committee implemented a policy of secrecy. It closed all records to the public and barred all nongovernmental personnel from attending meetings. Next, in a carefully reasoned document sent to the president, the panel described the impracticality of government ownership of communications. Its argument stressed that the existing arrangements had grown up under the policy developed by Congress in the Radio Act of 1927—a good act built upon sound fundamentals. It continued stressing that the American people liked the arrangement because they incurred no expense for programming. Furthermore, radio stations in general supported the administration and the president. Finally, the change over to government monopoly would disrupt the economy and impede recovery. In short, the members unanimously advised the president to reject Daniels' plan.[36]

By December the Roper Committee had filed its recommendations with FDR. Its report highlighted the division of authority and under-scored the existing lack of unified control and centralized responsibility. Moreover, the panel declared that divided rule had continued too long. Notwithstanding the wide differences among radio, telephone, telegraph, and cables, the lack of centralized supervision had increased government costs, contributed to inefficient service and duplication, and impeded economic recovery. In summation, the advisory board urged the president to create a single agency to develop a national policy and supervise communications.[37]

Accordingly, the White House sent Congress the report along with a simple eloquent message recommending creation of the Federal Communications Commission. By placing supervision in a new regulatory agency, Roosevelt hoped to centralize authority and unify control without disrupting established business practices and existing commercial relationships. To placate broadcasting's critics, he urged the lawmakers to grant the body full investigative powers. Because he felt it was extremely important for the government to adopt a definite communications policy, the new chief executive placed the Federal Communications Commission on his "must" legislative list, thereby guaranteeing it congressional attention and speedy action.[38]

Consequently, Secretary Roper worked closely with Senator Dill and Representative Rayburn to draw up a bill encompassing the president's recommendations. In order to avoid prolonged debate and secure early congressional approval, they opted to avoid all controversy. As Dill pointed out, "The oppposition to such legislation which existed in the last Congress is still apparent. . . . If we leave out the controversial matters the bill can be passed at this session; otherwise it cannot." To do so, they decided against preparing an intricate, complicated measure; instead, they drafted a short bill entrusting the FCC with wide discretionary powers.[39]

In early 1934, momentum for unification became almost irreversible. Backed by presidential strength, popularity, and resourcefulness, Senator Dill and Representative Rayburn introduced in their respective chambers similar bills establishing a communications commission. Then the House and Senate Commerce committees chaired by these two legislators took up the proposal. Because these congressional panels had been examining the concept of a communications commission since the late 1920s, their members faced the issue with confidence. All signs pointed to quick passage.[40]

In the Senate, however, the proposal once again encountered strong opposition from opponents of commercialism. Rallying around an amendment allocating one-fourth of all channels to university and college stations, religious institutions, and other nonprofit organizations, the reformers attempted to revamp the broadcasting structure. Quick action from the Roosevelt administration overwhelmed its opposition. A host of impartial, nontechnical experts from the Interstate Commerce Commission, the Federal Radio Commission, and the military services contained the attack. Moreover, to placate the critics, the lawmakers also granted the FCC full investigative powers. Consequently, in mid-May the bill passed the upper house without a roll call.[41]

Shortly thereafter, the House of Representatives also acted. In contrast to the Senate, opposition developed here along party lines as Republicans claimed radio censorship. After some complex parliamentary maneuvering, Rayburn disposed of these objections and the measure quickly passed. But, since several sections of the original proposal dealing with the FCC's organization and membership had been revised, the House version differed from the Senate's. Accordingly, a conference committee assembled to iron out the differences. In its final form, the act, following the House version, stipulated seven members instead of five and developing three divisions around radio, telegraph, and telephone to administer the act. In early June both legislative bodies passed the revised Dill-Rayburn communications control bill. On 19 June 1934, the president signed the Communications Act of 1934 into law. Through it the legislators unified control for radio, telephone, telegraph, and cables. In doing so, they retained substantial portions of the Radio Act of 1927; indeed, major sections were incorporated directly into the text of the new bill. Its adoption decisively quelled educators' and other dissenters' hopes for an improved situation. While the possibility for change did exist, the new law essentially represented little more than a repetition of the 1927 act for broadcasters.[42]

The New Deal legislation consolidating government supervision of communications under one federal bureau drew its inspiration from the "boom," years of the 1920s. The idea, originally suggested by Zenith president Eugene McDonald, received additional support from Representative Edwin Davis as an alternative to the Radio Act of 1927. In 1928 and 1929, the scheme gained wide-ranging support from congressmen, the business community, and others in the federal bureaucracy. Since the Communications Act of 1934 simply incorporated the 1927 act into its text, it confirmed the 1927 legislation as the basis for federal regulation of American broadcasting. Because the judiciary had unequivocally upheld the 1927 law and the FRC, the FCC relied upon its predecessor agency's routines to guide it in controlling wire and wireless. Paradoxically then, Franklin Roosevelt actually ensured the prolonged reign of Herbert Hoover's fourteen-year-old structure. Even today it serves as the foundation of American broadcasting regulation.[43]

11

CONSENSUS

The Communications Act of 1934 embodied a consensus between government and business on the ends and means of radio policy. Over the previous fourteen years, technological innovations, bureaucratic infighting, and industrial maneuvering had dramatically restructured broadcasting. In the process, giant network corporations encroached on the nation's airwaves, transforming disorder and uncertainty into oligopoly. Their growth sprang, in part, from an increased bureaucratization of both public and private institutions. This expansion, in turn, elicited a companion demand for a federal arbiter powerful enough to control the complex forces at work. The Federal Communications Commission completed the cycle.

To a considerable degree consensus had been produced by seven years of crisis. From 1920 to 1927, a host of interest groups battled for a place in the electromagnetic spectrum, and the resulting chaos threatened to destroy the medium. In order to surmount this state of perpetual instability, the radio giants sought economic equilibrium and effective federal control. The national government, too, expressed an abiding interest in resolving the dilemma while also promoting its own supervisory prowess. For different reasons, then, businessmen and bureaucrats recognized similar problems and began to move toward the same basic goals.

Against this critical backdrop, commercial broadcasters, network executives, and government officials formulated their agreement through traditional means. Using formal and informal political institutions, they lobbied, coerced, and compromised to shape the broad outlines of a national radio policy. As they interacted, Herbert C. Hoover, perhaps better than any other figure of the prosperity and Depression decades, recognized the new relationship between modern American government and the private sector. With remarkable sagacity he sketched a national regulatory policy which has served radio for fifty years.

The broadcasting consensus worked out between industry and government revealed precise areas of agreement. Its main thrust left the medium primarily in private hands but mandated public supervision. Despite the emphasis on private enterprise, it compelled the federal government to promote and protect communications. Finally, it empowered the federal authorities to solve business problems through the regulatory process.

After the passage of the Communications Act of 1934, the American broadcasting system took its place in the nation's mythology. In time, as the struggle among businessmen, bureaucrats, and reformers drew to a close, the strongest came to be regarded as purveyors of the unqualified truth, a sort of holy grail, if you will, of good judgment and sound vision. In the process, the participants embraced consensus history emphasizing evolutionary development.

Since commercial broadcasters and network executives had won, their view of the past became the authorized chronicle. In their interpretation of the truth, an enlightened business community had produced a broadcasting system reflective of the very best in American society. In addition, they extolled technological and scientific innovation as part of the American character. Senator Clarence C. Dill, one of the chief architects of the system, observed, "Since Marconi's feat of spanning the Atlantic . . . by far the greatest radio developments have been produced by American inventors and businessmen. Radio as we know it today is truly an American art." Equally important, their version highlighted the role of businessmen and private enterprise in creating radio. Once again Dill represented all the winners when he pointed out, "Private initiative, private capital, and most of all American business methods . . . have placed radio in this country far ahead of that of any in the world."[1]

Through such rhetoric, the power brokers of the broadcasting system extolled their domain. According to them, it produced national unity, prevented disintegration of the populace into classes, and cemented the country by common sources of entertainment, economic interests, ideals, problems, and dangers. Equally telling, broadcasting aided the government at critical times by fully and accurately informing the people. As FRC commissioner James Hanley pointed out, "Our dynamic President takes advantage of radio now and then to talk to the whole family." In short, the medium became an important part of the nation's folklore because it symbolized a national community and promoted uniformity.[2]

Any attempt to criticize or challenge the arrangement represented a direct assault on the larger society as well as a rejection of the nation's past. The favored sons rejected demands by noncommercial broadcasters for special privileges and government intervention because these modifications stood outside the American heritage; indeed, they were attacked as symbols of British or European solutions. Consequently, since these reforms violated the American experience, they were denied a place in the broadcasting system. In fact, any opposition to network radio, advertising, or commercialism was categorized as an attempt to undermine American society. William S. Paley spoke for the chosen when he equated all condemnations: "The real question now before you is whether we are to have the American or European system of radio broadcasting."[3]

The legislative saga, as the chronicle would have it, introduced a new dimension to the myth by extolling the wise, foresighted, American people. While broadcasters struggled to control the airwaves through voluntary agreements, self-restraint, and self-regulation, an enlightened populace had demanded congressional action. Under intense public pressure the lawmakers complied by passing the Radio Act of 1927. The new legislation guaranteed public interest by vesting supervision in the people's agent—the Federal Radio Commission. Congress, according to this version, had especially created the new agency to protect and represent the listener. In turn, the Supreme Court and the federal judiciary had also defended the public, its law, and its commission when they unequivocably upheld the constitutionality of the 1927 act.[4]

Adding the people's role in directing and guiding the radio control bill completed the mythololgy. The winning side thus erected a solid framework, anchored to the citizenry, emphasizing private enterprise and the American way. Evolution, continuity, and inevitability became synonymous with the broadcasting system. It made little difference that the interpretation was divorced from reality, for in time it came to influence persuasively the actions of the commissioners, broadcasters, network executives, and listeners alike. Indeed, so strong did the myths become that they set the tone for the next fifty years of radio history.

The Communications Act of 1934 and its creation, the Federal Communications Commission, fit nicely into the story. However, in their case, the myth assumed amazing accuracy. Since the 1934 legislation had merely reenacted the 1927 act, it maintained continuity. Even though in almost every session of Congress thereafter noncommercial groups and critics of the American system attempted to amend the 1934 measure, there has been little change. Even though almost a dozen alterations have been enacted, most of them showed minor significance especially with regard to the law as a whole or specific business practices. That the 1927 bill withstood attacks from almost every imaginable source attested to the strength of the mythology.[5]

Through association the commission form of supervision gained permanency. Closely following the practices of its predecessor agency, the Federal Communications Commission made no break with the past. At first, it was almost required to do so since its broadcast division staff came almost entirely from the Radio Division of the Commerce Department and the FRC, and its chairman, Eugene Sykes, and a commissioner, Thad Brown, also had served in that agency. With the court-tested FRC policies representing its precedent and FRC personnel filling its ranks, the FCC's supervisory procedures remained unchanged.[6]

Thus, the legal and regulatory foundations of the American system initially implemented by Herbert Hoover and the Republican administrations during the 1920s, gained permanency under the New Deal. Subsequently, the 1934 act and the FCC have proved adaptable to numerous technological innovations, including television, frequency modulation, and coaxial cables. From humble beginnings, then, the Radio Act of 1927 and the commission form of supervision have grown to form the present regulatory arrangement.

The business and economic foundations established during Hoover's New Era have also avoided interruption. Indeed, the

single most important element in the structure of broadcasting
—network radio—continued to dominate the medium. Logically
enough, when television commercially overwhelmed post-World
War II America, those same business practices and rules developed
during the 1920s and early 1930s were applied to it, too. Even though
a medium dependent upon sound alone cannot really be equated with
one using sight as well as sound, the network system supported by
commercialism has been altered only by a change in economic
scale fostered by the phenomenal growth of advertising income.
Through the long haul from crystal set to mini-transistor, from crackle
and hum to quadraphonic sound, the contributions of economic
idealists, realists, and even charlatans have poked and prodded the
expediencies of political reality to form a system unique to broadcasting history.[7]

Notes

The following abbreviations have been used in the notes for archival and manuscript collections.

Caldwell Papers, MSS, Wis. Hist. Soc.: O. H. Caldwell Papers, Wisconsin Historical Society.

Clark Collection, MSS, MHT: George Clark Collection, Museum of History and Technology, Smithsonian Institution.

Coolidge Papers, MSS, LC: Calvin Coolidge Papers, Manuscript Division, Library of Congress.

Couzens Papers, MSS, LC: James Couzens Papers, Manuscript Division, Library of Congress.

Daniels Papers, MSS, LC: Josephus Daniels Papers, Manuscript Division, Library of Congress.

Davis Papers, MSS, AIS: Harry P. Davis Papers, Archives of Industrial Society, University of Pittsburgh Libraries.

De Forest Papers, MSS, LC: Lee De Forest Papers, Manuscript Division, Library of Congress.

Hedges Papers, MSS, Wis. Hist. Soc.: William S. Hedges Papers, Wisconsin Historical Society.

HHPL: Collections of the Herbert Hoover Presidential Library.

Hooper Papers, MSS, LC: Stanford Caldwell Hooper Papers, Manuscript Division, Library of Congress.

James Papers, MSS, Wis. Hist. Soc.: E. P. H. James Papers, Wisconsin Historical Society.

NAB: Broadcast Pioneers History Project, National Association of Broadcasters.

NARG:The following record groups of the National Archives have been listed according to group number and shortened title.

NARG 12, Office of Education: Records of the Office of Education.

NARG 16, Sec. of Agriculture: Records of the Secretary of Agriculture, Radio News Service.

NARG 18, Army Air Force: Records of the Army Air Force.

NARG 19, Bureau of Ships: Records of the Bureau of Ships.

NARG 28, PMG Letterbooks: Records of the Post Office Department, Postmaster General Letterbooks.

NARG 38, Bullard: Records of the Office of the Chief of Naval Operations, W. H. G. Bullard Files.

NARG 38, DNC: Records of the Office of the Chief of Naval Opertaions, Director of Naval Communications.

NARG 38, Noyes: Records of the Office of the Chief of Naval Operations, L. Noyes Files.

NARG 38, Todd: Records of the Office of the Chief of Naval Operations, D. W. Todd Files.

NARG 40, Dept. of Commerce: General Records of the Department of Commerce.

NARG 45, Naval Records Collection: Naval Records Collection of the Office of Naval Records and Library.

NARG 51, Bureau of Budget: Records of the Bureau of the Budget.

NARG 60, Dept. of Justice: General Records of the Department of Justice.

NARG 80, Sec. of Navy, 1916–26: General Records of the Department of the Navy, Secretary of the Navy, 1916–26.

NARG 111, Chief Signal Officer: Records of the Office of the Chief Signal Officer.

NARG 122, FTC: Records of the Federal Trade Commission.

NARG 167, JHD Papers: Records of the National Bureau of Standards, J. Howard Dellinger Papers.

NARG 173, FCC: Records of the Federal Communications Commission, Records of Predecessor Agencies.

NARG 173, IRAC: Records of the Federal Communications Commission, Interdepartmental Radio Advisory Committee.

NBC Records, Wis. Hist. Soc.: National Broadcasting Company Records, Wisconsin State Historical Society.

Sarnoff Papers: David Sarnoff Papers, David Sarnoff Research Library, Princeton, New Jersey.

White Papers, MSS, LC: Wallace White Papers, Manuscript Division, Library of Congress.

INTRODUCTION

1. Oscar and Mary Handlin, *The Dimensions of American Liberty* (Cambridge, Mass.: Belknap Press, 1961); Louis Hartz, *The Liberal Tradition in America: An Interpretation of American Political Thought Since the Revolution* (New York: Harcourt Brace, 1955).

2. Elting E. Morison, *Men, Machines, and Modern Times* (Cambridge, Mass.: M.I.T. Press, 1966), pp. 9, 19.

3. Robert S. McMahon, "Federal Regulation of the Radio and Television Broadcast Industry in the United States, 1927–1959, With Special Reference to the Establishment and Operation of Workable Administrative Standards" (Ph.D. diss., Ohio State University, 1959), pp. 1, 4; Bernard S. Finn, "Electronic Communications," in *Technology in Western Civilization*, ed. Melvin Kranzberg and Carroll Pursell, 2 vols. (Madison: University of Wisconsin Press, 1967), 2: 293–310.

4. Gleason L. Archer, *History of Radio to 1926* (New York: American Historical Society, 1938), p. 189; Samuel Becker and Elmer W. Lower, "Broadcasting in Presidential Campaigns," in *The Great Debates*, ed. Sidney Kraus (Gloucester, Mass.: Peter Smith, 1968), p. 30; Editorial Record, Clipping (August 1928), Davis Papers, MSS, AIS, box 4, folder 47, news clippings.

5. Stanford Caldwell Hooper, "Selecting Wavelengths for Broadcasting, 1921–1922," *History of Radio*, vol. 1, Hooper Papers, MSS, LC, box 40, Hooper Misc. Woodworth to Bagley, 4 March 1919, NARG 38, DNC, file 21,7000-49; as quoted in Library of Congress, "Exhibit Commemorating 50th Anniversary of Radio Features Papers of Pioneer Scientists and Broadcasters," n.d., Press Release no. 70-33, Library of Congress.

6. Ellis W. Hawley, "Herbert C. Hoover, the Commerce Secretariat, and the Vision of an Associated State, 1921–28," *Journal of American History* 61 (June 1974): 121.

7. A. L. Ashby, "Legal Aspects of Broadcasting," Lecture delivered at New York University, School of Law, 22 April 1930, Davis Papers, MSS, AIS, box 3, folder 41.

8. Aylesworth to Brisbane, n.d., NBC Records, Wis. Hist. Soc., A. Brisbane, 1932, box 3.

CHAPTER 1

1. Westinghouse Engineering Department to Goldsmith, 8 July 1924, NAB, 351 K; Clark to Curtis, 2 June 1936, Clark Collection, MSS, MHT, CL 14, General History, 439 A.

2. Radio Corporation of America, *The First 25 Years of RCA* (New York: RCA, 1946), p. 25; Edgar H. Felix, "Dr. Alfred N. Goldsmith on the Future of Radio Telephony," *Radio Broadcast* 1 (May 1922): 44; Professor Robert A. Millikan, Address before the National Advisory Council on Radio in Education, 22 May 1931, Clark Collection, MSS, MHT, CWC 14, 458 A.

3. D.K.C. MacDonald, *Faraday, Maxwell, and Kelvin* (New York: Doubleday, 1964), pp. 9–101.

4. R. P. Clarkson, *The Hysterical Background of Radio* (New York: T. H. Sears, 1927), p. 121; W. Rupert Maclaurin, *Invention and Innovation in the Radio Industry* (New York: Macmillan, 1949), p. 20.

5. W. J. Baker, *A History of the Marconi Company* (London: Trinity Press, 1970), pp. 35–37; Maclaurin, *Invention and Innovation*, p. 37; Orrin E. Dunlap, Jr., *Marconi, the Man and His Wireless* (New York: Macmillan, 1937), p. 147; J. D. Tomlison, *The International Control of Radio Communications* (Ann Arbor, Mich.: J. W. Edwards, 1945), p. 12.

6. W. P. Jolly, *Marconi* (New York: Stein and Day, 1972), pp. 34–35, 321; Franklin M. Reck, *Radio from Start to Finish* (New York: Thomas Crowell, 1942), p. 14; Degna Marconi, *My Father Marconi* (New York: McGraw-Hill, 1962), pp. 6–7, 55; David Gunstan, *Guglielmo Marconi* (Geneva: Geron Books, 1962), pp. 8–9.

7. Dunlap, *Marconi*, p. 67; David Sarnoff, *Looking Ahead: The Papers of David Sarnoff* (New York: McGraw-Hill, 1968), p. 3; John L. Floherty, *On the Air: The Story of Radio* (New York: Doubleday, 1938), p. 6; Marvin R. Bensman, "The Regulation of Radio Broadcasting by the Department of Commerce, 1921–27," (Ph.D. diss., University of Wisconsin, 1969), p. 26.

8. L. S. Howeth, *History of Communications-Electronics in the United States Navy* (Washington, D.C.: Government Printing Office, 1963), p. 211; Lawrence Lessing, *Man of High Fidelity, Edwin Howard Armstrong* (New York: J. B. Lippincott, 1956), pp. 118–19; W. H. G. Bullard, "The Naval Radio Service: Its Development, Public Service, and Commercial Work," *Proceedings of the Institute of Radio Engineers* 3 (March 1915): 7–10; "Development and Activities of United States Naval Communications Service," Document no. 248, 66th Cong., 2d sess., Confidential Report, Radio Communications Facilities of United States Government, U.S. Bureau of Efficiency, 30 September 1921, NARG 167, JHD Papers, Box 6.

Some factions in the navy strongly resisted the development of radio communications, see Howeth, *History of Communications-Electronics*, p. 65; Josephus Daniels, *Wilson Era, Years of Peace* (Durham: University of North Carolina Press, 1944), pp. 497–98.

9. Howeth, *History of Communications-Electronics*, pp. 85–86; G. E. C. Wedlake, *SOS: The Story of Radio Communications* (New York:

Crane, Russak and Company, 1973), pp. 24, 37, 43, 53–59; Walter Lord, *A Night to Remember* (New York: Henry Holt, 1955), pp. 36–38, 171–72.

10. U.S. War Department, Bureau of Engineering, *Wireless Telegraph Stations of the World Including Shore Stations, Merchant Vessels, Revenue Cutters, and Vessels of the United States Navy, Corrected to Jan. 1, 1912* (Washington, D.C.: Government Printing Office, 1912); General Manager National Electric Signal Company to Hayden, 12 January 1912, Clark Collection, MSS, MHT, CL 5, History of Radio Companies; Ford to Daniels, 19 March 1912, Daniels Papers, MSS, LC, box 508, Subject File, Naval Communications Service, General, 1913–17.

11. Clarence C. Dill, *Radio Law Practice and Procedure* (Washington, D.C. National Book, 1938), p. 59; U.S., Department of Commerce, Bureau of Navigation, *Radio Communication Laws of the United States and the International Radio-Telegraphic Convention Regulations Governing Radio Operators and the Use of Radio Apparatus on Ships and on Land* (Washington, D.C.: Government Printing Office, 1919).

12. Tomlinson, *International Control of Radio*, p. 28; Paul Schubert, *The Electric Word* (New York: Macmillan, 1928), pp. 65–66; Thomas Porter Robinson, *Radio Networks and the Federal Government* (New York: Columbia University Press, 1943), pp. 47–48; Dallas W. Smythe, *The Structure and Policy of Electronic Communications* (Urbana: University of Illinois Press, 1957), p. 47; James M. Herring and Gerald C. Gross, *Telecommunications, Economics and Regulations* (New York: McGraw-Hill, 1936), pp. 239–40; Gilman G. Udell, comp., *Radio Laws of the United States*, (Washington, D.C.: Government Printing Office, 1962); Glenn A. Johnson, "The First Regulator of American Broadcasting, 1921–28, Secretary of Commerce Herbert Hoover" (Ph.D. diss., University of Iowa, 1970), p. 43; Pearl Augusta Drews, "Radio Broadcasting in the United States, 1920–29" (Master's thesis, University of Wisconsin, 1938), p. 90; "Harris Subcommittee Report: 50 Years of Broadcasting," *Journal of Broadcasting* 3 (Winter 1958–59): 56–57.

The figures on frequencies are my own assessment and have been derived from the following sources: Roy E. Thompson, "The Uni-Control Receiver," *Proceedings of the Institute of Radio Engineers* 7 (October 1919): 509–14; "Testimony of George Clark as to His Work with Navy Sets and with Design of Navy Receivers," Court of Claims Testimony C-26, 1934, Clark Collection, MSS, MHT, C/24, CVVC; Descriptive Catalogue no. 601–16, *Buy It from the Navy, Radio Apparatus Type CW-936, Telephone Set Short Range*, n.d. 1-14, Smithsonian Institution, Museum of History and Technology.

13. Daniels, *Wilson Era*, p. 106; Daniels to Page, 1 October 1919,NARG 80, Sec. of Navy 1916–26, File 26509; Daniels to Alexander, 29 December

1916, NARG 80, Sec. of Navy, 1916–26, file 26256-324; U.S. Naval Institute Release, Government Control of Radio Recommended, 1917, NARG 45, Naval Records Collection, box 76.

14. Hooper Diary, May 1904, Hooper Papers, MSS, LC; Bullard, Memo for Secretary of Navy, 18 Feb. 1915, Daniels Papers, MSS, LC, box 508, Subject File, Naval Communications Service, General, 1913–17; Hooper, Memo for Todd, 30 July 1917, NARG 38, Todd Files, box 2, G-Mc 1916–17; Proposed Government Monopoly, U.S. Naval Institute, 1916, NARG 45, Naval Records Collection, box 76.

15. Todd to Robinson, 3 March 1917, NARG 38, Todd Files, box 3; Memo on Radio Legislation Prepared by Todd, 12 September 1917, NARG 38, DNC, file 100 (1916–26); History of Radio, vol. 1, Hooper Papers, MSS, LC, box 40.

16. Howeth, History of Communications-Electronics, p. 227; Herring and Gross, Telecommunications, pp. 240–41; E. David Cronon, ed., Cabinet Diaries of Josephus Daniels (Lincoln: University of Nebraska Press, 1963), pp. 100–01; Todd to Bullard, 4 November 1916, NARG 38, Todd Files, box 1 (A-F 1916–17).

On the reaction of commercial companies, consult Daniels to President Atlantic Communications Company, 7 July 1915, Daniels Papers, MSS, LC, box 58, Subject File, Naval Communications Service, General, 1913–17; Gregory to Lansing, 16 September 1914, Daniels Papers, MSS, LC, box 58, Subject File, Naval Communications Service, General, 1913–17.

17. The war vastly changed the development of radio technology. On the vacuum tube and the Alexanderson high-frequency alternator, see Baker, Marconi Company, p. 177; Richard W. Hubbell, 4,000 Years of TV: The Story of Seeing at a Distance (New York: G. P. Putnam, 1942), pp. 80–81; Donald McNicol, Radio's Conquest of Space: The Experimental Rise of Radio Communications (New York: Murray Hill, 1946), pp. 236–37; General J. G. Harbord, "Radio in the World War and the Organization of an American Owned Transoceanic Radio Service," in The Radio Industry: The Story of Its Development as Told by Leaders of the Industry (New York: A. W. Shaw, 1928), pp. 8, 10.

On the lag in radio development in the United States, which the war dramatically affirmed, see Radio Corporation of America, The First 25 Years, p. 15; George C. Southworth, 40 Years of Radio Research (New York: Gordon and Breach, 1962), p. 38; Rexmond C. Cochrane, Measures for Progress: A History of the National Bureau of Standards (Washington, D.C.: National Bureau of Standards, 1966), p. 191.

For the most thorough account of naval radio during the conflict, consult Department of The Navy, History of the Bureau of Engineering of the Navy

Department During World War I (Washington, D.C.: Government Printing Office, 1922).

18. *Naval Communications*, Official Bulletin, no. 279, 9 April 1918, NARG 45, Naval Records Collection, box 76; Memo for Chief of Naval Operations, 28 May 1917, NARG 38, Todd Files, box 1 (A-F 1916-17).

Daniels varied his policies to achieve his objectives, see Cronon, *Cabinet Diaries*, p. 355; Daniels, *Wilson Years*, p. 496; *Report of Board of Organization, U.S. Naval Communications Service*, 10 December 1917, NARG 38, box 1, Newspaper Clippings, 1912–23; Daniels to Secretary of Commerce, 10 November 1918, NARG 80, Sec. of the Navy, 1916–26, file 12479–1165.

On purchase of commercial stations, consult Hooper Tape Recordings, 108, Hooper Papers, MSS, LC, box 37; Marconi Shore Radio Stations Purchased by Navy Dept., Naval Communications Service Release, 30 November 1918, NARG 45, Naval Records Collection, box 76; Egerton to Bureau of Supplies and Accounts, 29 November 1918, NARG 80, Sec. of Navy, 1916–26, box 543, file 10191.

19. A. Hunter Dupree, *Science in the Federal Government: A History of Policies and Activities to 1940* (Cambridge, Mass.: Belknap Press, 1957), pp. 324–25; Cronon, *Cabinet Diaries*, p. 372; Woodworth to Todd, 30 January 1919, NARG 38, Todd Files, box 4 (F-W 1918, A-Z 1919).

On appropriations bill, see Benson to Secretary of the Navy, 1 February 1919, NARG 45, Naval Records Collection, box 76; Todd to Director of Naval Communications, 9 February 1919, NARG 38, Todd Files, box 4; Hooper to Sweet, 24 June 1919, Hooper Papers, MSS, LC, box 2, January – April 1919.

Concerning Daniels' defense, see Todd, Memo for the Secretary of Navy, 1 April 1919, Daniels Papers, MSS, LC, box 509, Subject File, Naval Communications Service, General, January–December 1919; Daniels to Roper, n.d., NARG 40, Dept. of Commerce, file 80553, 13-G.

20. Lessing, *Man of High Fidelity*, p. 20; Hooper Tape Recordings, 119, 138, Hooper Papers, MSS, LC, box 37; Kinter to White, 10 February 1921, White Papers, MSS, LC, box 21.

21. Maclaurin, *Invention and Innovation*, p. 52; Baker, *Marconi Company*, p. 156; H. P. Davis, "History of Broadcasting," in *The Radio Industry: The Story of Its Development*, p. 3; Lee De Forest, *Father of Radio: Autobiography of Lee De Forest* (Chicago: Wilcox and Follett, 1950), p. 348; Kurt Borchardt, *Structure and Performance of the United States Communications Industry* (Cambridge: Harvard University Press, 1970), p. 4; C. W. Horn, "Ten Years of Broadcasting," Address before the Institute of Radio Engineers (1930), Davis Papers, MSS, AIS, box 3, folder 44.

22. "Organization of RCA," *Electrical World* 52 (10 January 1920): 93; Ida Tarbell, *Owen D. Young: A New Type of Industrial Leader* (New York: Macmillan, 1932); Robert J. Landry, *This Fascinating Radio Business* (Indianapolis: Bobbs-Merrill, 1946), p. 20; Federal Communications Commission, *Proposed Report Telephone Investigation, Pursuant to Public Resolution No. 8, 74th Congress, Federal Communications Commission* (Washington, D.C.: Government Printing Office, 1938); David Sarnoff. "Uncharted Roads of Radio Development," Address at St. Lawrence University, 10 December 1926, NARG 173, FCC, General Records, Radio Division, File 2640.

23. Maclaurin, *Invention and Innovation*, pp. 105–09; Bensman, "Regulation of Radio Broadcasting," p. 41; Otto Sorg Schairer, *Patent Policies of the Radio Corporation of America* (New York: RCA, 1939), pp. 7–8.

These maneuverings produced a group which became known as the big four: RCA, GE, AT&T, and Westinghouse. Baker, *Marconi Company*, p. 181; Hiram J. Jome, *Economics of Radio Industry* (Chicago: A. W. Shaw, 1925), p. 207; "The Background of Radio Development," Clark Collection, MSS, MHT, CL 4, General History, 541–600.

24. H. Frequency Allocation, n.d., NARG 19, Bureau of Ships, file 1084, Reorganization to Schnell; "General Activities of Naval Communications Service Including Its Organization and Operation," NARG 38, DNC, file 140–901.

25. Landry, *Fascinating Radio Business*, p. 33; Lessing, *Man of High Fidelity*, pp. 135–36; David Loth, *Swope of G.E.* (New York: Simon and Schuster, 1958), p. 247.

26. Cronon, *Cabinet Diaries*, pp. 123, 137; Keith Clark, *International Communications: The American Attitude* (New York: Ames Press, 1968) p. 239; Todd to Sweet, 2 October 1916, NARG 38, Todd Files, box 3 (N-Z 1916-1917, A-E 1918); Todd, Memo for Secretary of Navy, 18 November 1918, Daniels Papers, MSS, LC, box 509, General, October–December 1918.

27. Confidential Report, Radio Communication Facilities of the United States Government, U.S. Bureau of Efficiency, 30 September 1921, NARG 167, JHD Papers, box 6.

28. Will H. Hays, *The Memoirs of Will H. Hays* (New York: Doubleday, 1955), pp. v, 278–80, 283, 288–89, 302–04, 313; Francis Russell, *The Shadow of Blooming Grove: Warren G. Harding and His Times* (New York: McGraw-Hill, 1968), pp. 302, 359, 535.

29. Robert K. Murray, *The Harding Era: Warren G. Harding and His Administration* (Minneapolis: University of Minneapolis Press, 1969), pp. 413–16; Memo, Secretary of Commerce, 3 April 3 1922, HHPL, Sec. of Commerce, Official File, box 444, Radio Corresp.

On opening of stations and Agricultural Department cooperation with the Post Office, see "Department Heads Send First Messages From New Post Office Radio Stations," *Electrical World* 77 (30 April 1921): 1013; U.S. Department of Agriculture, Bureau of Markets and Crop Estimates Broadcasting Schedule, n.d., NARG 173, FCC, General Records, Radio Div., file 1600; Wheeler, Memo for Secretary of Agriculture, 8 July 1921, NARG 16, Sec. of Agriculture, Radio News Service.

Concerning Edgerton and his efforts, see Terrell, Memo for Files, 8 November 1921, NARG 173, FCC, General Records Radio Div., file 1474; James C. Edgerton, "Report on Possibilities of Air Mail Service," 1921, NARG 173, FCC, General Records, Radio Div., file 1474; Hooper to Bullard, 17 March 1927, Hooper Papers, MSS, LC, box 8, Corresp., March 1927.

30. Johnson, "First Regulator of American Broadcasting," p. 1; Cochrane, *Measures For Progress*, p. 287; Stephen B. Davis, "Law of the Air," *Radio Industry: Story of Its Development*, p. 165; "Radio Division, History and Functions," NARG 173, FCC, General Corresp., Radio Div., file 16–22.

31. Cochrane, *Measures for Progress*, p. 142; Confidential Report, Radio Communications Facilities of U.S. Government, U.S. Bureau of Efficiency, 30 September 1921, NARG 167, JHD Papers, box 6.

32. Redfield to U.S. Radio Inspectors, 22 November 1917, NARG 38, Todd Files, box 1 (A-F 1916-1917); Redfield to Alexander, 10 December 1918, NARG 173, FCC, General Corresp., Radio Div., File Legis.; Todd, Memo for Bullard, n.d., NARG 38, Bullard Files, box 1, B-Y, 1919–21.

33. Cochrane, *Measures for Progress*, pp. 229–30; Murray, *Harding Era*, p. 195; Joseph Brandes, *Herbert Hoover and Economic Diplomacy: Department of Commerce Policy 1921-28* (Pittsburgh: University of Pittsburgh Press, 1962), pp. 3, 25; as quoted in Robert Blake, *Disraeli* (London: Eyne and Spottiswoode, 1966), p. 477.

34. John D. Hicks, *Republican Ascendancy, 1921–33* (New York: Harper & Row, 1960), p. 67; Waste Eliminators Incorporated, War on Waste, n.d., HHPL, Sec. of Commerce, Official File, Elimination of Waste in Industry, folder 1; "Hoover Emerges as a Cabinet," *New York Times Magazine*, 19 September 1926, HHPL, Sec. of Commerce, Personal File, Personal Articles and Speeches, 1926; C.C. Dill, Oral History Collection, 2, HHPL.

35. White to Hoover, 7 March 1921, White Papers, MSS, LC, box 15, Dept. File, 66th Congress, Sec. of Commerce; West to Hooper, 15 February 1922, Hooper Papers, MSS, LC, box 4, Corresp., February–March 1922.

36. Hooper to Dodd, 11 July 1921, Hooper Papers, MSS, LC, box 3, May–August 1921; Bureau of Engineering to Secretary of Navy, 25 July 1921, NARG 80, Sec. of Navy, 1916–26, file 575403–600; Memo for the Secretary

of Navy, Chief of Naval Operations, 23 September 1921, NARG 38, DNC, file 100.

37. Egge to Bureau of Naval Communications, 7 October 1921, NARG 38, DNC, file 63700–64900; Hays to Secretary of Navy, 9 May 1921, NARG 28, PMG Letterbooks, 1 January 1921, to 30 June 1921; Hays to Secretary of Navy, 27 July 1921, NARG 28, PMG Letterbooks, 1 July 1921, to 31 December 1921.

38. *Congressional Record*, 66th Cong., 2d sess., 1920, 3865, 4113, 4115; "House Passes Bill," *Electrical World* 78 (9 July 1921): 83; Walcott to Daniels, 8 March 1917, NARG 80, Sec. of Navy, 1916–26; file 26256-324; C. B. Cooper, "Government Ownership of Radio Shore Stations," 4 June 1918, NARG 38, DNC, file 110; Daniels to Bullard, Copy of letter to Senate, Committee on Naval Affairs, 27 February 1920, NARG 38, Bullard Files, box 1 (B-Y 1919-21).

39. Todd, Memo for Bullard, 12 March 1919, NARG 38, Bullard Files, box 1 (B-Y 1919-21); Bullard to Young, 6 November 1919, NARG 38, Bullard Files, box 1 (B-Y 1919-21); Woodworth, Memo for Hooper, 2 April 1919, NARG 38, DNC, file 49-21, 700; Acting Secretary of Navy to Wilson, 12 January 1920, NARG 80. Sec. of Navy, 1916–26, file 26509-283:23.

40. Jewett to Hooper, 8 March 1921, Hooper Papers, MSS, LC, box 3, January–April 1921; Edwards to Hooper, 3 May 1921, Hooper Papers, MSS, LC, box 3, May–April 1921; Griffin to Edwards, 24 June 1921, Clark Collection, MSS, MHT, CL 5, M.W.T. Company-RCA Corresp., June 1921–December 1921.

For the navy position on coastal communications, consult Hooper to Todd 4 December 1919, Hooper Papers, MSS, LC, box 2, September–December 1919; Hooper, "Survey of Radio Situation, 1921, *"Journal of American Society of Naval Engineers*, Hooper Papers, MSS, LC, box 44, Speeches and Articles, 1921–28.

Sarnoff had attempted to join the Naval Communications Service in World War I. Todd contended, "His personality is very distasteful to us and we feel that we don't want him connected with the Naval Communications Service in any way." Todd, Report of Telephone Conference with Nally, 2 April 1917, NARG 38, Todd Files, box 3 (N-Z 1916-17, A—E 1918); Todd to Bullard, 17 September 1917, NARG 38, Todd Files, box 1 (A-F 1916-17).

41. Hooper to Young, 17 January 1921, Hooper Papers, MSS, LC, box 3, January–April 1921; Hooper Memo Regarding Owen D. Young, 11 November 1921, Hooper Papers, MSS, LC, box 3, Hooper Corresp., November–December 1921; Hooper to Young, 5 November 1921, Hooper

Papers, MSS, LC, box 3, Hooper Corresp., November–December 1921;
Hooper to Johnson, 6 June 1921, Hooper Papers, MSS, LC, box 3, Hooper
Corresp., May–August 1921.

42. Long Distance Radio Telephony Now Practicable," *Electrical World*
77 (15 January 1921): 142–43; *AT&T Annual Report* (1920): 23–24, NARG
173, FCC, General Corresp., Radio Div., Commercial Stations, file 1-3 A;
Bullard to Carty, 5 March 1920, NARG 38, Bullard Files, box 1 (B-Y 1919–
20); Holt to Noyes, 16 March 1921, NARG 38, Noyes Files, box 2, 1917–22.

43. Data on International Radio Conferences and Committees (1906–20),
20 May 1921, NARG 167, JHD Papers, box 1; Knapp to Secretary of Navy,
8 April 1919, NARG 45, Naval Records Collection, box 484; QR Interallied
Radio Telegraphic Commission and Protocol Technical Radio Telephone
Commission, 25 January 1919, NARG 45, Naval Records Collection, box
484; Hooper Tape Recordings, 37, 309, 311, Hooper Papers, MSS, LC.

44. Dellinger to Stratton, 28 May 1921, NARG 167, JHD Papers, box 39,
Washington Conference; Minutes, Meeting of Radio Conference Committee,
Engineering Society, 2–3 June 1921, NARG 167, JHD Papers, box 1; Kennelly
to Hoover, 28 May 1921, NARG 40, Dept. of Commerce, file 67032/3; RCA
Memo with Reference to the Proposed Universal Electrical Communica-
tions Union, 23 May 1921, NARG 40, Dept. of Commerce, file 67032/3.

45. Hoover to Goldsmith, 6 October 1921, NARG 40, Dept. of Commerce,
file 67032/3; Kennelly and Dellinger to Hoover, 22 August 1921, HHPL,
Sec. of Commerce, Official File, box 437.

46. Lessing, *Man of High Fidelity*, p. 131; Clark, *International Communications*, p. 187; Hoover to Maxim, 30 August 1921, NARG 167, JHD
Papers, box 6, File Radio Inspection Service; Hoover to Ferrell, 29 August
1921, NARG 173, FCC, General Records, Radio Div., file 460; Warner to
Bureau of Navigation, 28 September 1921, NARG 173, FCC, General
Records, Radio Div., file 1363; Tyrer to Warner, 4 October 1921, NARG
173, FCC, General Records, Radio Div., file 1363.

47. Hooper to Boucheron, 3 January 1921, Hooper Papers, MSS, LC,
box 3, General Corresp., January–April 1921; Roosevelt to Phelan, 29
August 1919, NARG 38, DNC, file 21,700–49; Denby to Edwards, 2 March
1922, NARG 80, Sec. of Navy, 1916–26, box 597, file 12479 (1678 to 1737).

48. U.S., Congress, House, *Congressional Record*, 66th Cong., 2d sess.,
1920, 4116; U.S., Congress, House, *Congressional Record*, 67th Cong., 1st
sess., 1921, 2918; New York *Times*, 25 July 1919, NARG 38, DNC, box 1,
Newspaper Clippings.

49. Chief Radio Inspector, Memo to Secretary of Commerce, 21 September
1921, NARG 40, Dept. of Commerce, file 67032/7; Dellinger, Confidential

Memo to Stratton, 18 October 1922, NARG 167, JHD Papers, box 39, File General Records; Chief Radio Inspector, Memo for Acting Commissioner of Navigation, 30 September 1921, NARG 173, FCC, General Records, Radio Div., file 1474.

CHAPTER 2

1. Glenn A. Johnson, "The First Regulator of American Broadcasting, 1921-28, Secretary of Commerce Herbert Hoover" (Ph.D. diss., University of Iowa, 1970), p. 301; James G. Harbord, "Commercial Uses of Radio," *Annals of the American Academy of Political and Social Science* 142 (March 1929): 57; Hampton Gary, "Regulation of Broadcasting in the United States," *Annals of the American Academy of Political and Social Science* 177 (January 1935): 15; Ray L. Wilbur and Arthur Masticke Hyde, *The Hoover Policies* (New York: Scribners, 1937), p. 207; Memo, Some Phases of Radio Telephone Broadcasting, 3 January 1924, NARG 38, DNC, file 350.

2. H. P. Davis, "Broadcasting Evolved from the Chaos of the War," New York *Times*, 2 November 1930; Carson, Memo for Secretary of Commerce, 30 January 1922, NARG 173, FCC, General Records, Radio Div., file 1179; Carson to Texas Radio Sales and Engineering Company, 13 February 1922, NARG 173, FCC, General Records, Radio Div., file 1175.

3. Joint Technical Advisory Committee IRE-RTMA, *Radio Spectrum Conservation: A Program of Conservation Based on Present Uses and Future Needs, A Report of the Joint Technical Advisory Committee IRE-RTMA* (New York: McGraw-Hill, 1952), pp. 10, 155; "Is Radio Only a Passing Fad,"*Literary Digest* 73 (3 June 1922): 3-4; Carson, Memo for Secretary of Commerce, 2 March 1922, HHPL, Sec. of Commerce, Personal File, box 72; Minutes, Meeting of Radio Conference Committee, Engineering Society, 23 June 1921, NARG 167, JHD Papers, box 1.

4. Carson to Radio Inspector, Detroit, 21 January 1922, NARG 173, FCC, General Records, Radio Div., file 1179; Hoover to Secretary of Navy, 15 June, 1922, NARG 80, Sec. of Navy, 1916–26, file 28576-28577.

5. "The Standing of the Amateur," *Radio Broadcast* 2 (February 1923): 268-69; J. L. Ray, "The Distribution and Merchandizing of Radio Equipment," in *The Radio Industry: The Story of Its Development as Told by Leaders of the Industry* (New York: A. W. Shaw, 1928), pp. 3–11; Clinton B. DeSoto, *Two Hundred Meters and Down: The Story of Amateur Radio* (West Hartford: American Radio Relay League, 1936), p. 75; Edwards to Commissioner of Navigation, 16 December 1921, NARG 173, FCC, General Records, Radio Div., file 1109.

6. "Hoover to Advise on Radio Control," New York *Times*, 10 February 1922; Carl Dreher, "Is the Amateur at Fault?" *Radio Broadcast* 4 (February 1924); Maxim to Terrell, 24 October 1922, NARG 173, FCC, General Records, Radio Div., file 1179; Supervisor of Radio, New York to Carson, 17 November 1923, NARG 173, FCC, General Records, Radio Div., file 1109; "Interference Problems Are Being Solved," *Radio News Bulletin*, 29 February 1924, NARG 173, FCC, General Records, Radio Div., file 570.

7. David C. Phillips; John M. Grogan; and Earl H. Ryan, *Introduction to Radio and Television* (New York: Ronald Press, 1954), p. 14; Tyrer to Radio Inspector, Detroit, 16 December 1921, NARG 173, FCC, Radio Div., file BC-15; Carson, Memo for Secretary of Commerce, 24 March 1922, NARG 173, FCC, Radio Div., file BC-15.

8. Maryland W. Wilson, "Broadcasting by the Newspaper Owned Stations in Detroit, 1920–27" (Ph.D., diss., University of Michigan, 1952), pp. 63–64; Tyrer, Memo for Secretary of Commerce, 3 May 1922, NARG 173, FCC, General Records, Radio Div., file 1675; Carson, Memo for Secretary of Commerce, 27 July 1922, NARG 173, FCC, General Records, Radio Div., file 1179; Hoover to Banning, 12 September 1922, NARG 173, FCC, General Records, Radio Div., file 2617.

9. Alfred N. Goldsmith and Austin C. Lescarboura, *This Thing Called Broadcasting* (New York: Henry Holt, 1930), pp. 54–55; Carson, Memo for Secretary of Commerce, 7 October 1922, NARG 173, FCC, General Records, Radio Div., file 1179; Dellinger, Notes on Radio Standardization Conference, 9 January 1923, HHPL, Sec. of Commerce, Official File, box 438; Herbert Hoover, "Simplified Practice What It Is and What It Offers," 26 November 1924, HHPL, Sec. of Commerce, Official File, box 116, folder 1.

10. "War Between Broadcasting Stations," *Radio Broadcast* 1 (October 1922): 457; Terrell, Memo for Files, 21 April 1922, NARG 173, FCC, General Records, Radio Div., file 1179; Appel to Hoover, 15 June 1922, NARG 173, FCC, General Corresp., Radio Div., file BC-15; Batcheller to Whittmore, 10 June 1922, NARG 167, JHD Papers, box 6, File Broadcasting Stations of 1922.

11. Rexmond C. Cochrane, *Measures for Progress: A History of the National Bureau of Standards* (Washington, D.C.: National Bureau of Standards, 1966), pp. 269–70; George C. Southworth, *40 Years of Radio Research* (New York: Gordon and Breach, 1962), pp. 36–37; "Regulation and Standardization of the National Radio Chamber of Commerce," *Radio Broadcast* 1 (October 1922): 459-60; J. H. Dellinger, "The Bureau of Standards Lends a Hand," *Radio Broadcast* 1 (November 1922): 41–48.

12. "Harding Moves to Limit Wireless Telephony; Asks Hoover to Call Conference of Experts," New York *Times*, 8 February 1922; C. M. Jansky,

"Contributions of Herbert Hoover to Broadcasting," *Journal of Broadcasting* 3 (Summer 1957): 241-47; Edward F. Sarno, Jr., "The National Radio Conferences," *Journal of Broadcasting* 13 (Spring 1966): 189-91; Hoover to Begg, 6 March 1922, NARG 173, FCC, General Records, Radio Div., file 1179; Huston to Gould, 18 March 1922, NARG 173, FCC, General Records, Radio Div., file 1179; Libbey to Sproul, 15 March 1922, NARG 40, Dept. of Commerce, file 67032/31.

13. Wilson, "Broadcasting by the Newspaper Owned Stations in Detroit," p. 190; "Hoover Set Up American System for Radio," *Broadcasting*, HHPL, reprint; Hoover to McCutchen, 3 February 1922, NARG 173, FCC, General Records, Radio Div., file 1179; Taylor, Memo for Secretary of Agriculture, 14 March 1922, NARG 16, Sec. of Agriculture, Radio Telephones, Wireless Telegrams; Huston to Silver, 23 March 1922, NARG 40, Dept. of Commerce, file 67032/32.

14. Hoover Address, First National Radio Conference, 27 February 1922, HHPL, Sec. of Commerce, Official File, box 437, Radio: Conference, Draft of Minutes, 27-28 February 1922.

15. "Radio Regulation Conference Opens in Washington," *Electrical World* 79 (4 March 1922): 446-47; "The Explosive Growth of Radio," *Outlook* 130 (29 March 1922): 489-90; "Wavelengths Recommended by the Washington Conference," *Radio Broadcast* 1 (May 1922): 92-93; Wheeler to Stratton, 21 March 1922, NARG 173, FCC, General Records, Radio Div., file 1179; First National Radio Conf., Appendix, HHPL, Sec. of Commerce, Official File, Radio Conf., Draft of Minutes.

16. "Urges Federal Rule Over Radiophones," New York *Times*, 11 March 1922; "Recommendations for Government Radio Control," *Electrical World* 79 (18 March 1922): 547; Terrell, Memo for Huston, 15 March 1922, NARG 173, FCC, General Records, Radio Div., file 1179; Memo, Some Phases of Radio Telephone Conference, 3 January 1924, NARG 38, DNC, file 350; Summary of Preliminary Report of the Technical Committee of the Radio Telephone Conf., HHPL, Sec. of Commerce, Official File, Radio: Conf.; Goldsmith to Stratton, Comments on Tentative Report, HHPL, Sec. of Commerce, Official File, Radio: Conf.

17. Clarence C. Dill, *Radio Law Practice and Procedure* (Washington, D.C.: National Book, 1938), p. 33; "Broadcasting Situation," *Literary Digest* 73 (8 April 1922): 30-31; "Proposes New Law for Radio Control," New York *Times*, 28 April 1922; Chief Radio Inspector, Memo for Huston, 15 March 1922, NARG 40, Dept. of Commerce, File 67032/31; *Radio Service Bulletin*, no 61, 1 May 1922, NARG 173, FCC, General Corresp., Radio Div., file Leg-3-a, Radio Act.

18. "Inter-Departmental Advisory Committee to Help Regulate All Government Radio," *Radio Broadcast* 1 (October 1922): 456–57; "Government Forms a Committee for Broadcasting," *Electrical World* 80 (22 July 1922): 191; Hoover to Secretary of War, 10 March 1922, NARG 111, Chief Signal Officer, National Radio Conf., folder No. 1, 337; History of the Interdepartmental Radio Advisory Committee, 27 March 1957, NARG 167, JHD Papers, box 5, IRAC History; Perrill, Wheeler, Terrell, IRAC Meeting, n.d., NARG 173, IRAC Files, Operation and Procedure, box 77.

19. Herbert I. Schiller, *Mass Communications and the American Empire* (New York: Augustus M. Kelley, 1969), p. 35; Donald Wilhelm, "Uncle Sam in Radio," *Radio Broadcast* 1 (May 1922): 21–27; Hoover to Smither, 24 May 1922, HHPL, Sec. of Commerce, Official File, box 447, Interdepartmental Problems, 1922–27; Press Release, Interdepartmental Advisory Committee on Government Radio Broadcasting, 17 July 1922, HHPL, Sec. of Commerce, Official File, Radio Corresp., Press Releases.

20. Dellinger, Memo for Strattton, 16 March 1922, NARG 173, IRAC Files, box 106, Commerce, 1922; Dellinger to Terrell, 20 March 1922, NARG 173, FCC, General Records, Radio Div., file 1179; Testimony of Dellinger, H.R. 6949, 15 February 1950, NARG 167, JHD Papers, box 5, IRAC History.

21. Elwood to Hoover, 24 July 1922, HHPL, Sec. of Commerce, Official File, box 444, Radio: Corresp., Press Releases, 1922; Carson to Hoover, 21 October 1922, HHPL, Sec. of Commerce, Official File, box 447, Radio: Interdepartmental Problems, 1922–27.

22. White to Carson, 20 June 1922, White Papers, MSS, LC, box 35, Commerce Legislation, 67th Cong.; Dodd to Hooper, 2 November 1922, Hooper Papers, MSS, LC, box 4, Corresp., October to November 1922; Pannill to Hooper, 3 November 1922, Hooper Papers, MSS, LC, box 4, Corresp., October to November 1922; Denby to Scott, 6 March 1922, NARG 80, Sec. of Navy, 1916–26, box 593, file 12479 (1253: 100 to 1253: 159-1).

23. Hooper Memo, 25 April 1922, Hooper Papers, MSS, LC, box 4, Corresp., April 1922; Denby to Postmaster General, 15 April 1922, NARG 38, DNC, File 350–RG; Secretary of Navy to Chief Coordinator, 11 May 1922, NARG 80, Sec. of Navy, 1916–26, box 598, file 12479 (1738 to 1784).

24. S. C. Hooper, "Keeping the Stars and Stripes in the Ether," *Radio Broadcast* 1 (June 1922): 125–32; Hooper to Coman, 15 April 1922, Hooper Papers, MSS, LC, box 4, Corresp., May 1922; Hooper to *Popular Radio*, 18 July 1922, Hooper Papers, MSS, LC, box 4, Corresp., June to July 1922; Robinson to Secretary of Navy, 12 April 1922, NARG 80, Sec. of Navy, 1916–26, file 28576-28577 (28576-1).

25. "Facilities Available in Post Office Department to Make Cross-Country Flying Less Hazardous," 15 February 1922, NARG 28, PMG Letterbooks, 1 January 1922 to 31 March 1922; Work to Wallace, 3 April 1922, NARG 16 Sec. of Agriculture, Radio Telephones, Wireless Telegrams; Work to Secretary of Agriculture, 15 April 1922, NARG 16, Sec. of Agriculture, Radio Telephones, Wireless Telegrams; Denby to Postmaster General, 12 May 1922, NARG 38, DNC, File 110, 1922-23; Work to Secretary of Commerce, 3 April 1922, HHPL, Sec. of Commerce, Official File, Radio Corresp., Press Releases.

26. Final Report of Temporary Committee, Recommendations on Governmental Radio Broadcasting, 17 April 1922, NARG 173, FCC, General Records, Radio Div., file 1179; Report of the Subcommittee on Technical Problems, 4 October 1922, NARG 173, IRAC Files, box 52; Rules of Procedure for the Guidance of the IACGB in Its Conduct of Business with the Executive Departments, 25 July 1922, NARG 40, Dept. of Commerce, file 67032/32; Ziegemeier to All Bureaus and Offices, 14 September 1922, NARG 38, DNC, file 350.

27. Edgerton, Memo on Data Covering Proposed Post Office Department Radio Broadcasting System, 7 April 1922, NARG 173, IRAC Files, box 106, Post Office Dept.; Edgerton to Dellinger, Reservations of Signatories to Report on Recommendations of Government Radio Broadcasting, 17 April 1922, NARG 173, IRAC Files, box 77, Subcommittee on Material for Broadcasting; Work to Secretary of Agriculture, 3 May 1922, NARG 16, Sec. of Agriculture, Radio Telephones, Wireless Telegrams, U.S. Congress, House, *House Resolution 357*, 67th Cong., 2d sess., 31 May 1922, NARG 173, FCC, General Corresp., Radio Div., file Leg-3-a; Excerpts from Discussion of the Plan for the Reorganization of Government Departments as Regards Efficiency of Naval Communications and the Establishment of Department of Communications, 18 September 1923, NARG 167, JHD Papers, box 6.

28. Adjutant General to Chiefs of all War Department Branches, 4 January 1922, NARG 18, Records of the Army Air Force, file 311.23A; Pershing to Hale, 19 August 1922, NARG 18, Army Air Force, file 350.001; Annual Report, Director of Naval Communications, 30 June 1921, pp. 4-5, NARG 38, DNC, file 140-901.

29. "The Work of the Interdepartmental Radio Advisory Committee," *Radio Broadcast*, 2 (August 1923): 278-79; Harbord to Davis, 19 October 1923,. NARG 173, IRAC Files, box 124, RCA; Huston to Secretary of Commerce, 12 February 1923, NARG 40, Dept. of Commerce, file 67032/32.

30. Hogg, Memo, 15 March 1923, NARG 38, DNC, file 110-120; IRAC Progress Report of Subcommittee on Policy and Legislation, 13 April 1923, NARG 40, Dept. of Commerce, file 67032/32; Chief Coordinator to Director,

Bureau of Budget, 18 May 1925, NARG 51, Bureau of the Budget, series 21.1, Radio no. 1, Prior to January 1932.

31. IRAC Meeting, 20 June 1924, NARG 173, IRAC Files, box 1, IRAC Meeting, 20 June 1924; Tentative Statement of Government Radio Policy Prepared by the IRAC, 15 August 1924, NARG 173, IRAC Files, box 104, Minutes.

32. Regulations Pertaining to Radio Broadcast of Information Furnished by Government Departments to Private Radio Broadcast Stations, 4 January 1923, NARG 40, Dept. of Commerce, file 67032/32; Hooper to Bryant, 2 February 1923, Hooper Papers, MSS, LC, box 5; Naval Communications Service Annual Report, 1922–23, NARG 38, file 140–901.

33. U.S., Congress, House, *House Resolution 14169*, 67th Cong., 4th sess., 2 February 1923, NARG 173, FCC, General Corresp., Radio Div., file Leg-3-a; Nagle to Hoover, 23 April 1923, HHPL, Sec. of Commerce, Official File, Interdepartmental Problems.

34. Harbord to Davis, 19 October 1923, NARG 173, IRAC Files, box 124, RCA.

CHAPTER 3

1. "For Regulating Radio," New York *Times*, 19 April 1921; White to Hoover, 12 April 1921, White Papers, MSS, LC, box 35, Dept. File, Commerce, Legis. 67th Congress; Memo for Sec. of Commerce, White's Draft Bill, 23 April 1921, NARG 173, FCC, General Corresp., Radio Div., file Leg-3; Hoover to Kellogg, 23 April 1921, HHPL, Sec. of Commerce, Official File, Radio: Legis.

2. Marvin R. Bensman, "The Regulation of Radio Broadcasting by the Department of Commerce, 1921–27" (Ph.D. diss., University of Wisconsin, 1969), p. 91; Terrell, Memo for Commissioner of Navigation, 25 February 1922, NARG 173, FCC, General Records, Radio Div., file 1179; Department of Commerce Release, 9 June 1922, NARG 173, FCC, General Records, Radio Div., file 1104; Stratton to George, 28 September 1922, NARG 173, FCC, General Records, Radio Div., file 1600.

3. "Radio Legislation," *Outlook* 131 (28 June 1922): 363–64; Herbert Hoover, "Development and Control of Radio Broadcasting," *Academy Magazine* (January 1953), reprint, HHPL; Hoover to White, 12 August 1922, White Papers, MSS, LC, box 35, Dept. File, Commerce; Hoover to Goldsmith, 18 January 1922, NARG 40, Dept. of Commerce, file 67032/3; Brown to Hoover, 14 February 1922, NARG 173, FCC, General Corresp., Radio Div., file Leg-3-a; U.S., Congress, House, *House Resolution 11964*, 67th Cong. 2d sess., 9 June 1922, NARG 173, FCC, General Corresp., Radio Div., file Leg-3-a.

4. Robert K. Murray, *The Harding Era: Warren G. Harding and His Administration* (Minneapolis: University of Minnesota Press, 1969), pp. 125–26; "Wanted: An American Radio Policy," *Radio Broadcast* 1 (May 1922): 29–33; "Do You Want Broadcasting,"*Radio Broadcast* 2 (December 1922); Radio Inspector, New York, to Commissioner of Navigation, 18 December 1922, NARG 173, FCC, General Records, Radio Div., file 1484; IRAC Report of Special Subcommittee on Material on Broadcasting, 13 November 1922, NARG 173, IRAC Files, box 77, Subcommittee on Broadcasting.

5. Jerome G. Kerwin, *The Control of Radio* (Chicago: University of Chicago Press, 1934), p. 6; Statement Issued by the Secretary of Commerce, August 1922, NAB; White to Maxim, 3 June 1922, White Papers, MSS, LC, box 35, Dept. File, 67th Congress; White to Elwood, 13 September 1922, White Papers, MSS, LC, box 35, Dept. File, 67th Congress.

6. Elwood to White, 12 September 1922, White Papers, MSS, LC, box 35, Dept File, 67th Congress; Elwood to White, 26 October 1922, White Papers, MSS, LC, box 35, Dept. File, 67th Congress; Young to Hoover, 6 March 1922, HHPL, Sec. of Commerce, Personal File, Young; "Memo of Radio Corporation of America with Reference to the Tentative Report of the Department of Commerce Radio Telephony Conference," 1922, HHPL, Sec. of Commerce, Official File, box 437, Radio: Conference Report.

7. White to Williams, 8 November 1922, White Papers, MSS, LC, box 35, Dept. File, 67th Congress; Memo to Carson, 27 November 1922, HHPL, Sec. of Commerce, Official File, Interdepartmental Problems; Commissioner of Navigation, Memo for Secretary of Commerce, 28 December 1922, NARG 173, FCC, General Records, Radio Div., file 1104; Radio Editors Conference Held at City Club, New York City, 6 November 1922, NARG 173, FCC, General Records, Radio Div., file 1179-2.

8. U.S., Congress, House, Committee on Merchant Marine and Fisheries, *To Amend the Radio Act of 1912; Hearings on H.R. 11964*, 66th Cong., 4th sess., 2 and 3 January 1923.

9. "Need for Law," *Literary Digest* 76 (13 January 1923): 25–26; Carson, Memo for Secretary of Commerce, 8 January 1923, NARG 173, FCC, General Records, Radio Div., file 1600; Klein to Hoover, 8 January 1923, NARG 40, Dept. of Commerce, file 67032/32.

10. "Hoover for Radio Control," New York *Times*, 3 January 1923; Ziegemeier, Memo for Chief of Naval Operations, 2 January 1923, NARG 80, Sec. of Navy 1916–26, file 12479 (1957 to 1987); Memo for Secretary of Navy, 4 January 1923, NARG 38, DNC, file 110 (1922–23).

11. Carson, Memo for Secretary of Commerce, 9 January 1923, NARG 173, FCC, General Corresp., Radio Div., file 1484; White to Godley, 25 October 1922, White Papers, MSS, LC, box 42, Dept. File, Commerce.

12. Glenn A. Johnson, "The First Regulator of American Broadcasting, 1921–28, Secretary of Commerce Herbert Hoover" (Ph.D. diss., University of Iowa, 1970), pp. 114-15; U.S., Congress, House, *Bill to Amend an Act to Regulate Radio Communications*, 67th Cong., 4th sess., 16 January 1923, White Papers, MSS, LC, box 64, Subject File, Radio; Tyrer, Memo for Herter, 8 February 1923, HHPL, Sec. of Commerce, Official File, box 447, Radio Legislation; Hoover to Harding, 31 January 1923, HHPL, Sec. of Commerce, Official File, box 235, President Harding; Brown, Memo for Huston, 20 February 1923, NARG 173, FCC, General Corresp., Radio Div., file 67032/32.

Concerning navy support, see Denby to Henning, 22 January 1923, NARG 38, DNC, file 110 (1922–23); "Naval Communications Service," Address by Admiral Ziegemeier, Army-Navy Club, 21 February 1923, NARG 38, DNC, File 110-120 (1924–26).

13. George F. Gurghard, "Eighteen Years of Amateur Radio,"*Radio Broadcast* 3 (August 1923): 290–98; "The Legislative Situation," *QST*, n.d., White Papers, MSS, LC, Dept. File, Merchant Marine and Fisheries Committee; Rogers to Hoover, 3 May 1922, HHPL, Sec. of Commerce, Official File, Radio Corresp., Press Releases; Carson, Memo for Secretary of Commerce, 1 March 1922, NARG 173, FCC, General Records, Radio Div., file 1179; IRAC Report, Meeting of 2 February 1923, NARG 173, IRAC Files, box 1, IRAC Meeting, Government Radio Broadcasting.

14. Herbert C. Hoover, "The Urgent Need for Radio Legislation," *Radio Broadcast* 2 (January 1923): 211; John V. L. Hogan, "Putting Through the White Bill," *Radio Broadcast* 2 (March 1923): 452–55; Charles H. Kesler, "This Radio Bill We're Hearing About," *Radio Broadcast* 2 (February 1923): 282–86; Davis to Greene, 20 January 1923, White Papers, MSS, LC, box 35, Dept. File Commerce; Geer to Hoover, 3 January 1923, HHPL, Sec. of Commerce, Official File, box 447, Radio Legislation, 1923; Petition from Selma, Alabama, Citizens Favoring Radio Legislation, 26 February 1923, HHPL, Sec. of Commerce, Official File, box 447.

Concerning congressional inaction, consult "Incompetent Senate," *Outlook* 133 (7 March 1923): 432–33; "News from the Capital," *Electrical World* 81 (24 February 1923): 468; IRAC Report of Subcommittee on Policy and Legislation, 13 March 1923, NARG 173, IRAC Files, box 104, Policy and Legislation, 1923.

15. Notes of American Telephone and Telegraph Radio Conference (Confidential), New York City, 26 February to 2 March 1923, NAB.

16. Clarence C. Dill, *Radio Law Practice and Procedure* (Washington, D.C.: National Book, 1938), pp. 68–69; "Hoover Is Summoned in a Wireless Case," New York *Times*, 17 November 1921; "Court Upholds Intercity Radio," New York *Times*, 19 November 1921; Hoover to Solicitor General,

Department of Justice, 17 February 1923, NARG 40, Dept. of Commerce, file 80524; Report of Investigation of Interference Caused by Intercity Radio Station, Bureau of Standards, 6 March 1922, NARG 173, FCC, General Records, Radio Div., file 1102; Intercity Radio Company File, NARG 173, FCC, General Records, Radio Div., file 1102.

17. F. C. James, *The Growth of Chicago Banks* (New York: Harper and Brothers, 1938), pp. 3–4; Forrest McDonald, *The Torch is Passed: The United States in the 20th Century* (Reading, Mass.: Addison-Wesley, 1968), pp. 4–7.

18. Carson, Memo for Secretary of Commerce, 14 April 1922, NARG 173, FCC, General Records, Radio Div., file 1179; Carson to Gates, 29 May 1922, NARG 173, FCC, General Records, Radio Div., file 307; Tyrer to Choate, 24 October 1922, NARG 173, FCC, General Records, Radio Div., file 1600.

19. Terrell to Emmet, 28 December 1922, HHPL, Sec. of Commerce, Official File, box 447, Radio Legislation, 1922.

20. Carson to Hill, 10 November 1922, NARG 173, FCC, General Records, Radio Div., file 1600; George Sterling, "Government in Broadcasting," 24 A (NAB).

21. IRAC Report, 2 March 1923, NARG 40, Dept. of Commerce, file 67032/32; Carson to Chief Signal Officer, 10 November 1922, NARG 173, FCC, General Corresp., Radio Div., file Com-3 (S-T); IRACGB Report of 16 February 1923, NARG 173, IRAC Files, IRAC Meeting, 16 February 1923; IRAC Report of 24 April 1925, NARG 173, IRAC Files, box 1.

22. Emmet to Terrell, 16 April 1923, HHPL, Sec. of Commerce, Official File, box 444, Radio: Corresp., Press Releases, 1923.

23. Murray, *Harding Era*, p. 409; Walter B. Emery, *Broadcasting and Government: Responsibilities and Regulations* (Lansing: Michigan State University Press, 1961), p. 18; "Calls Radio Conference," New York *Times*, 7 March 1923; Hoover to Secretary of Navy, 6 March 1923, HHPL, Sec. of Commerce, Official File, box 438, Radio: Conferences, Second National Radio Conference; Dept of Commerce, Press Release, 6 March 1923, HHPL, Secretary of Commerce, Official File, box 444, Radio: Corresp., Press Releases, 1923; Hoover to White, 6 March 1923, White Papers, MSS, LC, box 35, Dept. File, Commerce Legislation, 67th Congress; Terrell, Memo for Secretary of Commerce, 23 February 1923, NARG 173, FCC, General Records, Radio Div., file 1484.

24. Paul F. Godley, "A Kingdom for More Wavelengths," *Radio Broadcast* 2 (January 1923): 191–93; "Debate Plans to End Chaos in Radio," New York *Times*, 21 March 1923; "Urge Wide Reform in Broadcasting," New York *Times*, 25 March 1923; Chief Radio Inspector, Memo for Commissioner of Navigation, 17 March 1923, HHPL, Secretary of Commerce, Official File, box 438, Radio: Conferences; Carson, Memo for Davis, 19

February 1924, NARG 173, IRAC Files Corresp. and Reports, Commmerce Dept., 1924.

25. Department of Commerce Press Release, 2 April 1923, HHPL, Sec. of Commerce, Official File, box 438, Radio: Conferences; Lecture of S.C. Hooper, "Frequency Allocation," 1927, NARG 19, Bureau of Ships, file 1084; Carson, Memo for Secretary of Commerce, 27 January 1923, NARG 173, FCC, General Records, Radio Div., file 1179; Amendments to Regulations of Bureau of Navigation, General Letter no. 247, 2 April 1923, NARG 173, FCC, General Records, Radio Div., file 1179/8.

26. "Recommendations of Radio Conference," *Electrical World* 81 (31 March 1923): 765; Jack Binnis, "How Spark Interference Was Reduced," *Radio Broadcast* 4 (March 1924): 474; Carson to Supervisor of Radio, New York, 19 November 1923, NARG 173, FCC, General Records, Radio Div., file 1600; Tyrer to Radio Corporation of America, 3 October 1934, NARG 173, FCC, General Records, Radio Div., file 1600; Wilbur to Secretary of State, 2 June 1925, NARG 38, DNC, file 323–031; "Radio Laws and Regulations," 1926, National Radio Institute, NARG 173, FCC, Radio Div., file 1166.

27. Department of Commerce Release, Recommendations of the National Radio Conference, 24 March 1923, HHPL, Sec. of Commerce, Official File, box 438, Radio Conferences; McLean to Commander-in-Chief, U.S. Fleet, 16 June 1924, NARG 38, DNC, file 323–100; Tyrer to Orriss, 11 April 1923, NARG 173, FCC, General Records, Radio Div., file 1179; Report of Section 6, Division 1, Dept. of Commerce, 30 June 1923, NARG 167, JHD Papers, box 4.

28. "Plans New Classes for Radio Stations," New York *Times*, 2 April 1923; "Department of Commerce Acts on Radio Recommendations," *Electrical World* 81 (7 April 1923): 794; "Wavelengths and Lighthouse Keepers," *Outlook* 133 (11 April 1923): 645–46; "Wavelengths for Class B Stations," *Radio Broadcast* 3 (June 1923): 167; "Secretary Hoover Acts," *Radio Broadcast* 3 (August 1923): 277; Carson to Squier, 31 March 1923, NARG 111, Chief Signal Officer, box 337, National Radio Conference, folder 1; Carson to Anderson, 15 January 1923, NARG 173, FCC, General Records, Radio Div., file 1600; Bureau of Navigation, All Radio Supervisors, 27 March 1924, NARG 173, FCC, General Records, Radio Div., file 2666.

29. President, RCA, to Hoover, 4 April 1923, HHPL, Sec. of Commerce, Official File, box 438, Radio Conferences; *Department of Commerce Radio Regulatons*, Bulletin no. 5, AT&T, 30 July 1923, NARG 173, FCC, General Records, Radio Div., file 5000; Carson to Starkey, 22 September 1923, NARG 173, FCC, General Records, Radio Div., file 1600; IRAC Wave Frequency Assignments, 21 September 1923, NARG 173, IRAC Files, box 52.

30. Charles Saltzman, "The Radio Equipment Situation," *Infantry Journal* 25 (December 1924): 601–06; "Conference Discusses Radio Chaos," *Electrical World* 81 (24 March 1923): 708; Squier, Memo for Secretary of War, 12 April 1923, NARG 111, Chief Signal Officer, box 337, National Radio Conference, folder 1; IRAC Report of Subcommitte on Technical Problems, 17 May 1923, NARG 173, IRAC Files, Subcommittee on Technical Problems; Bender to IRAC, 4 August 1924, NARG 173, FCC, IRAC Flles, box 107.

31. Hooper Tape Recordings, 312–13, Hooper Papers, MSS, LC, box 37.

32. Concerning frequency allocation, see Hooper to McLean, 15 July 1924, Hooper Papers, MSS, LC, box 6; "Naval Communications," Lectures delivered by Ridley McLean, Naval War College, 31 October 1924, Hooper Papers, MSS, LC, box 6; Craven, Hooper Tape Recordings, 37, Hooper Papers, MSS, LC, box 37; Chief of Naval Operations to Naval Force Europe, Special Service Squadron, Transportation Service, 23 September 1923, NARG 38, DNC, file 323; Burgess to Smither, 28 September 1923, NARG 173, IRAC Files, box 106, Commerce Dept.; Bureau of Engineering to Chief of Naval Operations, Allocation of Radio Frequencies, 23 June 1925, NARG 173, IRAC Files, Corresp. and Reports, 1922–49.

On radio equipment, consult "Engineer Says Navy Needs More Up to Date Equipment," New York *Times*, 3 November 1926; Tawresey, Memo for Bingham, 9 August 1923, NARG 38, DNC, file 140–902; Chief of Naval Operations to Commander-in-Chief, U.S. Fleeet, 17 March 1924, NARG 38, DNC, file 323–100; Secretary of Navy to Carlson, 23 April 1925, NARG 80, Sec. of Navy, 1916–26; file 12479 (2060–2098:1).

33. As quoted in Llewellyn White, *The American Radio* (Chicago: University of Chicago Press, 1947), pp. 83–84.

34. Hoover Statement, U.S., Congress, House, Committee on Merchant Marine and Fisheries, *To Regulate Radio Communications; Hearings before Committee on Merchant Marine and Fisheries*, 69th Cong., 1st sess., 6, 7, 14, and 15 January 1926.

CHAPTER 4

1. Upton Close, *The Commentator's Story* (Palm Beach: Time for Truth Press, 1952), p. 2; U.S., Department of Commerce, *Commerce Yearbook, 1922* (Washington, D.C.: Government Printing Office, 1923), p. 418; Carson to Hogan, 1 December 1922, NARG 173, FCC, General Records, Radio Div., file 1179.

2. "Monopoly in Radio by 8 Concerns Charged in Action," New York *Times*, 28 January 1924; "Is Radio Corporation a Bad Trust," *Radio Broadcast* 4 (April 1924): 470–71; U.S., Congress, House, *Congressional Record*, 68th

Cong., 1st sess., 1924, 5056, 5122; Simmons to White, 15 February 1923, White Papers, MSS, LC, box 35,Dept. File, Commerce, 67th Congress.

Also see NARG 122, Records of the Federal Trade Commission, file no. 1–2728, box 455, and 456; U.S., Congress, House, *Report of the Federal Trade Commission on the Radio Industry,* House Resolution 548, 67th Cong., 4th sess., 1 December 1923 (Washington, D.C.: Government Printing Office, 1924).

3. Department of Commerce, Memo for White, 15 January 1923, NARG 173, FCC, General Corresp., Radio Div., file Leg-3.

Concerning radio manufacturers, see Thomas T. Eoyang, *An Economic Study of the Radio Industry* (New York: RCA, 1937), p. 103; Walter Kingsman; Rome Cowgill, and Ralph Levy, *Broadcasting: Television and Radio* (New York: Prentice-Hall, 1955), p. 141; Lawrence Wilson Lichty, "The Nation's Station: A History of Radio Station WLW" (Ph.D. diss., Ohio State University, 1964); "The Story of Powell Crosley," *Radio Broadcast* 6 (November 1924): 63–67.

For electrical companies, consult "Put Our Own Story on the Radio," *Electrical World* 82 (8 December 1922): 1,153; David Sarnoff, "What Radio Means to the Central Station," *Electrical World* 84 (22 November 1924): 1,094–95; "Radio Increases Use of Energy 40 per cent," *Electrical World* 84 (20 December 1924): 1,315.

For newspaper-owned stations, consult Jacquelin E. Morrison, "A Study of the Chronological Development of the Three Regional Radio Broadcasting Stations in Atlanta, Georgia" (Master's thesis, University of Georgia, 1954); Bruce A. Linton, "A History of Chicago Radio Station Programming 1921–31, With Special Emphasis on Stations WMAQ and WGN" (Ph.D. diss., Northwestern University, 1953); Orrin E. Dunlap, *Radio in Advertising* (New York: Harper and Brothers, 1931), p. 40; E. P. J. Shurick, *The First Quarter-Century of American Broadcasting* (Kansas City: Midland, 1946), pp. 19–20; Mitchell V. Charnley, *News By Radio* (New York: Macmillan, 1948), p. 4; Abel Green and Joe Laurie, *Show Biz from Vaude to Video* (New York: Henry Holt, 1951), p. 232.

4. Concerning religious broadcasters, see Linton, "History of Chicago Radio Station Programming," pp. 32, 99; Samuel L. Rothafel and Raymond F. Yates, *Broadcasting Its New Day* (New York: Century, 1925), p. 130; Statement of Dr. S. Parkes Cadman, 2 October 1928, Davis Papers, MSS, AIS, box 3, folder 44; "KRKD, Los Angeles, Formerly KFSG, Amy Semple McPherson," compiled by Dr. Raymond W. Becker, 6 February 1924, 441 (NAB).

For city government and broadcasting, see Saul N. Scher, "An Old City Hall Tradition: New York's Mayors and WNYC," *Journal of Broadcasting*

10 (Spring 1966): 137–47; Carson, Memo for Secretary of Commerce, 26 May 1922, NARG 173, FCC, General Records, Radio Div., file 1179.

For educational broadcasters, see Edgar E. Willis, *Foundations in Broadcasting: Radio and Television* (New York: Oxford University Press, 1951), p. 26; Barbara Joan Maurer, "History of Station WHA, 1926–31" (Master's thesis, University of Wisconsin, 1957); John Stanley Penn, "The Origin and Development of Radio Broadcasting at the University of Wisconsin to 1940" (Ph.D. diss., University of Wisconsin, 1959), "A Big Demand for Educational Radio?" *Radio Broadcast* 3 (June 1923): 94–97.

Also see, Ansel Harlan Resler, "The Impact of John Brinkley on Broadcasting in the United States" (Ph.D. diss., Northwestern University, 1958); Lillian Jones Hall, "A Historical Study of Program Techniques and Practices of Radio Station KWKH, Shreveport, Louisiana, 1922–1950" (Ph.D. diss., Louisiana State University, 1959).

5. Mary Ann Cusack, "Editorializing in Broadcasting," (Ph.D. diss., Wayne State University, 1959), pp. 34–35. David R. Mackey, "The National Association of Broadcasters: Its First Twenty Years" (Ph.D. diss., Northwestern University, 1956), David R. Mackey, "The Development of the NAB," *Journal of Broadcasting* 1 (Fall 1957): 305–26; Dr. Frank W. Elliot, Taped Interview, 155 (NAB); W. S. Hedges, "In The Beginning," Pamphlet, 9 C (NAB).

Concerning the ASCAP, consult "More Injunctions for the Broadcasters," *Radio Broadcast* 3 (July 1923): 180–81; "Will the Composer Pay for Broadcasting?" *Radio Broadcast* 3 (August 1923): 271–73; "With Justice for All," *"Radio Broadcast* 4 (February 1924): 273–74; Jennie Irene Mix, "How Shall We Get Great Artists to Broadcast?" *Radio Broadcast* 5 (May 1924): 11–17; Rosenthal to Department of Commerce, 6 September 1922, NARG 173, FCC, General Records, Radio Div., file 1600.

6. W. Rupert Maclaurin, *Invention and Innovation in the Radio Industry* (New York: Macmillan, 1949), pp. 113–14; Eoyang, *Economic Study of Radio Industry*, p. 155; "Radio Trust to Battle for Control of the Air," *American*, 14 November 1925, Davis Papers, MSS, AIS, box 3, folder 46; Carl Dreher, "How the Wasteland Began," *Atlantic Monthly*, 1966, 254 G (NAB); McLean to Davis, 19 March 1925, NARG 38, DNC, file 323–100; Sarnoff to Terrell, 10 December 1924, NARG 173, FCC, General Records, Radio Div., file 2678.

7. Schiller, *Mass Communications*, pp. 22–23; Eoyang, *Economic Study of Radio Industry*, p. 61; C. B. Rose, *National Policy for Radio Broadcasting* (New York: Harper and Brothers, 1940), p. 49; Sydney W. Head, *Broadcasting in America* (Boston: Houghton Mifflin, 1956), pp. 115–24; *Annual Report of Directors of Radio Corporation of America, 1921–1923*, NARG 173, FCC, General Corresp., Radio Div., file Com-3, M–R.

8. Brooke Graves, ed., *Readings in Public Opinion* (New York: Appleton, 1928), p. 533; Herman S. Hettinger, *The Use of Radio Broadcasting as an Advertising Medium in the United States* (Chicago: University of Chicago Press, 1933), pp. v, 107; William Peck Banning, *Commercial Broadcasting Pioneer, The WEAF Experiment, 1922-26* (Cambridge: Harvard University Press, 1946); Notes on AT&T Conference, 26 February to 7 March 1923 (NAB); Griswold Testimony, First National Radio Conference, 18-19, HHPL, Sec. of Commerce, Official File, box 437, Radio Conf., Draft of Minutes; Thayer to Hoover, 23 January 1922, NARG 173, FCC, General Records, Radio Div., file 1179.

9. Concerning AT&T's plans for monopoly, see Marvin R. Bensman, "Regulation of Radio Broadcasting by the Department of Commerce, 1921-27" (Ph.D. diss., University of Wisconsin, 1969), p. 130; Batcheller to Commissioner of Navigation 10 January 1922, NARG 173, FCC, General Records, Radio Div., file 1675.

For WEAF and network hook-ups, consult David C. Phillips; John M. Grogan; and Earl H. Ryan, *Introduction to Radio and Television* (New York: Ronald Press, 1954), p. 17; Franklin M. Reck, *Radio: From Start to Finish* (New York: Thomas Y. Crowell, 1942), pp. 62-63; Frank A. Arnold, *Broadcast Advertising: The Fourth Dimension* (New York: John Wiley, 1933), pp. 11-12; "Inaugural to Be Broadcast to All Parts of the Country," New York *Times*, 1 March 1925; *Report on Chain Broadcasting*, Federal Communications Commission, Order no. 37, Docket no. 5060, May 1941 (Washington, D.C.: Government Printing Office, 1941); NBC Press Bureau, Significant Dates in Broadcast History, 13 November 1931, Clark Collection, MSS, MHT, CL 134, 1051; *AT&T Annual Report, 1925*, NARG 173, FCC, General Records, Radio Div., File Commercial Stations, 1-3 A.

10. Maclaurin, *Invention and Innovation*, pp. 114-15; N. R. Danielan, *AT&T: The Story of Industrial Conquest* (New York: Vanguard, 1936), pp. 122-23; Pierre Boucheron, "Advertising Radio to the American Public: An Exposition of the Part Played by Advertising in the Development of the Radio Industry," in *The Radio Industry, Story of Its Development as Told by Leaders of the Industry* (New York: A. W. Shaw, 1928), pp. 3-46; *Commerce Yearbook, 1924* (Washington: Government Printing Office, 1925), 430.

11. Francis Chase, *Sound and Fury: An Informal History of Broadcasting* (New York: Harper and Brothers, 1942), p. 18; Ralph Adams Cram, "Radio City and After," *American Mercury* 23 (July 1923): 291-96; Director of Research to Sarnoff, 23 April 1923, Clark Collection, MSS, MHT, CL 5, M.W.T. Co. to RCA; Sarnoff to Heads of Departments, RCA, 1 May 1923, Clark Collection, MSS, MHT, CL 134, 701-800.

12. David Sarnoff, *Looking Ahead: The Papers of David Sarnoff* (New York: McGraw-Hill, 1968), pp. 29-71; Robert J. Landry, *This Fascinating*

Radio Business (Indianapolis: Bobbs-Merrill, 1946), p. 66; Eugene Lyons, *David Sarnoff* (New York: Harper & Row, 1966), p. 118; Julius Grodinsky, *Jay Gould, His Business Career, 1867–1892* (Philadelphia: University of Pennsylvania Press, 1957); Sarnoff's Views on Newspaper Owned Broadcasting Stations, 1922, Clark Collection, MSS, MHT, CL, 134, 801–930; Dora Albert, "How Did Sarnoff Become President of RCA," Clark Collection, MSS, MHT, CL 14, 001–680; Sarnoff Papers, vol. 1, Misc.

13. Allan Harding, "What Radio Has Done and What It Will Do Next, Interview with David Sarnoff," *American Magazine* 101 (March 1926): 46–47, 167–73; "Why Super Power Broadcasting Means Better Service," Sarnoff Address over KGO, 26 October 1924, Clark Collection, MSS, MHT, CL 134, 1051; Sarnoff to Goldsmith, 6 January 1922, Clark Collection, MSS, MHT, CL 134, 1051; Sarnoff Address Before Convention of Electrical Suppliers, 15 November 1923, NARG 173, FCC, General Records, Radio Div., file 2640; Carson to Horn, 3 April 1924, NARG 173, FCC, Radio Div., file KDKA; *Annual Report of Directors of RCA, 1924*, NARG 173, FCC, General Corresp., Radio Div., file Com-3, M-R.

Concerning difficulties with AT&T over wire service, consult Sarnoff to Goldsmith, 6 January 1922, Clark Collection, MSS, MHT, CL 134, 1051; Gifford to Harbord, 26 April 1923, Clark Collection, MSS, MHT, CL 134, 1051; Sarnoff to Brainard, 10 October 1923, Clark Collection, MSS, MHT, CL 134, 801–903.

14. McQuiston, Memo for Davis, n.d., Davis Papers, MSS, AIS, box 1, folder 13; Davis to Herr, 9 January 1924, Davis Papers, MSS, AIS, box 3, folder 36; Davis to Terrell, 9 April 1923, NARG 173, FCC, Radio Div., file KDKA.

15. "Fewer and Better Broadcasting Stations," *Radio Broadcast* 2 (February 1923): 272; "Saturation Point Has Been Reached in Broadcasting," Springfield *Daily Republican*, 10 October 1922, NARG 173, FCC, General Records, Radio Div., file 1179.

On national organization, see "Radio Broadcasting," Address by H. P. Davis Before Electrical Supply Jobbers' Association, 19 November 1925, Davis Papers, MSS, AIS, box 3, folder 44.

On advertising, see Clark to Bucher, 6 January 1922, Clark Collection, MSS, MHT, CL 134, 1051; H. P. Davis, 14 April 1922 Address, Davis Papers, MSS, AIS, box 1, folder 14 ; "How Radio Broadcasting Is Being Used as an Advertising Tool," *Advertising and Selling Fortnightly*, 22 April 1925, Davis Papers, MSS, AIS, box 3, folder 39; Associate Broadcasters to Jones, 18 December 1922, NARG 173, FCC, Radio Div., file WHN.

Concerning the considerable early opposition to advertising, see "Radio Currents An Editorial Interpretation," *Radio Broadcast* 1 (May 1922): 1–4; "Radio Men Oppose Ads in Programs," New York *Times*, 2 April 1924; "The

De Forest Anti-Ad," circa 1925–26, De Forest Papers, MSS, LC, box 1925–26; Tyrer to Radio Inspector, Boston, 25 April 1922, NARG 173, FCC, General Corresp., Radio Div., file BC-15, A.

16. "Standard Tests for Radio Receivers," *Radio Broadcast* 1 (September 1922): 376; G. Y. Allen, "How Radio Is Being Standardized," *Radio Broadcast* 6 (April 1925): 1035–36; Paul F. Peter, "The American Radio Listener in 1940," *Annals of the American Academy of Political and Social Science* 213 (January 1941): 1; Leslie J. Page, Jr., "Nature of the Broadcast Receiver and Its Market in the United States from 1922–27," *Journal of Broadcasting* 4 (Spring 1960): 174–82; Report of an Investigation Made Among Radio Owners of Missouri and Illinois Showing Individual Preferences, Davis Papers, MSS, AIS, box 4, folder 51; Goldsmith to Nally, 29 May 1922, Clark Collection, MSS, MHT, CL 134, 1179 A.

17. Shurick, *First Quarter Century*, 74–75; Green and Laurie, *Show Biz*, p. 233; John Gunther, *Taken At the Flood: The Story of Albert D. Lasker* (New York: Harper & Row, 1960), pp. 193–97; Donald W. Riley, "A History of American Radio Drama from 1919 to 1944" (Ph.D. diss., Ohio State University, 1944), pp. 9–36; William S. Paley, "Radio and the Humanities," *Annals of the American Academy of Political and Social Science* 179 (May 1935): 101; "Radio Broadcasting: Early Commercial History," Clark Collection, MSS, MHT, CWC 134, 1091 A; Department of Commerce Release, 1 January 1925, HHPL, Sec. of Commerce, Official File, box 444, Radio: Corresp., 1925; McDonald to Terrell, 15 January 1924, NARG 173, FCC, General Corresp., Radio Div., file BC-15, C.

For station management, see Penn, "Broadcasting at University of Wisconsin," p. 233; Arnold, *Broadcast Advertising*, pp. 22–32; Carl Dreher, "Pity the Poor Broadcaster," *Radio Broadcast* 5 (June 1924): 136–39.

18. Glenn A. Johnson, "The First Regulator of American Broadcasting, 1921-28, Secretary of Commerce Herbert Hoover" (Ph.D. diss., University of Iowa, 1970), p. 279; Address by Secretary Hoover to National Electric Light Association Convention, 21 May 1924, HHPL, Sec. of Commerce, Personal File, box 72; Edwards to Commissioner of Navigation, 24 January 1924, NARG 173, FCC, Radio Div., file WGN-WLIB; Carson to Bacon, 15 March 1924, NARG 173, FCC, General Records, Radio Div., file 1600.

Regarding experimentation, see "To Issue High Power Licenses For Experimental Stations," New York *Times*, 9 November 1924; Hoover to Hughes, 24 October 1924, NARG 173, FCC, General Records, Radio Div., file 1600; Hoover to Answell, 23 December 1924, NARG 173, FCC, General Records, Radio Div., file 1104.

Concerning advertising, consult Hoover to Banning, 2 May 1924, NARG 173, FCC, Radio Div., file 2617; Stokes to Editor, New York *Mirror*, 20

March 1925, HHPL, Sec. of Commerce, Official File, box 437, Radio Advertising.

19. For Hoover's position on monopoly, consult "Hoover Against Air Monopoly—Thayer Doesn't Want It," *Electrical World* 83 (15 March 1924): 542; "No Radio Monopoly, Declares Hoover," New York *Times*, 17 October 1924; Hoover to Weeks, 23 December 1925, NARG 173, FCC, General Records, Radio Div., file 1600.

Concerning radio legislation, see "Hoover Again Asks for Radio Regulation," *Electrical World* 82 (8 December 1923): 1186; "Urges Radio Regulation," New York *Times*, 8 December 1923; Coles to White, 11 December 1923, White Papers, MSS, LC, box 42, Dept. File, Commerce, Radio; IRAC Meeting, 12 February 1924, NARG 173, IRAC Files, box 1.

20. White to Cooper, 2 January 1924, White Papers, MSS, LC, box 42, Dept. File, Commerce, Radio; Statement by Secretary Hoover at Hearings Before the Committee on the Merchant Marine and Fisheries on H.R. 7357, "To Regulate Radio Communication and for other Purposes," 11 March 1924, HHPL, Sec. of Commerce, Official File, box 447, Radio Legislation; Acting Secretary of Commerce to White, 25 March 1924, NARG 173, IRAC Files, Corresp. and Reports, 1922–49.

For the navy position, see Bingham to Assistant Director of Naval Communications, 14 March 1924, NARG 38, DNC, file 110 (1924); Wilbur to Chairman, Senate Committee on Commerce, 10 May 1924, NARG 80, Sec. of Navy, 1916–26, file 26256–324.

21. Robert K. Murray, *The Harding Era: Warren G. Harding and His Administration* (Minneapolis: University of Minneapolis Press, 1969), p. 503. Stewart to White, 7 January 1924, White Papers, MSS, LC, box 42, Dept. File, Commerce, Radio; Scheverin to Perrill, 8 February 1924, NARG 173, IRAC Files, Corresp. and Reports, 1924; Radio Inspector, New York to Carson, 8 March 1924, NARG 173, FCC, General Records, Radio Div., file 1104.

22. Clipping, "Just Talks on Common Themes," 12 March 1924, White Papers, MSS, LC, box 42, Dept. File, Commerce, Radio.

23. "Hoover Calls Third National Radio Conference," *Electrical World* 84 (6 September 1924): 438; U.S. Foreign & Domestic Commerce Bureau, *Commerce Yearbook* (Washington, D.C.: Government Printing Office, 1924), p. 428; Department of Commerce Release, 29 August 1924, HHPL, Sec. of Commerce, Official File, box 438, Radio Conf., Third National Radio Conf.; Griffith to Sec. of IRAC, 9 August 1924, NARG 173, IRAC Files, box 107, U.S. Shipping Board; IRAC Report of Special Subcommittee on Broadcasting Stations, 10 September 1924, NARG 173, IRAC Files, Minutes of Committees.

24. "Hoover Proposes Radio Cooperation," New York *Times*, 7 October 1924; "What the Hoover Conference Did," *Radio Broadcast* 6 (December 1924): 252; National Association of Broadcasters, Letters to Members, n.d., #72 (NAB); Secretary Hoover Addresses Third National Radio Conference, Dept. of Commerce Release, 7 October 1924, HHPL, Sec. of Commerce, Official File, box 438, Radio Conference.

25. U.S. Department of Commerce, *Recommendations for Regulation of Radio Adopted by the Third National Radio Conference Called by Herbert Hoover Secretary of Commerce*, October 6 to 10, 1924 (Washington, D.C.: Government Printing Office, 1924); Third National Radio Conference, NARG 19, Bureau of Ships, folder 1084, Radio Stations, Reorganizaton to Schnell.

26. Carson to Jansky, 18 November 1924, NARG 173, FCC, Radio Div., file 2678; Chief of Naval Operations to All Ships and Stations, 3 January 1925, NARG 19, Bureau of Ships, folder 1084, Radio Conf., 1924.

CHAPTER 5

1. David Sarnoff, "Introduction," in *The Radio Industry: The Story of Its Development as Told by Leaders of the Industry* (New York: A. W. Shaw, 1928), p. 3; Radio Talk by Secretary Hoover, 26 March 1924, HHPL, Sec. of Commerce, Official File, box 444, Radio Corresp.; "Radio Problems," Address Before California Radio Exposition by Secretary Hoover, 16 August 1924, HHPL Sec. of Commerce, Official File, box 448, Radio, Speeches.

2. "Hoover Opposes Radio Control," New York *Times*, 6 December 1924; "Hoover on Radio Control," *Electrical World* 84 (13 December 1924): 1274; Hoover to White, 4 December 1924, HHPL, Sec. of Commerce, Official File, box 447, Radio.

3. "Claims Commission Needed to Control Broadcasting," New York *Times*, 28 December 1924; "Hoover's Suggestions for New Radio Regulations," *Radio Broadcast* 6 (March 1925): 891; NAB Bulletin no. 124, 24 December 1924, NAB library, Letters to Members (NAB); McLean to McDonald, 31 December 1924, NARG 38, DNC, file 110 (1925–26).

4. Stokes to Editor, *Herald Examiner*, 30 December 1924, HHPL, Sec. of Commerce, Official File, box 444, Radio Corresp., 1924; Report of the Subcommitteee on Policy and Legislation on Pending Radio Legislation, 5 November 1924, NARG 173, IRAC Files, box 1, Corresp. and Reports, 1922–49.

5. Herman S. Hettinger, *The Use of Broadcasting as an Advertising Medium in the United States* (Chicago: University of Chicago Press, 1933), p. 69; Speech of Wallace White in House of Representatives, 12 March, 1926, White Papers, MSS, LC, box 67, File Speeches; Secretary Hoover Reviews

Radio Situation, Department of Commerce Release, 8 February 1924, NARG 173, FCC, General Records, Radio Div., file 3536; Tyrer to Sills, 13 February, 1925, NARG 173, FCC, General Records, Radio Div., file 1600; Carson to Meenam, 13 September 1925, NARG 173, FCC, Radio Div., file WGY.

6. "158 New Broadcasters Add to Congestion in the Air," New York *Times*, 16 January 1927; Carson to All Supervisors of Radio, n.d., NARG 173, FCC, Radio Div., file 307; Davis to Goldsmith, 2 July 1925, NARG 173, FCC, General Records, Radio Div., file 1104.

7. "Problems Conference Must Face," New York *Times*, 13 September 1925; "To Seek Radio Regulation," New York *Times*, 16 September 1925; "Questions for Consideration by Fourth National Radio Conference," 9 November 1925, HHPL, Sec. of Commerce, Official File, box 438, Radio: Conferences; Davis to White, 22 October 1925, White Papers, MSS, LC, box 42, Dept. File, Commerce; Hoover to White, 14 November 1925, NARG 40, Dept. of Commerce, file 67032/42; Harkness to Davis, NARG 173, FCC, General Records, Radio Div., file 1600.

8. Marvin R. Bensman, "The Regulation of Radio Broadcasting by the Department of Commerce, 1921–1927" (Ph.D. diss., University of Wisconsin, 1969), p. 264; Hoover Address Over WRC, WJZ, and WGY on Opening of National Radio Conference, 12 September 1925, HHPL, Sec. of Commerce, Official File, box 438, Radio Conferences; NAB Release, To All Broadcasters, 21 October, 1925, NAB Letters to Members, NAB no. 72 (NAB).

9. "No More Licenses for Radio Stations," New York *Times*, 11 November 1925; Tyrer to Campbell, 5 December 1925, NARG 173, FCC, General Records, Radio Div., file 1600; Carson to Supervisor of Radio, Boston, 14 December 1925, NARG 173, FCC, General Corresp., file BC–15, U; White to Fernald, 6 April 1926, White Papers, MSS, LC, box 51, 69th Congress, Radio.

10. James M. Herring and Gerald C. Gross, *Telecommunications; Economics and Regulations* (New York: McGraw-Hill, 1936), pp. 242–43; "Wavelengths Will Not Be Changed," *Radio Broadcast* 6 (March 1925): 896–97; Hoover to Maxim, 14 November 1925, HHPL, Sec. of Commerce, Personal File, box 3, Amateur Radio; *Annual Report, Office of Chicago Supervisor of Radio*, 10 July 1926, NARG 173, FCC, General Corresp., Radio Div., file dept. 15, district 9.

11. Clarence C. Dill, *Radio Law Practice and Procedure* (Washington: National Book, 1938), p. 89; Walter B. Emery, *Broadcasting and Government; Responsibilities and Regulations* (Lansing: Michigan State University Press, 1961), p. 19; "Suggests a Program for Radio Reform," New York *Times*, 12 November 1925; "Radio Conference Adopts a Legislative Program," *Electrical World* 86 (14 November 1925): 1017; Frederick W. Ford, "The Meaning

of Public Interest, Convenience, or Necessity," *Journal of Broadcasting* 5 (Summer 1961): 205–19; Hoover to Klugh, 19 November 1925, 19 H (NAB); Proceedings of the Fourth National Radio Conference and Recommendations for the Regulation of Radio, 9-11 November 1925, NARG 111, Chief Signal Officer, file 337.

12. "Congress Expected to Pass New Bill Regulating Radio," New York *Times*, 6 December 1925; Young to Hoover, 2 December 1925, HHPL, Sec. of Commerce, Official File, box 438, Radio; Hoover to Walls, 14 November 1925, NARG 40, Dept. of Commerce, file 67032/42; Hoover to Harkness, 16 November 1925, NARG 40, Dept. of Commerce, file 67032/42.

13. Hoover to Broadley, 24 November 1925, HHPL, Sec. of Commerce, Official File, box 444, Radio, Corresp., 1925; "Hoover Is Czar of Radio Industry as Result of Washington Conference," *Crosley Radio Weekly*, 7 December 1925, NARG 173, FCC. General Records, Radio Div., file 3571; Weekly Radio Summary, 12, 19, and 26 December 1925, NARG 173, FCC, General Records, Radio Div., file 3600.

Concerning the controversy over WJZ, consult "Washington Gets Complaints that WJZ Blankets the Air," New York *Times*, 17 January 1926; U.S. Congress, Senate, *Congressional Record*, 69th Cong., 1st Sess., 1926, 5069; Harbord to Sanders, 10 December 1925, Coolidge Presidential Papers, MSS, LC, reel 80, 136.

14. David R. Mackey, "The National Association of Broadcasters: Its First Twenty Years" (Ph.D. diss., Northwestern University, 1956), pp. 323–24; White to Hutchinson, 23 December 1925, White Papers, MSS, LC, box 51, Dept. File, 69th Congress, Radio; Davis to White, 2 December 1925, White Papers, MSS, LC, box 50, Dept. File, 69th Congress, Radio Legislation; Purdy to Hoover, 27 December 1925, NARG 173, FCC, General Records, Radio Div., file 154.

Concerning Dill's position, see Burton K. Wheeler, *Yankee from the West* (Garden City, N.Y.: Doubleday, 1962), p. 196; "Decries Radio Regulation," New York *Times*, 17 September 1925; U.S., Congress, House, *Congressional Record*, 68th Cong., 1st sess., 1924, 3874.

15. Hoover Backs Radio Bill," New York *Times*, 7 January 1926; "No Vested Right in the Air If the White Bill Passed," New York *Times*, 28 February 1926; "Wavelengths and Politics," *Outlook* 142 (24 February 1926): 276–77; U.S., Congress, House, *Congressional Record*, 69th Cong., 1st sess., 1925–26, 2309; U.S., Congress, House, *Congressional Record*, 69th Cong., 1st sess., 1926, 5437–77; White to Cowles, 3 January 1926, White Papers, MSS, LC, box 50, Dept. Files, 69th Congress, Radio; Report of the Subcommittee on Policy and Legislation to the IRAC on House Resolution 5589, 9 January 1926, NARG 173, IRAC Files, box 104, Policy and Legislation.

16. "House Passes Bill for Radio Control," New York *Times*, 16 March 1926; Davis to Cooper, 8 March 1926, NARG 40, Dept. of Commerce, file 67032/7; Edwards to Carson, 13 March 1926, NARG 173, FCC, General Records, Radio Div., file 1104; House Resolution 9971, 15 March 1926, NARG 173, FCC, General Corresp., Radio Div., file Legis-3-a.

17. Statement of Secretary Hoover Before Committee on Merchant Marine and Fisheries, 6 January 1926, Dept. of Commerce Release, HHPL, Sec. of Commerce, Official File, box 447, Radio Legislation; U.S., Congress, House, *Congressional Record*, 69th Cong., 1st sess., 1926, 5474.

18. "Peace Terms Suggested for Radio and Composers," New York *Times*, 17 January 1926; "Radio Control Bill Stirs House Debate," New York *Times*, 13 March 1926; U.S., Congress, House, *To Regulate Radio Communications Hearings Before Committee of Merchant Marine and Fisheries, House of Representatives*, 69th Cong., 1st sess., 6, 7, 14 and 15 January 1926 (Washington, D.C.: Government Printing Office, 1926).

19. U.S., Congress, House, *Regulation of Radio Communications*, 69th Cong., 1st sess., 1926, H. Rept. 464; NARG 173, FCC, General Corresp., Radio Div., file Legis-3-a; U.S., Congress, House, *Congressional Record*, 69th Cong., 1st sess., 1926, 12451–53.

20. St. Louis-*Post Dispatch*, clipping, 20 October 1925, HHPL, Sec. of Commerce, Official File, box 9, Articles and Speeches, 1925; Hoover to Sanders, 29 March 1926, Coolidge Presidential Papers, MSS, LC, reel 80, 136.

21. Agricultural Radio Conference Under the Auspices of the Department of Agriculture, 4 December 1924, NARG 173, FCC, General Records, Radio Div., file 2727; "Use of Radio By Farmers, Department of Agriculture Survey, 1925," NARG 173, FCC, General Records, Radio Div., file 1406; Warburton to Peck. 13 January 1926, NARG 16, Sec. of Agriculture, Radio Legislation, Programs, 1924–27.

22. "Urges Inquiry on Radio," New York *Times*, 28 February 1926; "Dark Outlook for Passage of Radio Legislation," New York *Times*, 14 March 1926; Davis to White, 17 December 1925, NARG 40, Dept. of Commerce, file 67032/42; Circular, American Broadcasters, 30 December 1925, NARG 173, FCC, General Records, Radio Div., file 1104; White to Davis, 19 January 1926, White Papers, MSS, LC, box 51, Dept. File, 69th Congress.

23. Erling S. Jorgenses, "Radio Station WCFL: A Study in Labor Union Broadcasting" (Master's thesis, University of Wisconsin, 1949), p. 42; U.S., Congress, Senate, *Congressional Record*, 69th Cong., 1st sess., 1926, 5487; Merrill to Morrison, 11 February 1926, White Papers, MSS, LC, box 51, Dept. File, 69th Congress; White to Merrill, 13 February 1926, White Papers, MSS, LC, box 51, Dept. File, 69th Congress.

24. "White Radio Control Bill Lies Dormant in the Senate," New York *Times*, 11 April 1926; NAB Bulletin, 5 February 1926, Letters to Members,

no. 72 (NAB); Hall to White, 30 March 1926, White Papers, MSS, LC, box 51, Dept. File, 69th Congress, Radio.

25. "Radio Converts," *Literary Digest* 91 (4 December 1926): 26–27; J. G. Harbord, "Radio Progress in 1926," Clark Collection, MSS, MHT, CWC 14, 297 A; H. P. Davis, "How Can We Improve Radio Broadcasting," *Radio Digest* (31 October 1925), Davis Papers, MSS, AIS, box 38, Clippings, 1925; "Radio for All," Buffalo *Express*, 20 November 1925, Davis Papers, MSS, AIS, box 3, folder 46; Daggett to Hoover, 24 July 1925, NARG 173, FCC, General Records, Radio Div., file 1104.

26. George C. Southworth, *40 Years of Radio Research*, (New York: Gordon and Breach, 1962), p. 71; E. E. Bucher, "Radio and David Sarnoff," 56 parts (Manuscript deposited at the David Sarnoff Library), II: 474–75, 479, 482–83 (subsequent citations: Bucher," Radio and Sarnoff").

The following section on the industrial conflict relies heavily upon two secondary sources: Gleason Archer, *Big Business and Radio* (New York: American Historical, 1939), chaps. 1–13; Erik Barnouw, *A Tower in Babel: A History of Broadcasting in the United States, Vol. 1, to 1933* (New York: Oxford University Press, 1966), chaps. 2–4.

27. Director of Research to Sarnoff, 28 April 1923, Clark Collection, MSS, MHT, CWC 14, 1182 A; Director of Research to Sarnoff, 29 May 1923, Clark Collection, MSS, MHT, CWC 134, 1181 A.

28. White, Memo for Sarnoff, 28 June 1922, Clark Collection, MSS, MHT, CWC 134, 1180 A; Goldsmith to Sarnoff, 28 November 1922, Clark Collection, MSS, MHT CL 5, M.W.T. Co.-RCA Corresp., 1922; Horn to Weyrich, 24 December 1923, NARG 173, FCC, Radio Div., file KDKA.

29. Bucher, "Radio and Sarnoff," II: 477–500.

30. Ibid., II: 28–31, 504–06.

31. Southworth, *40 Years of Radio Research*, p. 74; W. Rupert Maclaurin, *Invention and Innovation in the Radio Industry* (New York: Macmillan, 1949), p. 116; William Peck Banning, *Commercial Broadcasting Pioneer, The WEAF Experiment, 1922–26* (Cambridge: Harvard University Press, 1946), p. xxvii.

32. Lloyd Espenschied, "Origin of Network Broadcasting," 458 A (NAB).

33. Hiram J. Jome, *Economics of the Radio Industry* (Chicago: A. W. Shaw, 1925), p. 206; "Radio New Social Force," *Outlook*, 136 (19 March 1924): 466; "Fight for Freedom," *Literary Digest* 80 (22 March 1924): 8–9; "Phone Company Denies Radio Monopoly," New York *Times*, 12 March 1924; Harkness to Moore, 5 February 1924, NARG 173, FCC, General Corresp., Radio Div., file BC–15, M.

34. Robert J. Landry, *This Fascinating Radio Business* (Indianapolis: Bobbs Merrill, 1946), p. 51; "Outlaw Station to Be Closed," *Radio Broadcast* 5 (June 1924): 130–31; "Licensing Broadcast Stations," *Radio Broadcast* 5

(August 1924): 300; Schubel to the Editor, 29 February 1924, NARG 173, FCC, General Corresp., file WHN; Batcheller to Commissioner of Navigation, 24 March 1925, NARG 173, FCC, General Records, Radio Div., file WEAF; Harkness to Davis, 19 August 1925, NARG 173, FCC, Radio Div., file WEAF.

35. Eugene Lyons, *David Sarnoff* (New York: Harper & Row, 1966), p. 134; Bucher, *Radio and Sarnoff*, II: 511–12, 534–37, 542; Plan for the Support of National Broadcasting Through Formation of the Public Broadcasting Company, David Sarnoff, n.d., Davis Papers, MSS, AIS, box 1, folder 12; Memo, Conference of Primary Committee on Broadcasting, 18 December 1925, Davis Papers, MSS, AIS, box 1, folder 12.

36. Goldsmith to Sarnoff, 4 November 1922, Clark Collection, MSS, MHT, CL 5, M.W.T. Co-RCA Corresp., 1922; Goldsmith to Gernsback, 9 December 1922, Clark Collection, MSS, MHT, CL 5, M.W.T. Co.-RCA Corresp., 1922; Davis, Memo of Proposed Organization of Mid-Continent Radio Chain, 27 June 1925, Davis Papers, MSS, AIS, box 1, folder 12; Clipping, New York *Herald Tribune*, 15 April 1926, Davis Papers, MSS, AIS, box 4, folder 49.

37. Young to Trip, 16 October 1925, Davis Papers, MSS, AIS, box 1, folder 6; Herr to Davis, 22 October 1925, Davis Papers, MSS, AIS, box 1, folder 6; Davis to Herr, 26 October 1925, Davis Papers, MSS, AIS, box 1, folder 6; Harbord to Herr, 4 December 1925, Davis Papers, MSS, AIS, box 1, folder 6; Davis to Herr, 12 December 1925, Davis Papers, MSS, AIS, box 1, folder 6.

38. Davis to Harbord, 15 September 1926, Davis Papers, MSS, AIS, box 1, folder 7; Davis, National Broadcasting Company, Prepared Plan, n.d., box 1, folder 7; President of Westinghouse to Aylesworth, 23 November 1926, Davis Papers, MSS, AIS, box 1, folder 8; Brown to Tripp, 24 November 1926, Davis Papers, MSS, AIS, box 1, folder 8; Brown to Tripp, 24 November 1926, Davis Papers, MSS, AIS, box 1, folder 8; Horn to Davis, 11 October 1926, Davis Papers, MSS, AIS, box 1, folder 8; Horn to Davis, 11 October 1926, Davis Papers, MSS, AIS, box 1, folder 8; Davis to Aylesworth, 25 October 1926, Davis Papers, MSS, AIS, box 1, folder 8.

39. Pearl Augusta Drews, "Radio Broadcasting in the United States, 1920–29" (Master's thesis, University of Wisconsin, 1938), p. 40; Thomas C. Cochrane and William Miller, *Age of Enterprise: A Social History of Industrial America* (New York: Harper & Row, 1961), pp. 338–39; David Sarnoff, *Principles and Practices of Network Radio Broadcasting, Testimony of David Sarnoff Before the Federal Communications Commission* (New York: RCA, 1939), pp. 8–9; Goldsmith to Rice, 8 January 1925, Davis Papers, MSS, AIS, box 1, folder 7; Subcommittee on Proposed Broadcasting Organization to Board of Directors, RCA, 22 January 1926, Davis Papers, MSS, AIS, box 1, folder 7.

40. Bucher, *Radio and Sarnoff*, II: 510, 526, 545–51.

41. "Hoover Sees Crisis of Radio Fading," New York *Times*, 30 July 1926; "Aylesworth to Head Broadcasting Company," *Electrical World* 88 (18 September 1926): 591; "They Made Radio History NBC's First Program, Nov. 15, 1926," NBC News Service, 13 October 1936, Clark Collection, MSS, MHT, CL 134, 801–903; Horn to Davis, 3 February 1927, Davis Papers, MSS, AIS, box 1, folder 9; Harkness to Batcheller, 4 November 1926, NARG 173, FCC, General Records, Radio Div., file WEAF.

42. David Sarnoff, *Looking Ahead: The Papers of David Sarnoff* (New York: McGraw-Hill, 1968), p. 38; "Multiplicity Means Destruction," New York *Times*, 14 February 1925; "Notes from Radio Broadcasting Stations," New York *Times*, 1 March 1925; Memo, Commissioner of Navigation, 20 March 1925, NARG 173, FCC General Corresp., Radio Div., file BC–15; McWilliams to Hoover, 18 October 1925, HHPL, Sec. of Commerce, Official File, box 444, Radio Corresp., 1925.

CHAPTER 6

1. Glenn A. Johnson, "First Regulator of American Broadcasting, 1921–28, Secretary of Commerce Herbert Hoover" (Ph.D. diss., University of Iowa, 1970), p. 200; "Air Piracy," *Literary Digest* 89 (1 May 1926): 13.

2. Clarence C. Dill, *Radio Law Practice and Procedure* (Washington, D.C.: National Book, 1938), p. 71; "Charge Radio Station Pirated Wavelengths," New York *Times*, 17 January 1926; Carson to Supervisor of Radio, Chicago, 21 March 1925, NARG 173, FCC, General Corresp., Radio Div., file BC–15; McDonald to Carson, 11 June 1925, NARG 173, FCC, General Corresp., Radio Div., file BC–15; Donovan to Olson, 14 January 1926, NARG 60, Dept. of Justice, file 230074; Davis to Attorney General, 12 January 1926, NARG 60, Dept. of Justice, file 230074; *United States of America* v. *Zenith Radio Corporation*, In the District Court of the U.S. Northern District of Illinois, Eastern Div., no. 14257, HHPL, Sec. of Commerce, Official File, box 448, Radio, Zenith.

3. Forrest McDonald, *Insull* (Chicago: University of Chicago Press, 1962); Forrest McDonald, *The Phaeton Ride: The Crisis of American Success* (Garden City, N.Y.: Doubleday, 1974), pp. 69–75; Gabriel Kolko, *Triumph of Conservatism: A Reinterpretation of American History, 1900–1916* (New York: Free Press, 1963); David R. Mackey, "The National Association of Broadcasters: Its First Twenty Years" (Ph.D. diss., Northwestern University, 1956), p. 63; "Hoover Asks Help to Avoid Chaos," New York *Times*, 10 July 1926; Acting Secretary of Commerce to Attorney General, 12 January 1926, NARG 173, FCC, General Corresp., Radio Div., file BC–15; McLean to McClatchy, 23 April 1926, NARG 38, DNC, file 110 (1925–26).

4. "Decision in Air Piracy Case Shows Need for New Laws," New York *Times*, 25 April 1925; *The Zenith Story*, 85 A (NAB); McDonald to White, 30 April 1926, White Papers, MSS, LC, box 51, Dept. File, 69th Congress, Radio; Statement by McDonald, Chicago *Daily News*, 16 January 1926, NARG 173, FCC, General Corresp., Radio Div., file BC–15; Irving Herriott, Radio Speech, n.d., NARG 173, FCC, General Corresp., Radio Div., file BC–15.

5. Francis Chase, *Sound and Fury: An Informal History of Broadcasting* (New York: Harper and Brothers, 1942), p. 22–23; "Hoover Sees Chaos Without Radio Law," New York *Times*, 21 April 1926; "Government Loses Suit Over Control of Radio," *Electrical World*, 87 (24 April 1926): 883; "Radio Confusion Worse," *Outlook*, 143 (5 May 1926): 9; Umberger to Frame, n.d., NARG 16, Sec. of Agriculture, Radio, 1926; Clipping, New York *Herald Tribune*, 12 February 1926, NARG 173, FCC, General Records, Radio Div., file 1204.

6. "New Dill Bill Advocates Commission to Regulate Radio," New York *Times*, 2 May 1926; U.S., Congress, Senate, *Congressional Record*, 69th Cong., 1st sess., 1926, 7948; Remarks by Paul B. Klugh, Fourth Annual Convention, National Association of Broadcasters, 13 September 1926, NARG 173, FCC, General Records, Radio Div., file 3601.

7. Paul A. Carter, *The Twenties in America* (New York: Thomas Y. Crowell, 1968), pp. 40–41; "Reports Bill Taking Radio from Hoover," New York *Times*, 9 May 1926; U.S., Congress, Senate, *Congressional Record*, 69th Cong., 1st. sess., 1926, 12351–12359; C. C. Dill, Interview, Oral History Collection, HHPL.

8. "Reports Bill to End Hoover Radio Power," New York *Times*, 7 May 1926; U.S., Congress, Senate, *Congressional Record*, 69th Cong., 1st Sess., 1926, 12335–51, 12959; U.S., Congress, Senate, *Report to Accompany H.R. 9971*, 69th Cong., 1st sess., 1926, S. Rept. 772; White Papers, MSS, LC, box 64, Subject File, Radio, 1925–48.

9. "Coolidge Radio Plan Looses in Committee," New York *Times* , 29 April 1926.

10. James E. Watson, *As I Knew Them* (Indianapolis: Bobbs-Merrill, 1936), pp. 257–59; "Senate Proposal Laid to Jealousy," Baltimore *Sun*, 18 May 1926, NARG 173, FCC, General Records, Radio Div., file 1484.

11. J. Joseph Hutchmacher, *Massachusetts People and Politics 1919–33* (Cambridge: Harvard University Press, 1959), p. 82; NAB Rush Bulletin, 5 May 1926, NARG 173, FCC, General Records, Radio Div., file 1104.

12. William Brooke Graves, *Readings in Public Opinion* (New York: D. Appleton & Co., 1928), pp. 550–53; Donald R. McCoy, *Calvin Coolidge: The Quiet President* (New York: Macmillan, 1967), pp. 285–86; Jules Abels,

In the Time of Silent Cal (New York: Putnam, 1969), p. 10; "Politics and Radio Legislation," *Literary Digest* 89 (22 May 1926): 12–13.

13. U.S., Congress, Senate, *Congressional Record*, 69th Cong., 1st sess., 1926, 12498–500; "Prominent Engineers Speak at Annual Dinner of RCA," New York *Telegram*, 15 May 1926, White Papers, MSS, LC, box 73, Scrapbooks, Political Clippings, Radio, 1925–48; "Senator Edwards Opposes Senate Radio Bureau," Buffalo *Evening News*, 13 May 1926, White Papers, MSS, LC, box 73: Joy to Edwards, n.d., NARG 173, FCC, General Records, Radio Div., file 1104.

14. "Hoover Sees Chaos Without Radio Law," New York *Times*, 21 April 1926; Hoover Interview, Philadelphia *Public Ledger*, 16 April 1926, HHPL, Sec. of Commerce, Personal File, box 72, Radio; Statement by Hoover, 20 April 1926, HHPL, Sec. of Commerce, Personal File, box 72, Radio; Hoover to Lockwood, 8 May 1926, HHPL, Sec. of Commerce, Official File, box 447, Radio Legislation, 1926.

15. "Let Hoover Do It," *Pennsylvania Farmer*, 15 May 1926, White Papers, MSS, LC, box 73, Scrapbooks, Political Clippings, Radio, 1925–48; Tyrer to Woertendyke, 13 May 1926, NARG 173, FCC, General Records, Radio Div., file 1484; Warner to Commissioner of Navigation, 5 June 1926, NARG 173, FCC, General Records, Radio Div., file 1109.

16. "Expect New Radio Law to Be Shaped This Month," New York *Times*, 7 November 1926; "Speculation Rife on Radio Law," New York *Times*, 21 November 1926; White to Raycroft, 27 November 1926, White Papers, MSS, LC, box 51, Dept File, 69th Congress, Radio; Broadcasters Protection, 18 April 1925, NAB Library, Letters to Members, no. 72 (NAB); Remarks by Paul Klugh, NAB Open Meeting, 13 September 1926, NARG 173, FCC, General Records, Radio Div., file 3601.

17. U.S., Congress, Senate, *Congressional Record, 69th Cong., 1st sess.*, 1926, 12497, 12617; McLean to White, 10 May 1926, NARG 38, DNC, file 110 (1925–26); Davis to Speaker of the House of Representatives, 2 July 1926, NARG 111, Chief Signal Officer, file 032; Bullard to Commissioner of Navigation, 16 November 1926, NARG 173, FCC, General Corresp., Radio Div., File Dept., 7; IRAC Subcommittee on Policy and Legislation, 5 October 1926, NARG 173, IRAC Files, box 104, Policy and Legislation, 1926.

18. White to Culver, 24 May 1926, White Papers, MSS, LC, box 50, Dept. File, 69th Congress, Radio; White to Tilson, 30 June 1926, White Papers, MSS, LC, box 50, Dept. File, 69th Congress, Radio.

19. Culver to White, 5 May 1926, White Papers, MSS, LC, box 50, Dept. File, 69th Congress, Radio; Jensen to Secretary Association of Colleges and University Broadcasting Stations, 5 May 1926, NARG 173, FCC, General

Records Radio Div., file 1484; Duncan to Warburton, 19 July 1926, Memo for Harvey, 29 July 1926, NARG 16, Sec. of Agriculture, Radio.

20. Mackey, "National Association of Broadcasters", pp. 327-28; "Congress Acts on Radio, Pensions, and Deficiency Measures," New York *Times*, 3 July 1926; White to Stewart, 3 July 1926, White Papers, MSS, LC, box 51, Dept. File, 69th Congress, Radio; White to Davis, 9 July 1926, White Papers, MSS, LC, box 51, Dept. File, 69th Congress, Radio.

21. "They Do Need a Ruler," New York *Times*, 21 July 1926; "Hoover on Broadcasting Control," *Radio Broadcast* 5 (June 1924): 127-28; "What Congress Did and Left Undone," *Outlook* 143 (14 July 1926): 374-75; Weekly Radio Summary, 13 July 1926, NARG 173, FCC, General Records Radio Div., file 3600; Clipping, *Ledger-Dispatch*, 14 July 1926, NARG 173, FCC, Radio Div., file 1484.

22. Solicitor General to Secretary of Commerce, 2 June 1926, NARG 60, Dept. of Justice, file 19-10-32; Donovan, Memo for Attorney General, 1 July 1926, NARG 60, Dept. of Justice, file 19-10-32; Solicitor General, Memo for Attorney General, NARG 60, Dept. of Justice, file 19-10-32.

23. "Text of Ruling Denying Radio Control," New York *Times*, 10 July 1926; Donovan to Hoover, 9 July 1926, HHPL, Sec. of Commerce, Official File, box 444, Radio Corresp., Press Releases; Davis to Sargent, 23 July 1926, NARG 173, FCC, General Records, Radio Div., file 2666; Radio Summary, 30 November 1926, NARG 173, FCC, General Records, Radio Div., file 3600.

24. S. E. Frost, Jr., *Is American Radio Democratic?* (Chicago: University of Chicago Press, 1937), p. 32; "Silver Linings Seen in Clouds Hanging Over Radio," New York *Times*, 18 July 1926; "Confusion Threatened in Radio Broadcasting," *Electrical World* 88 (17 July 1926): 136; Hoover to Wadsworth, 3 August 1926, HHPL, Sec. of Commerce, Official File, box 444, Radio Corresp., 1926; Carson to All Supervisors of Radio, 13 July 1926, NARG 173, FCC, General Records, Radio Div., file 2666.

25. Mackey, "National Association of Broadcasters," pp. 5, 331-32; "Organize to End Anarchy of the Air, " New York *Times*, 28 July 1926; NAB Bulletin, 15, 19 July and 5 November 1926, NARG 173, FCC, General Records, Radio Div., file 3601.

26. "Radio Undertakes Self-Control, " *Outlook* 143 (11 August 1926): 494; Dunlap to Coolidge, 17 July 1926, Coolidge Presidential Papers, MSS, LC reel 80, 136; Hoover to Sanders, 27 July 1926, Coolidge Presidential Papers, MSS, LC, reel 80, 136.

27. Statement, Chairman of Air Law Committee, American Bar Association, 2 December 1926, White Papers, MSS, LC, box 50, Dept. File, 69th Congress, Radio; Aylesworth to Davis, 28 October 1926, Davis Papers, MSS, AIS, box 1, folder 8; Carson to Kugler, 24 September 1926, NARG

173, FCC, Radio Div., file WGES; IRAC Meeting, 29 October 1926, NARG 173, IRAC Files, box 1, IRAC Meetings.

28. "Sees Deadlock in Radio Legislation," New York *Times*, 5 December 1926; Clipping, "Millions Interested in This Legislation," San Francisco *Chronicle*, 3 December 1926, NARG 173, FCC, General Records, Radio Div., file 1106.

29. Wood to Clark, 13 January 1927, Coolidge Presidential Papers, MSS, LC, reel 80, 136; Executive Secretary, Radio Protection Association to Borah, 14 December 1927, William E. Borah Papers, MSS, LC, box 295, Radio Legislation, General 1927-28; Arthur to White, 9 August 1926, White Papers, MSS, LC, box 51, Dept. File, 69th Congress, Radio; *Gold Medal Radio Station News* 2 (June 1926): 3, NARG 173, FCC, General Records, Radio Div., file 1484; Radio Summary, 17 November and 31 August 1926, NARG 173, FCC, General Records, Radio Div., file 3600.

Concerning the diversity among broadcasters, consult Statement of Position Taken by Association of Colleges and University Broadcasting Stations, 6 December 1926, White Papers, MSS, LC, box 51, Dept. File, 69th Congress, Radio; Caldwell to Davis, 15 October 1926, Davis Papers, MSS, AIS, box 1, folder 8; Davis to Aylesworth, 18 October 1926, Davis Papers, MSS, AIS, box 1, folder 8.

30. "Expect New Radio Law to Be Shaped This Month," New York *Times*, 7 November 1926; "President Coolidge's Message to the Short Session of the 69th Congress," New York *Times*, 8 December 1926; U.S., Congress, House, *Congressional Record*, 69th Cong., 2d sess., 1926-27, 106, 1272; White to Klugh, 3 September 1926, White Papers, MSS, LC, box 51, 69th Congress, Radio.

31. Robert E. Cushman, *The Independent Regulatory Commissions* (New York: Oxford University Press, 1941), pp. 302-09; "Tentative Radio Agreement Reached in Washington," *Electrical World* 89 (15 January 1927): 163; "Agree on Measure for Radio Control," New York *Times*, 23 January 1927; U.S., Congress, Senate, *Conference Report on Radio Act of 1927*, 69th Cong., 2d sess., S. Doc. 200, 1927.

32. Robert L. Hilliard, ed., *Radio Broadcasting, An Introduction to the Sound Medium* (New York: Hasting House, 1967), pp. 12-13; Frost, *Is American Radio Democratic?*, pp. 24-26; James M. Herring and Gerald C. Gross, *Telecommunications, Economics and Regulations* (New York: Mcgraw-Hill, 1926), p. 287; Dixon Merritt, "To Unscramble the Air," *Outlook* 145 (19 January 1927): 75-76.

33. Cushman, *Independent Regulatory Commissions*, pp. 302-09; "Radio Control Bill Passed," *Electrical World* 89 (26 February 1927): 468; White to

Nockels, 3 January 1927, White Papers, MSS, LC, box 50, Dept. Files, 69th Congress.

34. Edward W. Chester, *Radio, TV, and American Politics* (New York: Sheed and Ward, 1969), p. 223; White to Harbord, 27 January 1927, White Papers, MSS, LC, box 50, Dept. Files, 69th Congress, Radio; Coolidge to Hoover, 20 March 1927, Coolidge Presidential Papers, MSS, LC, reel 80, 136; Hooper to McNeely, 29 January 1927, Hooper Papers, MSS, LC, box 8, Hooper Corresp., 1927; Confidential Executive Order, Assignment of Frequencies to Government Radio Stations, 30 March 1928, NARG 40, Dept. of Commerce, file 67032/70.

35. Cushman, *Independent Regulatory Commissions*, pp. 309-10.

36. "House Approves New Radio Bill," New York *Times*, 30 January 1927; "Radio Control Bill Passed by Senate, Goes to Coolidge," New York *Times*, 19 February 1927; U.S., Congress, House, *Congressional Record*, 69th Cong., 2d sess., 1926-27, 3589.

CHAPTER 7

1. Alfred N. Goldsmith, "Progress in Radio Receiving During 1927," *General Electric Review* (January 1928), HHPL, Sec. of Commerce, Official File, box 444.

2. Gleason Archer, *Big Business and Radio* (New York: American Historical, 1939), p. 296; Edward W. Chester, *Radio, TV and American Politics*, (New York: Sheed and Ward, 1969), p. 217; Arthur Batcheller, "An Outline of the Radio Inspection Service," *Proceedings of the Institute of Radio Engineers* 17 (August 1929), NARG 173, FCC, Radio Div., General Corresp., file 820.

3. Thomas T. Eoyang, *An Economic Study of the Radio Industry* (New York: RCA, 1937), p. 157.

4. James M. Herring and Gerald C. Gross, *Telecommunications, Economics and Regulations* (New York: McGraw-Hill, 1936), pp. 246-48; "The Radio Law—An Experiment," *Outlook* 145 (9 March 1927): 291-92.

5. *Annual Report*, 1928, Radio Division, Dept. of Commerce, 1 July 1928, NARG 173, FCC, Radio Div., General Corresp., file 59.

6. Hooper to Firth, 12 July 1928, Hooper Papers, MSS, LC, box 9; Hooper to Loftin, 16 March 1934, Hooper Papers, MSS, LC, box 16; Gruen to Coolidge, 19 February 1927, HHPL, Sec. of Commerce, Official File, box 447, Radio, FRC.

7. "Coolidge Appoints Radio Commission," New York *Times*, 2 March 1927; Lawrence Wilson Lichty, "A Study of the Careers and Qualifications of Members of the Federal Radio Commission and the Federal Communica-

tions Commission 1927 to 1961," (Master's thesis, Ohio State University, 1961), pp. 26–27, 83–84, 87–89, 101, 150–51; Hooper to Bullard, 17 March 1927, Hooper Papers, MSS, LC, box 8.

8. C. B. Rose, *National Policy for Radio Broadcasting* (New York: Harper and Brothers, 1940), p. 8; *Annual Report of the Federal Radio Commission*, 30 June 1927 (Washington, D.C.: Government Printing Office, 1927), p. 1 (subsequent citiations: FRC, *Annual Report*).

9. "Fight on Nominations Indicated," New York *Times*, 2 March 1927; Lichty, "Study of the Careers and Qualifications of Members of the FRC and FCC," pp. 89–92; Clipping, New York *Herald Tribune*, 1 January 1928, White Papers, MSS, LC, box 75.

10. "Coolidge Fills Radio Commission," New York *Times*, 6 March 1927; "Bloom Sounds Radio Warning" New York *Times*, 20 March 1927; In the Matter of the Nomination and Confirmation of Federal Radio Commissioners, Opinion of the General Counsel of the FRC, no. 26, 12 February 1929, NARG 173, FCC, Radio Div., General Corresp., File Dept. FRC.

11. "The Federal Radio Commission," *Electric World* 89 (19 March 1927): 622; "The Radio Commission," *Outlook* 145 (23 March 1927): 355–56.

12. "Hoover to Maintain Radio Status Quo," New York *Times* 25 February 1927; "Coolidge Will Start Radio Board at Work," New York *Times*, 5 March 1927; Lichty, "A Study of the Careers and Qualifications of Members of the FRC and FCC," pp. 26–27, 200; FRC, *Annual Report*, 1927, p. 3.

13. George Sterling, *The Radio Manual* (New York: D. Van Nostrand, 1928), pp. 331–94; A. Hoyt Taylor, *Radio Reminiscences: A Half Century* (Washington, D.C.: U.S. Naval Research Laboratory, n.d.), pp. i–xii. For information on scientific and technical developments, consult O. H. Caldwell Broadcasts, Caldwell Papers, MSS, Wis. Hist. Soc., box 1.

14. G. Y. Allen, How Radio Is Being Standardized," *Radio Broadcast* 6 (April 1925): 1035–36; Leslie J. Page, "Nature of the Broadcast Receiver and Its Market in the United States from 1922–27," *Journal of Broadcasting* 4 (Spring 1960): 174–82.

15. W. Rupert Maclaurin, *Invention and Innovation in the Radio Industry* (New York: Macmillan, 1949), pp. 106, 123–29; G. E. C. Wedlake, *SOS: The Story of Radio Communications* (New York: Crane, Russak and Company, 1973), pp. 71, 174.

16. Charles Saltzman, "The Radio Equipment Situation," *Infantry Journal* 25 (December 1924): 601–06; Sterling, *Radio Manual*, p. 110.

17. Maclaurin, *Invention and Innovation in the Radio Industry*, pp. 129, 131, 136, 162, 165, 169, 175, 254.

18. Gleason Archer, *Big Business and Radio* (New York: American Historical, 1939), pp. 296–99; Edgar E. Willis, *Foundations in Broadcasting:*

Radio and Television (New York: Oxford University Press, 1951), pp. 37-9; A History of the National Broadcasting Company prepared by Horton Heath, NAB, 11. A; NBC History, *Sponsor Magazine*, 16 May 1966, NAB, 260 A.

19. *Principles and Practices of Network Radio Broadcasting, Testimony of David Sarnoff Before the FCC* (New York: RCA Press, 1939), pp. 8-10; Twenty Years of NBC, 1926-1946, NAB, 11. B; NBC Press Release, 31 December 1927, NAB, 130. K; Basic Red Network, sheets 1 and 2, n.d., NBC Records, Wis. Hist. Soc., box 17.

20. Little Books on Broadcasting published by NBC, 1927 through 1932, NAB, 11. TT; Q and A on NBC Organization and Facilities, July 1931, NAB, 11. 000; Federal Radio Commission, *Commercial Radio Advertising, Letter from Chairman of the FRC in Response to Senate Resolution 129*, 72nd Cong., 1st sess., S. Doc. 137 (Washington, D.C.: Government Printing Office, 1932), pp. 13-14 (Subsequent citations, FRC *Commercial Radio Advertising*).

21. Willis, *Foundations in Broadcasting*, p. 58; Report on Chain Broadcasting, FCC, pp. 34-44.

22. Ned Midgley, *The Advertising and Business Side of Radio* (New York: Prentice-Hall, 1948), pp. 55-65, 67-68; Report and Recommendations: KDKA, July 1933, Hedges Papers, MSS, Wis. Hist. Soc., box 1, 1926-35.

23. Herman S. Hettinger, *The Use of Broadcasting as an Advertising Medium, in the United States* (Chicago: University of Chicago Press, 1933), pp. 112-13; *Broadcasting Magazine*, 19 May 1966, Special Report on NBC, NAB, 260. B; Commercial Representative to Wood, 7 July 1927, NBC Records, Wis. Hist. Soc., General Corresp. W. box 15; NBC Memo, Sales Dept., 31 December 1929, National Lumbermen's Association Account, NBC Records, Wis. Hist. Soc., box 15.

24. A History of NBC, NAB, 11. A; The NBC Story, 1926-56, NAB, 11. C; NBC—A Documentary, NAB, 11. JJ.

25. Midgley, *Advertising and the Business Side of Radio*, pp. 89-103; Aylesworth to Sarnoff, 9 May 1932, NBC Records, Wis. Hist. Soc., David Sarnoff file, box 18.

26. Robert Metz, *CBS: Reflections in a Bloodshot Eye* (Chicago: Playboy Press, 1975), pp. 13-17; Reminiscences of Arthur Judson for Oral History Research, Columbia University, November 1950, NAB, 302. A.

27. Archer, *Big Business and Radio*, pp. 301-02; Judson, Reminiscences, NAB, 302. A; "CBS—Documenting 38 Years of Exciting History," *Sponsor Magazine* (13 September 1965) NAB, 12. E.

28. Clippings of Bob Considine's series on William S. Paley, *Journal-American*, 23-30 May 1965, NAB, 12. B; C. Dreher, "How the Wasteland

Began," *Atlantic Monthly*, 1966, NAB, 254. G; "Broadcast Advertising—
The Sales Voice of America, Issued by CBS," June 1929, NAB, 12. L.

29. CBS—Documenting 38 Years of Exciting History," NAB, 12. E; Archer,
Big Business and Radio, pp. 301–21.

30. Erik Barnouw, *A Tower in Babel: A History of Broadcasting in the
United States, vol. 1 to 1933* (New York: Oxford University Press, 1966),
pp. 219–24; Judson, Reminiscences, NAB, 302. A.

31. "CBS—Documenting 38 Years of Exciting History,"NAB, 12. E; Bob
Considine's Series on William S. Paley, NAB, 12. B.

Concerning the Levys and WCAU, see Powell to FRC, 14 April 1928,
NARG 173, FCC, file WCAU; Sterling to Department of Commerce, 26
November 1930, NARG 173, FCC, file WCAU; Federal Radio Commission,
Minutes, 13 March 1931, NARG 173, FCC, reel 1 (subsequent citations: FRC,
Minutes).

32. Metz, *CBS*, p. 20.

33. U.S. Government Proposals, September 1926 and July 1927, NARG
167, JHD Papers, box 41; Whittemore to Dellinger, 27 August 1927, NARG
167, JHD Papers, box 41; Hooper to Sykes, 21 March 1928, Hooper Papers,
MSS, LC, box 9.

34. H. H. Buttner, "International Radiotelegraph Convention at Washington," *International Telephone Review*, NARG 167, JHD Papers, box 1;
Address of Secretary Hoover at Opening Session of Radiotelegraph Convention, 4 October 1927, NARG 167, JHD Papers, box 41.

35. W. D. Terrell, "The International Radiotelegraph Conference of
Washington, 1927," *Institute of Radio Engineers* (February 1928) NARG 167,
JHD Papers, box 41; Final Report of the Executive Officer and Secretary of
the American delegation, 8 December 1927, NARG 167, JHD Papers, box 41.

36. International Radio Conference, Report of Subcommittee of Committee
no. 1, Session no. 6, 25 October 1927, NARG 167, JHD Papers, box 41; Text
of Washington Radio Conference, 25 November 1927, NARG 167, JHD
Papers, box 41; U.S., Congress, Senate, Commission on Communications,
Hearings Before Senate Committee on Interstate Commerce, 71st Cong., 1st
sess., 4 December to 26 February 1930 (Washington, D.C.: Government
Printing Office, 1930), p. 1353.

37. Report of Participation in the Radio Conference at Washington, 4
October to 25 November 1927, NARG 167, JHD Papers, box 41; Summary
of Important Facts of Convention Signed at Washington, 25 November 1927,
NARG 167, JHD Papers, box 41.

38. "Inquiry into Radio," *Outlook* 148 (18 April 1928): 616; FRC, *Second
Annual Report*, 1928, pp. 23, 223–24.

39. U.S., Congress, House, *Congressional Record*, 69th Cong., 2d sess., 1927, 3032; In the Matter of the Construction of Section 1 with Reference to Amateur Licenses, Opinion of the General Counsel of FRC, no. 11, September 1928, NARG 173, FCC, Radio Div., General Corresp., File Dept. 4-c; FRC, *First Annual Report*, 1927, p . 12.

For the best discussion of the various radio services and their place in the spectrum, consult testimony of Lieutenant Commander Craven, U.S., Senate, Commission on Communications, *Hearings Before the Senate Committee on Interstate Commerce,* 71st Cong., 1st sess., 18, 20, 22 May 1929 (Washington, D.C.: Government Printing Office, 1929), pp. 282–303.

40. Address by Admiral Bullard before National Press Club, 30 April 1927, NARG 173, FCC, Radio Div., General Corresp., Dept. 4-e; Bullard to Gove, 6 May 1927, NARG 173, FCC, file WHK: J. H. Dellinger, "The Empery of the Empyrean," NARG 167, JHD Papers, box 28, Publications; Statement by Secretary Hoover, 24 February 1927, HHPL, box 72, Personal File: Radio.

41. Radio Summary, 11 March 1927, NARG 173, FCC, Radio Div., General Records, file 3600; Akerson to Wright, 10 March 1927, HHPL, Sec. of Commerce, Official File, box 444, Radio: Corresp.; FRC, Minutes, 29 November 1927, NARG 173, FCC, reel 1.1.

42. "Radio Board Calls Public Hearings," New York *Times*, 16 March 1927 "Radio Control Board Begins to Unravel Wave Tangle," New York *Times*, 20 March 1927; Docket Cases Number 4870, 4871, 4880, NARG 173, FCC, Radio Div., General Corresp., Dept. 4-c; FRC, *First Annual Report*, 1927, pp. 3–16; Circular Letter Explaining Questionaire Regarding Broadcast Reception—Form 67, 20 April 1927, NARG 173, FCC, Radio Div., General Corresp., Dept. 4.

For the Canadian situation, see Hoover to Secretary of State, 24 May 1928, HHPL, Sec. of Commerce, Official File, box 444, Radio Corresp.: 1928; Radio Broadcasting, Arrangement Between the United States and Canada, 5 May 1932 (Washington, D.C.: Government Printing Office, 1932), pp. 1–3.

43. "Consolidation of Stations Urged to Cure Ills of Ether," New York Times, 20 March 1927; White to Treadway, 7 December 1926, White Papers, MSS, LC, box 51, Dept. File, Radio, 69th Congress; Plan for Frequency Allocation, 29 April 1927, FRC, Minutes, NARG 173, FCC, reel 1.1.

44. "Bullard's Death Removes Prominent Figure from Radio," New York *Times*, 27 November 1927; Lichty, "Study of the Careers, and Qualifications of Members of FRC and FCC," 27-28, 123, 139–44; FRC, *Second Annual Report*, 1928, p. 2.

45. "Clearing the Air," New York *Times*, 18 March 1927.

CHAPTER 8

1. Lawrence F. Schmeckebier, *The Federal Radio Commission: Its History, Activities and Organization* (Washington, D.C.: Brookings Institution, 1932), pp. 76–77; U.S., Congress, Senate, *Congressional Record*, 69th Cong. 2d sess., 1927, 3258; Field to Hoover, 25 September 1927, HHPL, box 447, Radio: FRC, 1927.

2. Press Release, 7 January, 1928, White Papers, MSS, LC, box 67.

3. "Radio Commission Assailed in Senate," New York *Times*, 28 February 1928; Clipping, Portland *Post Herald*, 1928, White Papers, MSS, LC, box 75; Scrapbooks, Radio and Shipping, White Papers, MSS, LC, box 75;

4. Herman S. Hettinger, *The Use of Broadcasting as an Advertising Medium in the United States* (Chicago: University of Chicago Press, 1933), pp. 46–47; Clarence C. Dill, *Radio Law Practice and Procedure* (Washington, D.C.: National Book, 1938), pp. 106–07, 179–80.

5. "Effect of New Radio Law," *Electrical World* 91 (7 April 1928): 695; "Congressional Delay on Radio Said to Threaten Chaos," *Electrical World* 91 (18 February 1927): 369; C. B. Rose, *National Policy for Broadcasting* (New York: Harper and Brothers, 1940), p. 27.

6. "Hoover Lets Board Keep Radio Control," New York *Times*, 16 March 1928; Hoover to FRC, 15 March 1928, HHPL, Sec. of Commerce, Official File, Radio: FRC.

7. Schmeckebier, *Federal Radio Commission*, pp. 102–03; Terrell to Kail, 26 March 1928, NARG 173, FCC, file WORD; Hoover to Coolidge, 27 March 1928, HHPL, Sec. of Commerce, Official File, box 233.

8. "Radio Commission Assailed in Senate," New York *Times*, 28 February 1928; Cowles to Caldwell, 10 February 1928, Caldwell Papers, MSS, Wis. Hist. Soc., box 1, Letters and Editorials: In Answer to Recent Statements Made Against O. H. Caldwell, Caldwell Papers, MSS, Wis. Hist. Soc., Box 1, Letters and Editorials; New York *Times*, Clippings, 1–27–29, White Papers, MSS, LC, box 75.

For Commissioner Caldwell's financial arrangements with McGraw-Hill, see Vice-President, McGraw-Hill, to Caldwell, 8 April 1927, Caldwell Papers, MSS, Wis. Hist. Soc., box 1, Letters and Editorials.

9. Hooper to Robinson, 4 January 1928, Hooper Papers, MSS, LC, box 9; Hooper to Dodd, 12 January 1928, Hooper Papers, MSS, LC, box 9; Firth to Hooper, 11 July 1928, Hooper Papers, MSS, LC, box 9.

10. "Confirmations Fill Radio Commisssion," New York *Times*, 31 March 1928; Batcheller to Department of Commerce, 3 March 1928, NARG 173, FCC, Radio Div., General Corresp., file 402-2; In the Matter of the Construc-

tion of the Radio Act of 1927 Involving Action by the Commission as Licensing Authority, Opinion of the FRC General Counsel, no. 12, 18 May 1929, NARG 173, FCC, Radio Div., Dept. 4-c.

11. Schmeckebier, *Federal Radio Commission*, pp. 66–67; FRC, Minutes, 6 September 1929, NARG 173, FCC, reel 1.1; Federal Radio Commission, *Second Annual Report* (Washington, D.C.: Government Printing Office, 1928), pp. 2–3, 5; Recommendations to the Congress by Directors of the NAB, 7 January 1929, NARG 167, JHD Papers, Bureau of Standards, box 13; In the Matter of the Relationship of FRC to the Dept. of Justice Under Section 16 of the Act, Opinion of the FRC General Counsel, no. 25, 11 June 1929, NARG 173, FCC, Radio Div., General Corresp., Dept. 4-c.

12. Robert G. Cushman, *The Independent Regulatory Commissions* (New York: Oxford University Press, 1941), p. 320; "Stations Adopt Code of Ethics," New York *Times*, 7 April 1929; Portland *Evening News*, Clippings, August 1929, White Papers, MSS, LC, box 75; Secretary of Commerce to Caldwell, 31 July 1931, NARG 40, Dept. of Commerce, file 84053-84075.

13. Lawrence Wilson Lichty, "A Study of the Careers and Qualifications of Members of the Federal Radio Commission and the Federal Communications Commission" (Master's thesis, Ohio State University, 1961), p. 33; Schmeckebier, *Federal Radio Commission*, pp. 104–05; Portland *Press Herald*, clipping, 16 December 1929, White Papers, MSS, LC, box 75.

14. Rose, *National Policy for Broadcasting*, p. 6; Federal Radio Commission, *Commercial Radio Advertising, Letter from the Chairman of the Federal Radio Commission in Response to Senate Resolution, No. 129*, 72d Cong., 1st sess., S. doc. no. 137 (Washington, D.C.: Government Printing Office, 1932), p. 3; Terrell to Supervisor of Radio, New Orleans, 16 April 1928, NARG 173, FCC, Radio Div., file WWL; Starbuck to Baruch, 29 June 1929, NARG 173, FCC, Radio Div., file WAWZ.

15. James M. Herring and Gerald C. Gross, *Telecommunications, Economics and Regulations* (New York: McGraw-Hill, 1936), pp. 270–79; A Statement on Engineering Principles Prepared for FRC by Committee on Radio Broadcasting, Engineering Council, 30 March 1927, NARG 173, FCC, Radio Div., General Corresp., Dept. 4; Memo for High Frequency Committee, FRC, 21 May 1928, NARG 173, FCC, Radio Div., General Corresp., Dept. 4.

16. Orrin E. Dunlap, Jr., *Radio in Advertising* (New York: Harper and Brothers, 1931), pp. 258–59; Herbert I. Schiller, *Mass Communications and the American Empire* (New York: Augustus M. Kelly, 1969), p. 24; FRC, *Commercial Radio Advertising*, 36; Terrell to Field, 28 March 1931, NARG 173, FCC, Radio Div., General Corresp., Dept. 4.

17. Statement by H. A. Bellows, "Straightening out Chicago's Radio Tangle," 4 May 1927, NARG 173, FCC, Radio Div., General Corresp., Dept. 4; Address by Major General Saltzman, "Radio and the Federal Government," 15 December 1930, NARG 173, FCC, Radio Div., General Corresp., Dept. 4; In the Matter of the Necessity for a Hearing When Frequency Is to Be Changed in a Renewed License, Opinion of the FRC General Counsel, no. 31, 28 May 1929, NARG 173, FCC, Radio Div., General Corresp., Dept. 4-c.

18. Dellinger to Radio Manufacturers Association, 5 January 1928, NARG 167, JHD Papers, box 13; FRC, Minutes, 4 April 1928, NARG 173, FCC, reel 1.1; Summary of Recommendations of Engineers for Broadcast Allocation, 11 April 1928, FRC, Minutes, NARG 173, FCC, reel 1.1.

19. Herring and Gross, *Telecommunications*, p. 254; "Less Noise," *Outlook* 149 (6 June 1928): 205; General Order no. 32, FRC, Minutes, 25 May 1928, NARG 173, FCC, reel 1.1; Lafount Memo for Commissioners, FRC, Minutes, 24 July 1928, NARG 173, FCC, reel 1.1.

20. Dill, *Radio Law*, pp. 180–82; O. H. Caldwell, "The Administration of Federal Radio Legislation," *Annals of the American Academy of Political and Social Science* (May-June 1929): 45–56; FRC, Minutes, 11 September 1928, NARG 173, FCC, reel 1.1.

21. J. H. Dellinger, "Analysis of Broadcasting Station Allocation," 14 September 1928, NARG 173, FCC, Radio Div., General Corresp., Dept. 4, Press Release folder; Report of Ellis A. Yost, Supplemental to Report no. 40, 16 October 1930, NARG 173, FCC, Radio Div., General Corresp., Dept. 4–e; FRC, Minutes, 24 July 1928, NARG 173, FCC, reel 1.1

22. Herring and Gross, *Telecommunications*, p. 255; U.S., Congress, House, *Hearing Before Committee on Merchant Marine and Fisheries on H.R. 8825*, 1st sess., 26, 27, 30, 31 January 1928 and 1, 7, 8, 9, 10, 11, 13 and 14 February 1928 (Washington, D.C.: Government Printing Office, 1928), pp. 105, 184; Statement by J. H. Dellinger, 4 September 1928, NARG 173, FCC, Radio Div., General Corresp., Dept. 4-e; FRC, *Second Annual Report*, 1928, pp. 17–18, 48–50.

23. U.S., Congress, House, *Hearings Before Committee on Merchant Marine and Fisheries on H.R. 8825*, 70th Cong., 1st sess., 26, 27, 30, 31 January 1928 and 1, 7, 8, 10, 11, 13 and 14 February 1928 (Washington, D.C.: Government Printing Office, 1928), p. 107; Confidential Memo, FRC, n.d., NARG 173, FCC, Radio Div., General Corresp., Dept. 4.

24. John Stanley Penn, "The Origin and Development of Radio Broadcasting at University of Wisconsin to 1940" (Ph.D. diss., University of Wisconsin, 1959), p. 292; E. Pendleton Herring, *Federal Commissioners: A*

Study of Their Careers and Qualifications (Cambridge: Harvard University Press, 1936), p. 168; FRC, Minutes, 8 September 1928, NARG 173, FCC, reel 1.1.

25. "Confirmations Fill Radio Commission," New York *Times*, 31 March 1928; Report of Meeting of Draft Committee no. 8, International Radio Conference at Washington, 24 October 1927, NARG 167, JHD Papers, box 41; In the Matter of Rights Reserved by the Countries Subscribing to the International Radiotelegraph Convention 1927, Opinions of the FRC General Counsel, no. 9, NARG 173, FCC, Radio Div., General Corresp., Dept. 4-c.

26. Minutes of Conference of National Electrical Manufacturers Association, February 1929, NARG 167, JHD Papers, box 13; IRE Report no. 8, 4 September 1929, NARG 167, JHD Papers, box 13; Linden to Department of Commerce, 1 December 1930, NARG 173, FCC, Radio Div., General Corresp., Dept. 4; Baldwin to KFKJ, 28 November 1931, NARG 173, FCC, file KFKJ.

27. U.S., Congress, House *Hearings Before Committee on Merchant Marine and Fisheries on H.R. 8825*, 70th Cong., 1st sess., 26, 27, 30, 31 January 1928, and 1, 7, 8, 9, 10, 11, 13 and 14 February 1928 (Washington, D.C.: Government Printing Office, 1928), p. 104; Sykes to Westinghouse, 1 October 1927, NARG 173, FCC, file KDKA; McDonald to FRC, 19 January 1928, NARG 173, FCC, file WJAZ; Federal Radio Commission Rules and Regulations, part 111, Broadcast Service, NARG 173, FCC, Radio Div., General Corresp., Dept. 4.

28. Edward W. Chester, *Radio, TV and American Politics* (New York: Sheed and Ward, 1969), p. 28; In the Matter of Construction of Section 11 in Regard to Whether Advertising and Slander of the Air May Be Made the Basis for Refusing a Renewal of License, Opinion of the FRC General Counsel, no. 3, September 1928, NARG 173, FCC, Radio Div., General Corresp. Dept. 4-c; In the Matter of the Construction of Sections 9 and 19 of the Radio Act of 1927, Opinion of the General Counsel, no. 29, 29 January 1929, NARG 173, FCC, Radio Div. General Corresp., Dept. 4-c.

29. U.S., Congress, Senate, *A Bill to Provide for the Regulation of Intelligence by Wire or Wireless, Hearings Before the Committee on Interstate Commerce*, 71st Cong., 1st sess., 1929 (Washington, D.C.: Government Printing Office, 1929), p. 1060; Banta to Batcheller, 10 November 1928, NARG 173, FCC, file WEAF: Memo to All Supervisors of Radio, 7 July 1930, NARG 40, Dept. of Commerce, file 67032/59.

30. Chester, *Radio, TV and American Politics*, p. 218; Linden to Director of Radio, 29 February 1931, NARG 173, FCC, file KTAB; Kearney to All Supervisors of Radio, 31 May 1932, NARG 173, FCC, Radio Div., General

Corresp., Dept. 4; Klein to Saltzman, 17 December 1931, NARG 40, Dept. of Commerce, file 88739/8.

31. David C. Philips; John M. Grogan; and Earl H. Ryan, *Introduction to Radio and Television*, (New York: Ronald Press, 1954), pp. 220–21; U.S., Congress, House, *A Bill to Amend an Act Entitled an Act for the Regulation of Radio Communications, Approved February 23, 1927, Hearings Before Committee on Merchant Marine and Fisheries*, 1928 (Washington, D.C.: Government Printing Office, 1928), pp. 103, 108–09; In the Matter of Jurisdiction of Radio Commission Over Broadcasting Stations in Regard to Private Debts and Claims, Opinion of the FRC General Counsel, no. 14, 12 September 1928, NARG 173, FCC, Radio Div., General Corresp., Dept. 4–c.

32. Schiller, *Mass Communications and the American Empire*, p. 25; Herring and Gross, *Telecommunications*, pp. 280–81; Horn to Bellows, 30 August 1927, NARG 173, FCC, file KDKA; N.Y. Radio Inspector's Report on WMBO, n.d., NARG 173, FCC, file WMBO.

33. S. E. Frost, Jr., *Is American Radio Democratic?* (Chicago: University of Chicago Press, 1937), p. 34; Don R. LeDuc and Thomas A. McCain, "The Federal Radio Commission in Federal Court: Origins of Broadcast Regulatory Doctrines," *Journal of Broadcasting* 14 (Fall 1970): 393–411.

34. Dill, *Radio Law*, p. 15; Rose, *National Policy for Broadcasting*, p. 11; U.S., Congress, Senate, *A Bill to Provide for the Regulation of the Transmission of Intelligence by Wire or Wireless, Hearings Before Committee on Interstate Commerce*, 10 May 1929 (Washington, D.C.: Government Printing Office, 1929), pp. 117–34; FRC, *Third Annual Report*, 1928–29, pp. 31–38.

35. Dill, *Radio Law*, p. 196; In the Matter of the Delegation of Power to the Federal Radio Commission and Validity of the Standard to Be Applied, Opinion of the FRC General Counsel, no. 6, October 1928, NARG 173, FCC, Radio Div., General Corresp., Dept. 4–c; FRC, Minutes, 12 May 1930, General Broadcasting System v. FRC, NARG 173, FCC, reel 1.2; FRC, Minutes, 26 January 1934, *FRC* v. *Nelson Bros.*, NARG 173, FCC, reel 1.7.

36. Andrew G. Haley, "The Law on Radio Programs," *George Washington Law Review* 5 (January 1937): 1–46; Edward A. Doering, *Federal Control of Broadcasting Versus Freedom of the Air* (Washington, D.C.: Georgetown Law School, 1939), pp. 33–50; FRC, Minutes, 20 February 1931, KFKB Case, NARG 173, FCC, reel 1.2; FRC, *Fifth Annual Report*, 1931, pp. 67–68.

37. Court of Appeals of the District of Columbia, *G.E.* vs. *FRC*, NARG 173, FCC, file WGY; Caldwell to Rice, 24 September 1928, NARG 173, FCC, file WGY; FRC, Minutes, Applications Designated for Hearings, WGY, 22 November 1928, NARG 173, FCC, reel 1.1.

38. "D.C. Court of Appeals," *Electrical World* 95 (25 January 1930): 184; Dill, *Radio Law*, p. 95; Cushman, *Independent Regulatory Commissions*, pp. 313–14.

39. Schmeckebier, *Federal Radio Commission*, p. 39; Herring and Gross, *Telecommunications*, p. 252; Wallace White Speech before NAB, 26 October 1931, White Papers, MSS, LC, box 67.

40. FRC, *Third Annual Report*, 1928–29, pp. 5–10; FRC, *Sixth Annual Report*, 1932, p. 5; In the Matter of the Right of the FRC to Compel the Attendance of Witnesses to Testify or Produce Documentary Evidence Before It, Opinions of the FRC General Counsel, no. 38, NARG 173, FCC, Radio Div., General Corresp., Dept. 4–c.

41. Sydney W. Head *Broadcasting in America* (Boston: Houghton Mifflin, 1956), p. 133; Federal Radio Commission, Rules and Regulations, NARG 173, FCC, Radio Div., General Corresp., Dept. 4.

42. Lichty, "Study of the Careers and Qualifications of Members of the FRC and FCC," pp. 85–86, 146, 187–88, 200–01; FRC, Minutes, 25 April 1933, NARG 173, FCC, reel 1.7.

43. Penn, "Development of Broadcasting at the University of Wisconsin," pp. 288–89.

CHAPTER 9

1. Gleason Archer, *Big Business and Radio* (New York: American Historical, 1939), pp. 314–18; Erik Barnouw, *A Tower in Babel* (New York: Oxford University Press, 1966), p. 222–25.

2. Robert Metz, *CBS: Reflections in a Bloodshot Eye* (Chicago: Playboy Press, 1975), p. 23; "Documenting 38 Years of Exciting History," *Sponsor Magazine* (13 September 1926): 52–53, NAB, 12. E; William S. Paley, "Early CBS History," *Broadcast Pioneer Bulletin* (May 1959), NAB, 12. G.

3. Eugene Lyons, *David Sarnoff* (New York: Harper & Row, 1966), pp. 38–71, 166; Bob Considine's Series on William S. Paley, *Journal-American*, 23–30 May 1965, NAB, 12. B.

4. Ned Midgley, *Advertising and the Business Side of Radio* (New York: Prentice-Hall, 1948), p. 89; Federal Communications Commission, *Report on Chain Broadcasting*, Order no. 37, Docket no. 5060, May 1941, pp. 22–23.

5. William S. Paley, *Why We Need a New Radio Law, Statement by William S. Paley Before Senate Committee on Interstate Commerce*, June 16, 1941 (New York: CBS, 1941), p. 69; Bob Considine's Series on William S. Paley, *Journal-American*, 23–30 May 1965, NAB, 12. B.

6. Sydney W. Head, *Broadcasting in America* (Boston: Houghton Mifflin, 1956), 144; Herman S. Hettinger, *The Use of Broadcasting as an*

Advertising Medium in the United States (Chicago: University of Chicago Press, 1933), p. 89; Metz, *CBS: Reflections in a Bloodshot Eye*, p. 25; U.S., Congress, Senate, *A Bill to Provide for the Regulation of the Transmission of Intelligence by Wire or Wireless, Hearings Before Committee on Interstate Commerce*, 71st Cong., 2d sess., 1930, 1783–1808.

7. "Broadcast Advertising—the Sales Voice of America," CBS Booklet, June 1929, NAB, 12. L; "That Wonderful Year of 1931," Mason Escher, CBS Radio, NAB, 254. B; Columbia Broadcasting System, Rate Card, NBC Records, Wis. Hist. Soc., box 5, CBS.

8. Edgar G. Willis, *Foundations in Broadcasting* (New York: Oxford University Press, 1951), pp. 40–41; Midgley, *Advertising and the Business Side of Radio*, p. 90; Bob Considine's Series on William S. Paley, *Journal-American*, 23–30 May 1965, NAB, 12. B.

9. FCC, *Report on Chain Broadcasting*, pp. 24–25; "CBS—Documenting 38 Years of Exciting History," *Sponsor Magazine* (13 September 1965): 53–54, NAB, 12. E; Arnold to Royal, 10 May 1932, NBC Records, Wis. Hist. Soc., box 5, CBS Mailing List.

10. Thomas T. Eoyang, *An Economic Study of the Radio Industry* (New York: RCA, 1937), p. 101; Comparison, NBC/CBS, n.d., NBC Records, Wis. Hist. Soc., box 23, CBS.

11. C. B. Rose, *National Policy for Broadcasting* (New York: Harper and Brothers, 1940), p. 50; U.S., Congress, Senate, *A Fee System for Radio Licenses, Pursuant to Senate Resolution No. 351*, 70th Cong., 2d sess., 4 December 1929 (Washington, D.C.: Government Printing Office, 1929), p. 17.

12. W. Rupert Maclaurin, *Invention and Innovation in the Radio Industry* (New York: Macmillan, 1949), pp. 132–52; Robert C. Bitting, Jr., "Creating an Industry," *Journal of the SMPTE* 74 (November 1965): 1016–17; FCC, Report on Chain Broadcasting, pp. 9–12.

13. Archer, *Big Business and Radio*, pp. 339–51; Eugene Lyons, *David Sarnoff* (New York: Harper and Brothers, 1966), pp. 130, 160–61; Head, *Broadcasting in America*, p. 142; A History of NBC prepared by Horton Heath, NAB, 11. A.

14. Archer, *Big Business and Radio*, pp. 353–63; Secretary of Navy to FRC, 11 January 1929, Hooper Papers, MSS, LC, box 10; Memo for Assistant Secretary of Navy, 31 October 1931, Hooper Papers, MSS, LC, box 13; Memo for Director of Naval Communications, 2 November 1931, Hooper Papers, MSS, LC, box 13.

15. Young to Hooper, 9 July 1928, Hooper Papers, MSS, LC, box 9; Sarnoff to Hooper 25 February 1931, Hooper Papers, MSS, LC, box 13; Sarnoff to Hooper, 4 November 1931, Hooper Papers, MSS, LC, box 13.

16. Bitting, "Creating an Industry," p. 1017; Hooper to Sarnoff, 1 December 1932, Hooper Papers, MSS, LC, box 14.

17. Maclaurin, *Invention and Innovation in the Radio Industry*, pp. 146–47; Archer, *Big Business and Radio*, pp. 365–86; Sarnoff to Hooper, 5 December 1932, Hooper Papers, MSS, LC, box 14.

18. Thomas Porter Robinson, *Radio Networks and the Federal Government* (New York: Columbia University Press, 1943), p. 167; A History of NBC prepared by Horton Heath, NAB, 11. A; Hedges to Codel, 7 April 1932, Hedges Papers, MSS, Wis. Hist. Soc., box 1, Corresp. 1926–35; Aylesworth to Brown, 15 February 1932, NBC Records, Wis. Hist. Soc., box 17, Radio-Keith-Orpheum Corp.; Ashby to Aylesworth, 11 April 1932, NBC Records, Wis. Hist. Soc., box 15, Northwest Broadcasting System.

19. Report and Recommendations, KDKA, July 1933, Hedges Papers, MSS, Wis. Hist. Soc., box 1, Corresp. 1926–35; NBC, Summary of Operations, NBC Records, Wis. Hist. Soc., box 18, Sarnoff; Northwest Broadcasting System, Consolidated Balance Sheet and Summary of Operations, 31 July 1932, NBC Records, Wis. Hist. Soc., box 15.

20. Midgley, *Advertising and the Business Side of Radio*, pp. 67–88; National Broadcasting Company, *Broadcasting in the Public Interest* (New York: NBC, 1939), pp. 15–17; FCC, *Report on Chain Broadcasting*, pp. 44–79; Engles to Amos 'n Andy, 11 November 1933, NBC Records, Wis. Hist. Soc., box 21; Clippings, Radio City Music Hall, NBC Records, Wis. Hist. Soc., box 17.

21. Robinson to Shipherd, 2 December 1929, NARG 12, Office of Education, box 44; Witner to Aylesworth, 17 February 1932, NBC Records, Wis. Hist. Soc., file Coca Cola; Aylesworth to Paley, 2 November 1933, NBC Records, Wis. Hist. Soc., file CBS.

22. Hettinger, *Use of Broadcasting as an Advertising Medium*, p. 133; Eoyang, *Economic Study of the Radio Industry*, pp. 176–77; Witmer to McClelland, 6 May 1932, NBC Records, Wis. Hist. Soc., box 10, Great A&P Tea Company.

23. Witmer to Richardson, 10 June 1932, NBC Records, Wis. Hist. Soc., box 1, Absorbine Junior; The Effectiveness of the A&P Morning Program, 21 July 1932, NBC Records, Wis. Hist. Soc., box 10, Great A&P Tea Company.

24. Client Testimonials, NAB, 315. A-M; Overall to Hacket, 4 April 1932, NBC Records, Wis. Hist. Soc., box 1, American Tobacco Company; Director of Sales Promotion, CBS, to Secretary of Commerce, 19 September 1935, NARG 40, Dept. of Commerce, file 86420.

25. Lewis H. Avery, *The Elements of a Successul Radio Program* (Washington, D.C.; NAB, 1943), p. 6; Hugh E. Agnew and Warren B. Dygert,

Advertising Media (New York: McGraw-Hill, 1938), pp. 292–323; Witmer to Aylesworth, 16 November 1932, NBC Records, Wis. Hist. Soc., box 19, Standard Oil of New Jersey; Facts and Figures, Early NBC Demographic Summary, 1927–1930, James Papers, MSS, Wis. Hist. Soc., Facts and Figures.

26. Metz, *CBS: Reflections in a Bloodshot Eye*, pp. 50–56; Kesten to Klein, 13 July 1931, NARG 40, Dept. of Commerce, file 86420; Kesten to Brown, 1 March 1932, NBC Records, Wis. Hist. Soc., box 17, Radio-Keith-Orpheum. For CBS's results, consult McClelland to Sarnoff, 29 September 1931, NBC Records, Wis. Hist. Soc., box 24, CBS; President, General Motors, to Aylesworth, 29 September 1933, NBC Records, Wis. Hist. Soc., box 24, General Motors; Royal to Aylesworth, 28 September 1933, NBC Records, Wis. Hist. Soc., box 24, General Motors.

27. Cuthbert to Royal, 19 August 1931, NBC Records, Wis. Hist. Soc., box 9, Ford Account; Hitz to Greene, 18 April 1932, NBC Records, Wis. Hist. Soc., box 4, Canada Dry; Peterson to Royal, 1 August 1932, NBC Records, Wis. Hist. Soc., General Motors.

28. Brainard to Rainey, 11 January 1932, NBC Records, Wis. Hist. Soc., box 1, American Tobacco Company; "Lasker Agency First Deliberate Placing of Account on CBS," Clipping, n.d., NBC Records, Wis. Hist. Soc., box 13, Lord, Thomas, and Logan; Aylesworth to Hill, 16 December 1933, NBC Records, Wis. Hist. Soc., box 21, American Tobacco Company.

29. Francis Chase, *Sound and Fury; An Informal History of Broadcasting* (New York: Harper and Brothers, 1942), pp. 199–200; Head, *Broadcasting in America*, pp. 136–37.

30. Hettinger, *The Use of Broadcasting as an Advertising Medium*, p. 216; A Brief Study of Appeal and Popularity of the Goldbergs, NBC Statistical Dept., 25 July 1932, NBC Records, Wis. Hist. Soc., Goldbergs.

31. Owens to Angus, 4 January 1931, NBC Records, Wis. Hist. Soc., box 17, Robertson.

32. Barnouw, *A Tower in Babel*, pp. 225–31; Bruce A. Linton, "A History of Chicago Radio Station Programming, 1921–31, with Special Emphasis on Stations WMAQ and WGN" (Ph.D. diss., Northwestern University, 1953), p. 232; Sprague to McKeon, 5 December 1932, NBC Records, Wis. Hist. Soc., box 16, Pepsodent, Amos 'n Andy.

33. Wilkins to Roberts, 24 August 1933, NBC Records, Wis. Hist. Soc., box 21, Amos 'n Andy; Witmer to McClelland, 19 July 1932, NBC Records, Wis. Hist. Soc., box 16, Pepsodent Company; Freeman to Aylesworth, 4 August 1933, NBC Records, Wis. Hist. Soc., box 21, Amos 'n Andy.

34. Barnouw, *A Tower in Babel*, pp. 244–45; Head, *Broadcasting in America*, pp. 136–37, 139–40; Report on Accounts Moving from One Network to Another, NBC Statistical Dept., 18 August 1932, NBC Records,

Wis. Hist. Soc., box 13, Lord, Thomas, and Logan; CBS Program Schedule, 28 December 1932, NBC Records, Wis. Hist. Soc. box 5, CBS; Present Clients of CBS, November 1932, NBC Records, Wis. Hist. Soc., box 5, CBS.

35. Willis, *Foundations in Broadcasting*, pp. 55–56; *Time* Cover Stories of Broadcasting Notables, 1938, William S. Paley, NAB, 349; FCC, *Report on Chain Broadcasting*, pp. 5, 39; Myers to Allen, 23 May 1932, NBC Records, Wis. Hist. Soc., box 1, Absorbine.

36. U.S., Congress, Senate, *A Bill to Provide for the Regulation of the Transmission of Intelligence by Wire or Wireless, Hearings before Committee on Interstate Commerce*, 71st Cong., 2d sess., 1930, 1699–1732; Comparison NBC/CBS, n.d., NBC Records, WIS. Hist. Soc., box 23, CBS.

37. National Broadcasting Company, *A Working Manual on NBC Program Policies* (New York: NBC, 1948), pp. 5–33; Aylesworth to Patterson, 15 February 1933, NBC Records, Wis. Hist. Soc., box 23, CBS; Klauber to Aylesworth, 14 February 1933, NBC Records, Wis. Hist. Soc., box 23, CBS; Columbia Reviews Half-Year's Achievements, 29 June 1932, NBC Records, Wis. Hist. Soc., box 5, CBS.

38. *Broadcasting in the Public Interest*, pp. 25–26, 33–35; Paley to Secretary of Commerce, 13 May 1935, NARG 40, Dept. of Commerce, file 86420; McLeod to Program Builders, 13 May 1932, NBC Records, Wis. Hist. Soc., box 13, Lindberg; List of Songs Banned by CBS, n.d., NBC Records, Wis. Hist. Soc., box 4, CBS.

39. Advertisers Using NBC/CBS, Month by Month Record, 1933–1937, NBC Sales-Research Div., NAB, 76. D; "Broadcast Advertising in Latin America," Dept. of Commerce, 1931, p. 1, NARG 40, Dept. of Commerce, file 67032/53; James to Carol, 17 November 1932, NBC Records, Wis. Hist. Soc., box 5, CBS; Aylesworth to Richey, 20 August 1932, NBC Records, Wis. Hist. Soc., box 10, General Motors.

CHAPTER 10

1. John E. Benton, "Should the Congress Create a Federal Communications Commission," *Congressional Digest* 9 (April 1930): 111; Hooper to Offley, 21 February 1929, Hooper Papers, MSS, LC, box 10.

2. William C. Green, "Proposed Federal Communications Commission: Pros and Cons on Couzens Bill," *Congressional Digest* 9 (April 1930); Louis G. Caldwell Testimony Before Interstate Commerce Committee on Couzens Bill to Create Communications Commission to Regulate Cables, Telephone, Telegraph, and Radio, 11 May 1929, NARG 173, FCC, Radio Div., General Corresp., Dept. 4; Hooper to Carty, 11 March 1930, Hooper Papers, MSS, LC, box 11.

3. Clipping, New York *Daily News*, 27 May 1927, NARG 173, FCC, Radio Div., General Corresp., Dept. 4; Bulletin, National Radio Club of Washington, D.C., 9 January 1928, NARG 173, FCC, Radio Div., General Corresp., Dept. 4.

4. U.S., Congress, Senate, *Hearings Before Committee of Interstate Commerce*, 71st Cong., 2d sess., 17, 18, 20, 21, 22, 23, 27, 29, 30, and 31 January 1930 (Washington, D.C.: Government Printing Office, 1930), p. 1850; Pearce to Secretary of Commerce, 11 December 1928, NARG 40, Dept. of Commerce, file 84095; McKeown, Extension of FRC, 10 March 1928, NARG 173, FCC, Radio Div., General Corresp., file 1106; In the Matter of the Construction of Sections 13, 15, and 17 of the Radio Act of 1927 in Reference to Whether a Violation of These Sections May Be the Basis for Revoking the License of a Broadcasting Station, Opinion of the FRC General Counsel, no. 2, 13 August 1928, NARG 173, FCC, Radio Div., General Corresp., Dept. 4-e.

5. U.S., Congress, House, *Congressional Record*, 69th Cong., 2d sess., 1927, 4112; Clipping, *Radio Digest*, 15 March 1927, NARG 173, FCC, Radio Div., General Corresp., Dept. 4; Bulletin, National Radio Club of Washington, D.C., 28 January 1928, NARG 173, FCC, Radio Div., General Corresp., Dept. 4.

6. National Advisory Council on Radio in Education, *Four Years of Network Broadcasting, A Report by the Committee on Civic Education by Radio of the National Advisory Council on Radio in Education and the American Political Science Association* (Chicago: University of Chicago Press, 1936), pp. 49-73; Robert M. Hutchins "Radio and Public Policy," *Education by Radio* 4 (6 December 1934):57-58; NARG 16, Dept. of Agriculture, Radio General Corresp.

7. Sydney W. Head, *Broadcasting in America* (Boston: Houghton Mifflin, 1956), p. 123; Hooper to Perry, 31 March 1933, Hooper Papers, MSS, LC, box 15.

8. In the Matter of the Petition of Adrien M. Kelly, Chairman, National Food Products Committee, Opinions of the FRC General Counsel, no. 32, 15 April 1929, NARG 173, FCC, Radio Div., General Corresp., Dept. 4; Clipping, Washington *Star*, 6 May 1929, NBC Records, Wis. Hist. Soc., box 2, American Tobacco Company, 1929; Grace to McClelland, April 25, 1929, NBC Records, Wis. Hist. Soc., box 2, American Tobacco Company, 1929.

9. Federal Radio Commission, *Commercial Radio Advertising, Letter from the Chairman of the Federal Radio Commission in Response to Senate Resolution No. 129*, 72d Cong., 1st sess., S. Doc. 137 (Washington, D.C.: Government Printing Office, 1932), p. 13; Federal Radio Commission, *Second*

Annual Report 376 (Washington, D.C.: Government Printing Office, 1928), p. 21; In the Matter of the Right of Broadcasting Stations to Contract for Exclusive Service Involving the Policy of Block Booking, Opinions of the FRC General Counsel, no. 27, 20 May 1929, NARG 173, FCC, Radio Div., General Corresp., Dept. 4-e.

10. James M. Herring and Gerald C. Gross, *Telecommunications, Economics and Regulations* (New York: McGraw-Hill, 1926), pp. 279–80; Gilman to Aylesworth, 3 March 1932, NBC Records, Wis. Hist. Soc., American Tobacco Company, 1932. Also see file on American Radio Audience League, 1933, NBC Records, Wis. Hist. Soc., box 21.

11. FRC, *Commercial Radio Advertising*, pp. 14, 33, 36–39; Reber to Aylesworth, 21 January 1932, NBC Records, Wis. Hist. Soc., box 19, J. Walter Thompson; Peter to Withycomb, 20 January 1932, NBC Records, Wis. Hist. Soc., box 8, FRC; Contributions of FRC to Education by Radio, Commissioner Harold Lafount, delivered before Institute for Education by Radio, 8 June 1931, NARG 173, FCC, Radio Div., General Corresp., Dept. 4-c.

12. Heitmezer to Elwood, 27 October 1929, NARG 12, Office of Education, box 43; Data Sheet, Educational Broadcasting, WFAA, 1 February 1930, NARG 12, Office of Education, box 47; Commercial Broadcasting and Education, Address delivered by Henry A. Bellows, 22 May 1931, NBC Records, Wis. Hist. Soc., box 14, Advisory Council on Radio in Education.

13. Supervisor of Radio to Smith, 10 June 1929, NARG 12, Office of Education, box 42; University of Chicago, Broadcasts over WMAQ, Visited by JMR, 20 December 1929, NARG 12, Office of Education, box 40.

14. Eastman to Shipherd, 12 September 1929, NARG 12, Office of Education, box 35; Assistant to President (WCAE) to Elwood, 21 October 1929, NARG 12, Office of Education, box 44; Burton to Division of Education, Boston, 3 December 1929, NARG 12, Office of Education, box 47.

15. H. O. Davis, *The Empire of the Air: The Story of the Exploitation of Radio for Private Profit, with a Plan for the Reorganization of Broadcasting* (Ventura, Calif.: Ventura Free Press, 1932); Davis to Assistant Secretary of Commerce, 12 December 1933, NARG 40, Dept. of Commerce, file 88739; Clipping, Ventura *Free Press*, 10 June 1932, NBC Records, Wis. Hist. Soc., box 20.

For NBC's reaction, see Gilman to Aylesworth, 1 October 1931, NBC Records, Wis. Hist. Soc., box 20, Ventura *Free Press*; Confidential Memo, Sarnoff to Aylesworth, 21 October 1931, NBC Records, Wis. Hist. Soc., box 20; Aylesworth to Sarnoff, 23 October 1931, NBC Records, Wis. Hist. Soc., box 20.

16. James Rorty, *Our Master's Voice* (New York: John Day, 1934), and *Order on the Air!* (New York: John Day, 1934), pp. 8–9, 27–32.

17. Jerome G. Kerwin, *The Control of Radio* (Chicago: University of Chicago Press, 1934), pp. 19–27.

18. WHAZ, Rensselaer Polytechnic Institute, 19 November 1927, NARG 12, Office of Education, box 47; Futrall to Russell, 18 November 1929, NARG 12, Office of Education, box 40.

19. Eisenhower to Secretary of Agriculture, 18 June 1929, NARG 16, Dept. of Agriculture, Radio, General Corresp.; Hyde to Aylesworth, 14 January 1930, NARG 16, Dept. of Agriculture, Radio, General Corresp.; Hyde to Palmer, 22 January 1930, NARG 16, Dept. of Agriculture, Radio, General Corresp.; Wallace to NBC and CBS, NARG 16, Dept. of Agriculture, Radio, General Corresp.

20. Memo, Funds for National Committee on Education by Radio, 25 November 1929, NARG 12, Office of Education, box 36; Report of Committee on Education by Radio, 30 December 1929, NARG 12, Office of Education, box 30; Perry to Presidents of Colleges and Universities, 31 July 1930, NARG 12, Office of Education, box 32; Secretary of Interior to New York *Times* (editor), n.d., NARG 12, Office of Education, box 36.

21. Analysis of Broadcasting on Adult Education, 1 September to 1 December 1929, NARG 12. Office of Education, box 35; Radio in the Service of Education, 22 January 1930, NARG 12, Office of Education, box 36,

22. Eric Barnouw, *The Golden Web: A History of Broadcasting in the United States, 1933–1953* (New York: Oxford University Press, 1968), pp. 22–26; "The Fess Bill," New York *Times*, 22 May 1931; Clipping, *U.S. Daily*, 10 March 1931, White Papers, MSS, LC, box 75; Perry to Hooper, 1 April 1933, Hooper Papers, MSS, LC, box 15; Perry to Pitman, 5 October 1930, NARG 12, Office of Education, box 33.

23. "The Forgotten Listener," *Outlook* 149 (1 August 1928): 53; Henry T. Volkening, "Abuses of Radio Broadcasting," *Current History* 33 (December 1930): 396–400; Ashby to Aylesworth, 30 June 1932, NBC Records, Wis. Hist. Soc., box 1, ASCAP; Remarks Made by Commissioner Lafount at Assembly of National Advisory Council on Radio in Education, 17 May 1933, NBC Records, Wis. Hist. Soc., box 23, FRC; Supplementary Statement by NAB, 14 May 1934, Hedges Papers, MSS, Wis. Hist. Soc., box 1, Corresp., 1926–1935.

24. Lawrence Wilson Lichty, "A Study of the Careers and Qualifications of Members of the Federal Radio Commission and the Federal Communications Commission, 1927 to 1961" (Master's Thesis, Ohio State University, 1961),

p. 36; Richey to Secretary of Commerce, 29 June 1932, NARG 40, Dept. of Commerce, file 84035–84075; Couzens to Director of Radio, 9 March 1932, NARG 173, FCC, Radio Div., file BC–WWJ.

25. Report of the Subcommittee on Policy and Legislation, 11 December 1928, IRAC, NARG 167, JHD Papers, box 56; Payne to the Secretary of Commerce, 30 September 1930, NARG 167, JHD Papers, box 17; Confidential Report of JHD, Activities of Government Radio Stations, 19 January 1931, NARG 167, JHD Papers, box 17; Vallance to Hoover, 29 October 1931, NARG 167, JHD Papers, box 17.

26. Report of Army and Navy Radio Stations, Committee on Duplication, 30 January 1931, NARG 167, JHD Papers, box 17; Burgess to Secretary of Commerce, 11 March 1931, NARG 167, JHD Papers, box 17; Draft Report on Committee on Technical Problems, 27 March 1931, NARG 167, JHD Papers, box 56.

27. FRC, *Annual Report*, 1933, pp. 7, 35; FRC, Minutes, 31 October 1932, NARG 173, FCC, reel 1.6.

28. Craven, Memo for Hooper, 11 May 1929, Hooper Papers, MSS, LC, box 10.

29. Memo, Hooper, 14 November 1928, Hooper Papers, MSS, LC, box 9; Hooper to Chief Signal Officer, 3 June 1929, Hooper Papers, MSS, LC, box 10; Hooper to Jewett, 14 June 1929, Hooper Papers, MSS, LC, box 10; Hooper to Wheeler, 18 October 1932, Hooper Papers, MSS, LC, box 14; Hooper to Chairman, President's Communication Policy Committee, 7 December 1933, Hooper Papers, MSS, LC, box 15.

30. Harbord to Hooper, 17 April 1929, Hooper Papers, MSS, LC, box 10; Aylesworth to Russell, 15 February 1932, NBC Records, Wis. Hist. Soc., box 5, Couzens; Ashby to Aylesworth, 30 June 1932, NBC Records, Wis. Hist. Soc., box 1, ASCAP; Sarnoff to Roper, 24 January 1934, NAB, 123 A.

31. New York *Times*, 27 December 1933; David R. Mackey, "The National Association of Broadcasters: Its First Twenty Years" (Ph.D. diss., Northwestern University, 1956), pp. 198–200; Walter B. Emery, *Broadcasting and Government* (Lansing: Michigan State University Press, 1961), p. 23; Robert E. Cushman, *The Independent Regulatory Commissions* (New York: Oxford University Press, 1941), pp. 320–21; Supplementary Statement by National Association of Broadcasters, 14 May 1934, Hedges Papers, MSS, Wis. Hist. Soc., box 1; Roper to Dixon, 6 May 1933, NARG 40, Dept. of Commerce, file 80553.

32. Roper to Dorn, 18 September 1933, NARG 40, Dept. of Commerce, file 80553; Statement by Secretary Roper, 25 October 1933, NARG 167, JHD Papers, box 17; Clipping, Washington *Post*, 26 October 1933, NARG 167, JHD Papers, box 17.

33. Roper to Guffery, 3 October 1933, NARG 40, Dept. of Commerce, file 80553, 13–D; Roper to Fulmer, 9 November 1933, NARG 40, Dept. of Commerce, file 80553, 13–D.

34. Morgan to Tyler, 19 December 1933, NARG 40, Dept. of Commerce, 80553, 13–D; Cameron to Howe, 7 April 1933, NARG 40, Dept. of Commerce, 80553, 13–D. Daily Washington Merry-Go-Round, 30 November 1933, NARG 40, Department of Commerce 80553, 13-G.

35. Roper to FDR, 15 August 1933, NARG 40, Dept. of Commerce, file 80553, 13-D; Daniels to Roper, 4 December 1933, NARG 40, Dept. of Commerce, 80553, 13-D.

36. Report of Committee on Communications Appointed by Secretary of Commerce, 8 September 1933, NARG 167, JHD Papers, Communications Comm., 1933; Roper to Duffy, 1 May 1933, NARG 40, Dept. of Commerce, file 80553, 13–D; Saltzman to Dill, 14 December 1933, NARG 40, Dept. of Commerce, 80553.

37. Report of Committee on Reorganization of Department of Commerce, 29 April 1933, NARG 40, Dept. of Commerce, 80553; Report of Communications Committee, 3 December 1933, NARG 167, JHD Papers, box 17; Department of Commerce Release, 13 December 1933, NARG 40, Dept. of Commerce, 80553, 13-D.

38. New York *Times*, 27 February 1934; Message from President Recommending Congress Create New Agency to Be Known as the Federal Communications Commission, 26 February 1934, NARG 40, Dept. of Commerce, 96261–96345.

39. Roper to McCartney, 13 January 1934, NARG 40, Dept. of Commerce, 80553, 13-D; Roper to Dill and Rayburn, 15 December 1933, NARG 40, Dept. of Commerce, 80553, 13-D.

40. New York *Times*, 31 January 1934; U.S., Congress, Senate, *Communications Act of 1934, Senate Report 781*, 73rd Cong., 2d sess., 19 April 1934, NARG 40, Dept. of Commerce, 96345.

41. New York *Times*, 11 April 1934; New York *Times*, 9 May 1934; Gleason Archer, *Big Business and Radio* (New York: American Historical Company, 1939), p. 426.

42. Thomas Porter Robinson, *Radio Networks and the Federal Government*, (New York: Columbia University Press, 1943), pp. 60–61; Hedges Address before Engineers Society of Western Pennsylvania, 20 March 1934, Hedges Papers, MSS, Wis. Hist. Soc., box 1.

43. Lichty, "Study of the Careers and Qualifications of Members of the FRC and FCC," p. 16; Report of Subcommittee on Policy and Legislation, 27 May 1929, IRAC Meeting, NARG 167, JHD Papers, box 56; Investigation of Executive Agencies of the Government, n.d., NARG 40, Dept. of Commerce, 80553.

CHAPTER 11

1. James H. Hanley, "Radio in the United States," n.d., NBC Records, Wis. Hist. Soc., box 23, FRC; Hooper, Tentative Survey, Principles Involved in Legislating for Radio Communications, n.d., Hooper Papers, MSS, LC, box 10.

2. Hanley, "Radio in the United States"; Couzens to Folman, 16 August 1933, Couzens Papers, MSS, LC, box 97, Corresp.; Tyson to Couzens, 13 September 1933, Couzens Papers, MSS, LC, Corresp., box 97.

3. William S. Paley, *Freedom of Radio, The Statement of William S. Paley, President of CBS, Before Interstate Commerce Committee, Concerning S. 814, November 9, 1943* (New York: CBS, 1944), p. 14; National Association of Broadcasters, *Code Manual, Issued by Code Compliance Committee* (Washington, D.C.: NAB, 1944), p. 1.

4. Walter B. Emery, *Broadcasting and Government* (Lansing: Michigan State University Press, 1961), pp. 8, 19; Robert J. Landry, *This Fascinating Radio Business* (Indianapolis: Bobbs-Merrill, 1947), p. 50.

5. Sydney W. Head, *Broadcasting in America* (Boston: Houghton Mifflin, 1956), p. 134.

6. Federal Communications Commission, Minutes, 11 July 1934, NARG 173, FCC, reel 2.1.

7. Hedges Speech, "Has Radio a Future," September 1951, Hedges Papers, MSS, Wis. Hist. Soc., box 2, Speeches, 1929–1961.

BibliogRAphy

MANUSCRIPT SOURCES

United States Official Papers, National Archives

National Archives Record Group 12, Records of the Office of Education.

National Archives Record Group 16, Records of the Office of the Secretary of Agriculture.

National Archives Record Group 18, Records of the Army Air Force.

National Archives Record Group 19, Records of the Bureau of Ships.

National Archives Record Group 28, Records of the Post Office Department, Postmaster General Letterbooks.

National Archives Record Group 38, Records of the Office of the Chief of Naval Operations, Director of Naval Communications.

National Archives Record Group 40, General Records of the Department of Commerce.

National Archives Record Group 45, Naval Records Collection of the Office of Naval Records and Library.

National Archives Record Group 51, Records of the Bureau of the Budget.

National Archives Record Group 60, General Records of the Department of Justice.

National Archives Record Group 80, General Records of the Department of the Navy, Secretary of the Navy.

National Archives Record Group 111, Records of the Office of the Chief Signal Officer.

National Archives Record Group 122, Records of the Federal Trade Commission.

National Archives Record Group 167, Records of the National Bureau of Standards, J. H. Dellinger Papers.

National Archives Record Group 173, Records of the Federal Communications Commission, Records of Predecessor Agencies.

Private Papers

Borah, William E. Papers. Manuscript Division, Library of Congress.

Broadcast Pioneers History Project. Broadcast Pioneers Library. National Association of Broadcasters.

Caldwell, Orestes H. Papers. Archives Division, The State Historical Society of Wisconsin, Madison.

Clark, George. Collection. Museum of History and Technology, Smithsonian Institution.

Coolidge, Calvin. Papers. Manuscript Division, Library of Congress.

Couzens, James. Papers. Manuscript Division, Library of Congress.

Daniels, Josephus. Papers. Manuscript Division, Library of Congress.

Davis, Harry P. Papers. Archives of Industrial Society, University of Pittsburgh Libraries.

De Forest, Lee. Papers, Manuscript Division, Library of Congress.

Hedges, William S. Papers. Archives Division, The State Historical Society of Wisconsin, Madison.

Hooper, Stanford C. Papers. Naval Historical Foundation Collection, Manuscript Division, Library of Congress.

Hoover, Herbert C. Papers. Presidential Library, West Branch, Iowa.

James, E. P. H. Papers. Archives Division, The State Historical Society of Wisconsin, Madison.

National Broadcasting Company. Records. Archives Division, The State Historical Society of Wisconsin, Madison.

Sarnoff, David. Papers. Sarnoff Research Library, Princeton, New Jersey.

White, Wallace. Papers. Manuscript Division, Library of Congress.

Unpublished Manuscripts

Bensman, Marvin R. "The Regulation of Radio Broadcasting by the Department of Commerce, 1921–1927." Ph.D. dissertation, University of Wisconsin, 1969.

Bucher, E. E. "Radio and David Sarnoff." Manuscript. David Sarnoff Research Library.

Cusack, Mary Ann. "Editorializing in Broadcasting." Ph.D. dissertation, Wayne State University, 1959.

Drews, Pearl Augusta. "Radio Broadcasting in the United States, 1920–29." Master's thesis, University of Wisconsin, 1938.

Hall, Lillian Jones. "A Historical Study of Program Techniques and Practices of Radio Station KWKH, Shreveport, Louisiana, 1922–1950." Ph.D. dissertation, Louisiana State University, 1959.

Johnson, Glenn A. "The First Regulator of American Broadcasting, 1921–28, Secretary of Commerce Herbert Hoover." Ph.D. dissertation, University of Iowa, 1970.

Jorgenses, Erling S. "Radio Station WCFL: A Study in Labor Union Broadcasting." Master's thesis, University of Wisconsin, 1949.

Lichty, Lawrence Wilson. "The Nation's Station: A History of Radio Station WLW." Ph.D. dissertation, Ohio State University, 1964.

_____. "A Study of the Careers and Qualifications of Members of the Federal Radio Commission and the Federal Communications Commission, 1927 to 1961." Master's thesis, Ohio State University, 1961.

Linton, Bruce A. "A History of Chicago Radio Station Programming 1921–31, With Special Emphasis on Stations WMAQ and WGN." Ph.D. dissertation, Northwestern University, 1953.

Mackey, David R. "The National Association of Broadcasters: Its First Twenty Years." PH.D. dissertation, Northwestern University, 1956.

Maurer, Barbara Joan. "History of Station WHA, 1926–31." Master's thesis, University of Wisconsin, 1957.

McMahon, Robert S. "Federal Regulation of the Radio and Television Broadcasting Industry in the United States, 1927–1959, With Special Reference to the Establishment of Workable Administrative Standards." Ph.D. dissertation, Ohio State University, 1959.

Morrison, Jacquelin E. "A Study of the Chronological Development of the Three Regional Radio Broadcasting Stations in Atlanta, Georgia." Master's thesis, University of Georgia, 1954.

Penn, John Stanley. "The Origin and Development of Radio Broadcasting at the University of Wisconsin to 1940." Ph.D. dissertation, University of Wisconsin, 1959.

Resler, Ansel Harlan. "The Impact of John Brinkley on Broadcasting in the United States." Ph.D. dissertation, Northwestern University, 1958.

Riley, Donald W. "A History of American Radio Drama from 1919 to 1944." Ph.D. dissertation, Ohio State University, 1944.

Wilson, Maryland W. "Broadcasting by the Newspaper Owned Stations in Detroit, 1920–27." Ph.D. dissertation, University of Michigan, 1952.

PUBLISHED SOURCES

United States Official Papers

Congress, *Congressional Record.* 66th Congress to 69th Congress.

Congress, House. *Hearings Before the Committee on Merchant Marine and Fisheries on H.R. 11964, To Amend the Radio Act of 1912.* 66th Congress, 4th Session, January 2, 3, 1923.

———. *Hearings Before the Committee on Merchant Marine and Fisheries on H.R. 5589, To Regulate Radio Communications.* 69th Congress, 1st Session, 6, 7, 14, and 15 January 1926.

———. *Hearings Before the Committee on Merchant Marine and Fisheries on H.R. 8825.* 70th Congress, 1st session, 26, 27, 30, 31 January 1928 and 1, 7, 8, 9, 10, 11, 13, and 14 February 1928.

———. *Report of the Federal Trade Commission on the Radio Industry.* House Resolution 548, 67th Congress, 4th session, Submitted December 1923.

Congress, Senate. *Conference Report on Radio Act of 1927.* Document No. 200, 69th Congress.

———. *Hearings Before the Committee of Interstate Commerce, Commission on Communications.* 71st Congress, 1st Session, 18, 20, and 22 May 1929.

———. *Hearings Before the Committee of Interstate Commerce on a Bill to Provide for the Regulation of the Transmission of Intelligence by Wire or Wireless.* 71st Congress, 2nd Session. 1930.

Department of Commerce. *Commerce Yearbook.* 1922, 1923, 1924, 1927.

———. *Radio Communications Laws of the United States and the International Radiotelegraphic Convention Regulations Covering Radio Operators and the Use of Radio Apparatus on Ships and on Land.* August 1919.

———. *Recommendations for Regulation of Radio Adopted by the Third National Radio Conference Called by the Secretary of Commerce.* October 1924.

Federal Communications Commission. *Proposed Report, Telephone Investigation.* Pursuant to Public Resolution no. 8, 74th Congress. 1938.

———. *Report on Chain Broadcasting.* Order no. 37, Docket no. 5060. May 1941.

Federal Radio Commission. *Annual Reports.* Nos. 1–7, 1927–33.

———. *Commercial Radio Advertising, Letter from Chairman of the Federal Radio Commission in Response to Senate Resolution, no. 129.* 72nd Congress, 1st Session. Document no. 137. 1932.

Navy Department. *History of the Bureau of Engineering of the Navy Department During World War I.* 1922.

War Department, Bureau of Engineering. *Wireless Telegraph Stations of the World Including Shore Stations, Merchant Vessels, Revenue Cutters, and Vessels of the United States Navy.* January 1912.

Books and Pamphlets

Agnew, Hugh, and Dygert, Warren. *Advertising Media.* New York: McGraw-Hill, 1938.

Archer, Gleason. *Big Business and Radio.* New York: American Historical, 1939.

_____.*History of Radio to 1926.* New York: American Historical Society, 1938.

Arnold, Frank A. *Broadcast Advertising: The Fourth Dimension.* New York: John Wiley, 1933.

Baker, W. J. *A History of the Marconi Company.* London: Trinity Press, 1970.

Banning, William Peck. *Commercial Broadcasting Pioneer, The WEAF Experiment, 1922–26.* Cambridge: Harvard University Press, 1946.

Barnouw, Erik. *The Golden Web: A History of Broadcasting in the United States, Vol. II, 1933 to 1953.* New York: Oxford University Press, 1968.

_____. *A Tower in Babel: A History of Broadcasting in the United States, Vol. 1 to 1933.* New York: Oxford University Press, 1966.

Borchardt, Kurt. *Structure and Performance of the United States Communications Industry.* Cambridge: Harvard University Press, 1970.

Charnley, Mitchell V. *News By Radio.* New York: Macmillan, 1948.

Chase, Francis. *Sound and Fury: An Informal History of Broadcasting.* New York: Harper and Brothers, 1942.

Chester, Edward W. *Radio, TV and American Politics.* New York: Sheed and Ward, 1969.

Clark, Keith. *International Communications: The American Attitude.* New York: Ames Press, 1968.

Clarkson, R. P. *The Hysterical Background of Radio.* New York: T. H. Sears, 1927.

Close, Upton. *The Commentator's Story.* Palm Beach: Time for Truth Press, 1952.

Cochrane, Rexmond C. *Measures for Progress: A History of the National Bureau of Standards.* Washington, D.C.: National Bureau of Standards, 1966.

Committee on Civic Education by Radio and the American Political Science Association. *Years of Network Broadcasting, A Report by the Committee on Civic Education by Radio and the American Political Science Association.* Chicago: University of Chicago Press, 1936.

Cronon, E. David, ed. *Cabinet Diaries of Josephus Daniels.* Lincoln: University of Nebraska Press, 1963.

Cushman, Robert E. *The Independent Regulatory Commissions.* New York: Oxford University Press, 1941.

Danielian, N. R. *AT&T: The Story of Industrial Conquest.* New York: Vanguard, 1936.

Davis, H. O. *The Empire of the Air: The Story of the Exploitation of Radio for Private Profit, With a Plan for the Reorganization of Broadcasting.* Ventura, Calif.: Ventura Free Press, 1932.

DeForest, Lee. *Father of Radio: Autobiography of Lee De Forest.* Chicago: Wilcox and Follett, 1950.

De Soto, Clinton B. *Two Hundred Meters and Down: The Story of Amateur Radio.* West Hartford: American Radio Relay League, 1936.

Dill, Clarence C. *Radio Law Practice and Procedure.* Washington, D.C.: National Book, 1938.

Doering, Edward A. *Federal Control of Broadcasting Versus Freedom of the Air.* Washington, D.C.: Georgetown Law School, 1939.

Dunlap, Orrin E., Jr. *Marconi: The Man and His Wireless.* New York: Macmillan, 1937.

———. *Radio in Advertising.* New York: Harper and Brothers, 1931.

Dupree, A. Hunter. *Science in the Federal Government: A History of Policies and Activities to 1940.* Cambridge: Belknap Press, 1957.

Emery, Walter B. *Broadcasting and Government: Responsibilities and Regulations.* Lansing: Michigan State University Press, 1961.

Eoyang, Thomas T. *An Economic Study of the Radio Industry.* New York: Radio Corporation of America, 1937.

Floherty, John L. *On the Air: The Story of Radio.* New York: Doubleday, 1938.

Frost, S. E., Jr. *Is American Radio Democratic?* Chicago: University of Chicago Press, 1937.

Goldsmith, Alfred N., and Lescarboura C., Austin. *This Thing Called Broadcasting.* New York: Henry Holt, 1930.

Green, Abel, and Laurie, Joe. *Show Biz from Vaude to Video.* New York: Henry Holt, 1951.

Gunstan, David. *Guglielmo Marconi.* Geneva: Geron Books, 1962.

Gunther, John. *Taken at the Flood: The Story of Albert D. Lasker.* New York: Harper & Row, 1960.

Harvard University Graduate School of Business Administration. *The Radio Industry: The Story of Its Development as Told by Leaders of the Industry.* New York: A. W. Shaw, 1928.

Hays, Will H. *The Memoirs of Will H. Hays.* New York: Doubleday, 1955.

Head, Sydney W. *Broadcasting in America.* Boston: Houghton Mifflin, 1956.

Herring, James M., and Gross, Gerald C. *Telecommunications, Economics and Regulations.* New York: Mc Graw-Hill, 1936.

Hettinger, Herman S. *The Use of Broadcasting as an Advertising Medium in the United States.* Chicago: University of Chicago Press, 1933.

Hilliard, Robert L., ed. *Radio Broadcasting, An Introduction to the Sound Medium.* New York: Hasting House, 1967.

Howeth, L. S. *History of Communications-Electronics in the United States Navy.* Washington, D.C.: Government Printing Office, 1963.

Hubbell, Richard W. *4,000 Years of TV: The Story of Seeing at a Distance.* New York: G. P. Putnam, 1942.

Joint Technical Advisory Committee IRE-RTMA, *Radio Spectrum Conservation: A Program of Conservation Based on Present Uses and Future Needs, A Report of the Joint Technical Advisory Committee IRE-RTMA.* New York: McGraw-Hill, 1952.

Jolly, W. P. *Marconi.* New York: Stein and Day, 1972.

Jome, Hiram H. *Economics of Radio Industry.* Chicago: A. W. Shaw, 1925.

Kerwin, Jerome G. *The Control of Radio.* Chicago: University of Chicago Press, 1934.

Kingsman, Walter; Cowgill, Rome; and Levy, Ralph. *Broadcasting: Television and Radio.* New York: Prentice-Hall, 1955.

Landry, Robert J. *This Fascinating Radio Business.* Indianapolis: Bobbs-Merrill, 1946.

Lessing, Lawrence. *Man of High Fidelity, Edwin Howard Armstrong.* New York: J. B. Lippincott, 1956.

Leuchtenberg, William E. *The Perils of Prosperity, 1914–32.* Chicago: University of Chicago Press, 1967.

Library of Congress. *Exhibit Commemorating 50th Anniversary of Radio Features Papers of Pioneer Scientists and Broadcasters.* Press Release no. 70–73. n.d.

Lord, Walter. *A Night to Remember.* New York: Henry Holt, 1955.

Loth, David. *Swope of G.E.* New York: Simon and Schuster, 1958.

Lyons, Eugene. *David Sarnoff*. New York: Harper & Row, 1966.

_____. *Herbert Hoover, A Biography*. New York: Doubleday, 1964.

Maclaurin, W. Rupert. *Invention and Innovation in the Radio Industry*. New York: Macmillan, 1949.

MacDonald, D. K. C. *Faraday, Maxwell, and Kelvin*. New York: Doubleday, 1964.

McDonald, Forrest. *Insull*. Chicago: University of Chicago Press, 1962.

_____. *The Phaeton Ride: The Crisis of American Success*. Garden City, N.Y.: Doubleday, 1974.

McNicol, Donald. *Radio's Conquest of Space: The Experimental Rise of Radio Communications*. New York: Murray Hill, 1946.

Marconi, Degna. *My Father Marconi*. New York: McGraw-Hill, 1962.

Metz, Robert. *CBS: Reflections in a Bloodshot Eye*. Chicago: Playboy Press, 1975.

Midgley, Ned. *The Advertising and the Business Side of Radio*. New York: Prentice-Hall, 1948.

Morison, Elting E. *Men, Machines, and Modern Times*. Cambridge: Massachusetts Institute of Technology Press, 1966.

Murray, Robert K. *The Harding Era: Warren G. Harding and His Administration*. Minneapolis: University of Minnesota Press, 1969.

National Advisory Council on Radio in Education. *Four Years of Network Broadcasting, A Report by the Committee on Civic Education by Radio of the National Advisory Council on Radio in Education and the American Political Science Association*. Chicago: University of Chicago Press, 1936.

Paley, William S. *Freedom of Radio, the Statement of William S. Paley, President of Columbia Broadcasting System, Before Interstate Commerce Committee, Concerning S. 814, November 9, 1943*. New York: CBS, 1944.

Phillips, David C.; Frogan, John M.; and Ryan, Earl H. *Introduction to Radio and Television*. New York: Ronald Press, 1954.

President's Research Committee on Social Trends. *Recent Social Trends in the United States*. 2 vols. New York: McGraw-Hill, 1933.

Radio Corporation of America. *The First 25 Years of RCA*. New York: RCA, 1946.

Reck, Franklin M. *Radio: From Start to Finish*. New York: Thomas Y. Crowell, 1942.

Robinson, Thomas Porter. *Radio Networks and the Federal Government*. New York: Columbia University Press, 1943.

Rorty, James. *Order on the Air!* New York: John Day, 1934.

_____. *Our Master's Voice: Advertising*. New York: John Day, 1934.

Rose, C. B. *National Policy for Radio Broadcasting*. New York: Harper and Brothers, 1940.

Rothafel, Samuel L., and Yates, Raymond F. *Broadcasting Its New Day*. New York: Century, 1925.

Sarnoff, David. *Looking Ahead: The Papers of David Sarnoff*. New York: McGraw-Hill, 1968.

_____. *Principles and Practices of Network Radio Broadcasting, Testimony of David Sarnoff Before the Federal Communications Commission*. New York: RCA, 1939.

Schairer, Otto Sorg. *Patent Policies of the Radio Corporation of America*. New York: RCA, 1939.

Schiller, Herbert I. *Mass Communications and the American Empire*. New York: Augustus M. Kelley, 1969.

Schmeckebier, Lawrence R. *The Federal Radio Commission: Its History, Activities, and Organization*. Washington, D.C.: Brookings Institution, 1932.

Schubert, Paul. *The Electrical Word*. New York: Macmillan, 1928.

Shurick, E. P. J. *The First Quarter-Century of American Broadcasting*. Kansas City, Kansas: Midland, 1946.

Smythe, Dallas W. *The Structure and Policy of Electronic Communications*. Urbana: University of Illinois Press, 1957.

Southworth, George C. *40 Years of Radio Research*. New York: Gordon and Breach, 1962.

Stein, Herbert. *Fiscal Revolution in America*. Chicago: University of Chicago Press, 1969.

Sterling, George. *The Radio Manual*. New York: D. Van Nostrand, 1928.

Tarbell, Ida. *Owen D. Young: A New Type of Industrial Leader*. New York': Macmillan, 1932.

Tomlinson, J. D. *The International Control of Radio Communications*. Ann Arbor: J. W. Edwards, 1945.

Udell, Gilman, G., comp. *Radio Laws of the United States*. Washington, D.C.: Government Printing Office, 1962.

U.S. Navy, *Descriptive Catalogue No. 601-16, Buy It from the Navy, Radio Apparatus Type CW-936 Telephone Set Short Range*. Smithsonian Institution, Museum of History and Technology, n.d.

Watson, James E. *As I Knew Them*. Indianapolis: Bobbs-Merrill, 1936.

Wedlake, G. E. C. *SOS: The Story of Radio Communications*. New York: Crane, Russak and Company, 1973.

Wheeler, Burton K. *Yankee from the West*. Garden City, N.Y.: Doubleday, 1962.

White, Llewellyn. *The American Radio*. Chicago: University of Chicago Press, 1947.

Wilbur, Ray L., and Hyde, Arthur Masticke. *The Hoover Policies*. New York: Scribners, 1937.

Willis, Edgar E. *Foundations in Broadcasting: Radio and Television*. New York: Oxford University Press, 1951.

Articles

Allen, G. Y. "How Radio Is Being Standardized." *Radio Broadcast* 6 (April 1925): 1035–36.

Barton, Winfield. "What Broadcasting Does for a Newspaper." *Radio Broadcast* 4 (February 1924): 344–46.

Bensman, Marvin R. "The Zenith-WJAZ Case and the Chaos of 1926–27," *Journal of Broadcasting* 14 (Fall 1970): 423–41.

Binnis, Jack. "How Spark Interference Was Reduced." *Radio Broadcast* 4 (March 1924): 446.

Bitting, Robert C. "Creating an Industry." *Journal of SMPTE* 74 (November 1965): 1016–17.

Bullard, W. H. G. "The Naval Radio Service: Its Development, Public Service, and Commercial Work." *Proceedings of the Institute of Radio Engineers* 3 (March 1915): 7–10.

Chase, Stuart. "An Inquiry into Radio." *Outlook* 148 (18 April 1928): 616–19.

Cram, Ralph Adams. "Radio City and After." *American Mercury* 23 (July 1923): 291–96.

Dellinger, J. H. "The Bureau of Standards Lends a Hand." *Radio Broadcast* 1 (November 1922): 41–48.

Dreher, Carl. "Is the Amateur at Fault?" *Radio Broadcast* 4 (February 1924): 293–96.

Ford, Frederick W. "The Meaning of Public Interest, Convenience, or Necessity." *Journal of Broadcasting* 5 (Summer 1961): 205–19.

Gary, Hampton. "Regulation of Broadcasting in the United States." *Annals of the American Academy of Political and Social Science* 177 (January 1935): 15–21.

Haley, Andrew F. "The Law on Radio Programs." *George Washington Law Review* 5 (January 1937): 1–46.

Harbord, James G. "Commercial Uses of Radio." *Annals of the American Academy of Political and Social Science* 142 (March 1929): 57–63.

Harding, Allan. "What Radio Has Done and What It Will Do Next, Interview with David Sarnoff." *American Magazine* 101 (March 1926): 46–47, 167–73.

Hawley, Ellis W. "Herbert Hoover, the Commerce Secretariat, and the Vision of an Associated State, 1921–28." *Journal of American History* 61 (June 1974): 116–40.

Jansky, C. M. "Contributions of Herbert Hoover to Broadcasting." *Journal of Broadcasting* 3 (Summer 1957): 241–47.

McDonald, Eugene, F. "What We Think The Public Wants." *Radio Broadcast* 4 (March 1924): 382–84.

Mackey, David R. "The Development of the NAB." *Journal of Broadcasting* 1 (Fall 1957): 305–26.

Merritt, Dixon. "To Unscramble the Air." *Outlook* 145 (19 January 1927): 75–76.

Olson, James S. "The End of Voluntarism: Herbert Hoover and the National Credit Corporation." *Annals of Iowa* 41 (Fall 1972): 1104–13.

Page, Leslie J. "Nature of the Broadcast Receiver and Its Market in the United States from 1922–27." *Journal of Broadcasting* 4 (Spring 1960): 174–82.

Paley, William S. "Radio and the Humanities." *Annals of the American Academy of Political and Social Science* 179 (May 1935): 94–104.

Saltzman, Charles. "The Radio Equipment Situation." *Infantry Journal* 25 (December 1924): 601–06.

Sarno, Edward F., Jr. "The National Radio Conferences." *Journal of Broadcasting* 13 (Spring 1966): 183–202.

Sarnoff, David. "What Radio Means to the Central Station." *Electrical World* 84 (22 November 1924): 1094–95.

Thompson, Roy E. "The Uni-Control Receiver." *Proceedings of the Institute of Radio Engineers* 7 (October 1919): 509–14.

Index

A&P, 154, 155, 159
Abernethy, Charles L., 164
Advertisers, 108, 118, 145, 148–49, 157–58, 159
Advertising: adopted, 69, 72; agencies, 158, 164; effects of, 108, 153–56, 167; opposed, 68, 87, 164–65; revenue from, 10, 11, 89, 117–18, 146, 174, 159; rights to, 86; support for, 73, 133, 139
Affiliates, 116, 119, 120, 145, 146, 148–49. *See also* Stations
Agriculture Department, U.S., 27, 44, 169
Air Wave Piracy, 93, 102–03
Alexanderson, Ernst Frederick Werner, 24
Amateurs, 16; consulted, 31–32; frequencies for, 21; oppose U.S. Navy, 9, 20, 31; problems of, studied, 75, 80, 122, 123; restricted, 23, 36, 37; support Hoover, 98. *See also* American Radio Relay League
American Bond and Mortgage Company v. *United States*, 141
American Medical Association, 165

American Physical Education Association, 165
American Political Science Association, 164
American Radio Relay League, 31–32, 37–38, 52, 74, 102. *See also* Amateurs
American Telephone and Telegraph Co. *See* AT&T
American Tobacco Company, 154, 155–56, 159, 164–65. *See also* Lucky Strike Cigarettes
"Amos 'n Andy," 157
Anti-trust statutes, 73
Anti-trust suits, 145, 151
Appeals: court cases, 141–44; legislative provisions for, 53, 73, 82, 106
Appropriations, FRC, 111–12
Armstrong, Edwin H., 113, 115
Artists Bureaus, 118–19, 149
AT&T: in conference, 31; on national broadcasting 65–66; opposes Navy, 30; v. radio group, 10, 25, 64–69, 86–91; on regulation, 9–10, 53; telephone lines of, 90, 121

Army, U.S. (War Department), 44,
    58, 99
ASCAP (American Society of Com-
    posers, Authors, and Publishers),
    64
Associated Manufacturers of Electri-
    cal Supplies, 102
Atwater Kent, 118, 120
Audiences, 108, 116, 154, 164. *See
    also* Listeners
Aylesworth, Merlin, 108, 119, 146,
    173

Baker, Norman, 84, 103
Batcheller, Arthur, 50
Batteries, 69, 113, 114
Bellows, Henry A., 103, 110-11, 125
Benny, Jack, 158
Bingham, Hiram, 97
Bloom, Sol, 83, 94, 112
Blue Network, 116-17, 154-55
Boyden, Roland W., 87-88
Boy Rangers of America, 165
Branly, Edouard, 18, 19
Broadcast band. *See* Radio spectrum,
    broadcasting band in
Broadcasters: composition of, 62-63;
    cooperation of, 38-39; reduction
    of, 134, 135-38; opposition of,
    31, 42, 50, 97; rivalry among,
    103. *See also* Commercial broad-
    casters; NAB; Noncommercial
    broadcasters
Broadcasting: American v. European,
    121-23, 146, 168, 170; commer-
    cial, 3, 9, 161-71; disruption by,
    25; educational, 164; govern-
    ment, 45, 105-06; growth of, 7,
    9, 101-02; national, 65-69,
    72-73; nature of, 3, 7, 13-14,
    15, 80, 86-91, 153; public ser-

vice of, 36, 158-59, 167, 169;
    regulation of, 4-5, 103-06, 123,
    125, 133-44, 178-79; toll, 40,
    65, 86, 87, 88. *See also* Com-
    munications; Regulation
Brown, Thad, 144, 182
Bullard, William H. G., 22, 24,
    110-12, 125, 131
Bureau of Navigation, 27, 54. *See
    also* Carson, David B;
    Commerce Department
Bureau of Standards, 27, 32, 39,
    41, 112, 124. *See also* Commerce
    Department
Burleson, Albert S., 26
Burns and Allen, 157

Caldwell, Louis G., 162
Caldwell, Orestes H. 110-11, 131,
    132, 134, 139
Cameron, George Carter, 175
Campbell Soup, 154
Canada Dry, 158
Cantor, Eddie, 157, 158
Carnegie Corporation, 166, 169
Carson, David B., 51, 54, 101
Carty, J. J., 65
CBS, 12, 119-21, 145-60, 163, 169
Cellers, Emanuel, 163
Censorship, 4-5, 105, 138-39, 142,
    178
Chamberlain, Eugene T., 28
Channels. *See* Radio spectrum
Chase and Sanborn, 157
Chesterfield, 158
Chevrolet, 157
Chicago Federation of Labor, 85
Cities Service Gasoline, 155
City of New York v. *FRC*, 141
Clear channel stations. *See* Stations,
    clear channel

Clicquot Club Soda, 155
Coats, George Arthur, 119
Columbia Broadcasting System. *See*
    CBS
Columbia Concert Corporation,
    149–50
Columbia Phonography Record
    Company, 120
Commerce Department, U.S.: confer-
    ences, 39–41, 55, 56, 121–23;
    and FRC, 109, 131, 138, 172;
    regulation by, 27, 49, 54, 57,
    74, 93–104, 162; strategy of,
    8, 9, 31, 35–42, 44–85. *See
    also* Hoover, Herbert C.;
    National Radio Conferences;
    Regulation, by Commerce
    Department; Secretary of
    Commerce
Commercial broadcasters, 59; advan-
    tages of, 9, 12–13, 133, 136,
    139; and Commerce Depart-
    ment, 31, 36, 57; corporate,
    53, 77–85, 108, 128, 133–34,
    150; independent, 64, 84, 153,
    163; opposition of, 9–10, 30,
    177; proliferation of, 61. *See
    also* AT&T; General Electric;
    Networks; RCA; Westinghouse
Commissioner, FRC, 109–11, 125,
    129, 143–44
Commissions: National communica-
    tions, 8, 26, 43, 84, 132, 171,
    176; national radio, 9, 78, 81,
    98–103. *See also* FCC; FRC
Communications Act of 1934,
    13–14, 162, 176–78, 179, 180,
    182
Competition: between radio and tele-
    phone groups, 87; among radio
    users, 108

Components, 114
Confiscation, 140
Congress, U.S., 47, 109, 94–106,
    111, 127–30
Connecticut State College, 168
Contracts, 145, 148–49, 153
Control of Radio, The, 168
Coolidge, Calvin, 74, 104; Commerce
    Department, support for, 96, 97,
    104; and FRC, 106, 110, 111,
    112, 125; and Washington Radio
    Conference, 122
Cooper, William John, 169
Correll, Charles J., 157
Court cases: anti-trust, 145, 151–52;
    post-FRC, 128, 140–42; pre-
    FRC, 7, 53–54, 93, 102–03
Court of Appeals of the District of
    Columbia, 106, 142–43
Couzens, James, 132, 162, 171, 172,
    173, 174
Cowles, W. G., 97
Crosby, Bing, 149
Crosley, Powell, 62–64, 71
Cross-licensing agreements, 25, 64,
    86–90, 151
Crystal sets, 69, 70

Daggett, John D., 85–86
Daniels, Josephus, 21–22, 23–24,
    52, 175, 176
Davis Amendment, 127, 130, 134
Davis, Edwin L, 83–84, 130, 131,
    163, 170
Davis, Harry P., 52, 68–69, 86,
    89–90
Davis, H. O., 167
Davis, Stephen B., 44, 103
De Forest, Lee, 164
De Forest stations, 23
Dellinger, J. Howard, 41, 174

Denby, Edwin C., 32, 42
Dill, Clarence C.: on broadcasting, 163, 180; and FCC, 175, 177; and FRC, 111, 129, 131, 171; and radio regulation, 81, 95–106, 174
Dillon, John F., 110–11, 125
Dill-Rayburn Communications Control Bill, 177–78
Discrimination: geographic, 129; racial. *See* Racism
District of Columbia Court of Appeals, 106, 142–43
Donnelley, Thorne, 63–64
Donovan, William J., 101
Downey, Morton, 149
Dunlap, Orrin E. Jr., 102

Edgerton, James C., 27, 29, 44
Educational Band. *See* Radio Spectrum, educational band
Edward (Prince of Wales), 18
Edwards, Edward I., 97
Electric companies, 9, 63, 150. *See also* AT&T; Western Electric
Electromagnetic waves, 17
Elliot, Frank, 63–64
Elwood, John W., 50
Emerson, Radio Corp., 150, 151
Empire of the Air, 167
Enforcement, 128, 137
Entertainers, 157–58. *See also* Talent
Equal time, 105
Ervin, Edwin, 119
EU-F-GB-I Commission, 30
Eveready Batteries, 155
Expansion, 9, 101–02

Faraday, Michael, 17
Favoritism, 163–71
FCC, 13, 161–62, 170–78, 182

Federal Radio Commission. *See* FRC
Federal Trade Association, 134
Fess, Simon S., 170
Finances: CBS, 120, 146–48; industrial, 77, 140; NBC, 153; network, 117, 146, 150, 158, 159. *See also* Advertising
Fleischman's Yeast, 157
Fortunetelling, 139
FRC: creation of, 11, 103–06, 181; favors commercial broadcasters, 12–13; operations of, 109–12, 123–44, 172; problems of, 107, 165–67; proposed, 82–85, shared authority of, 162
Frequencies: allocation of, 38, 40, 51, 54, 56, 58, 75, 79, 104, 123, 124, 134, 135; amateur, 37; Canadian, 93, 124; government, 99, 106; Navy, 21; regulation of, 78, 82, 137. *See also* Air wave piracy; Radio spectrum; Stations, clear channel
Futrall, J. C., 169

General Electric: 64–69; advertising, 159; and FRC, 129, 163, 167; and RCA, 24–25, 150–52; and regulation, 10, 31
General Electric v. *FRC*, 141, 142
General Foods Corporation, 159
General Mills, 159
General Motors, 118, 159
General Oats Company, 159
Geographic Distribution of Stations. *See* Stations, geographic distribution of
Gilbert, James C., 55
Goldsmith, Alfred N., 31, 49, 99, 107
Gooding, Frank R., 104
Goodrich Tires, 118

Goodwin Sands Lightship, 18
Gosden, Freeman Fisher, 157
Great Atlantic and Pacific Tea Corp.
    See A&P
Great Britain, 3, 18, 108, 122, 123
Grebe Radio Manufacturing
    Company, 148

Hanley, James H., 144, 181
Hanson, Elisha, 111
Happiness Boys, 138–39
Harbord, James G., 46, 94, 173
Harding, Warren G., 8, 15, 26, 32,
    39, 49
Hays, Will, 26
Hedges, William, 63–64
Hertz, Heinrich R., 17
Heterodyning, 114
Hill, George Washington, 154,
    155–56
Holland, E. O., 100
Holmes, Mrs. Christian, 120
Hooper, Stanford C., 28; on broad-
    casting, 164, 172–73; on broad-
    casting band, 58; and FRC,
    110, 131; and GE, 24; on gov-
    ernment monopoly, 22; on IRAC,
    45, 51; on RCA, 30; and Roper
    Committee, 174
Hoover, Herbert C.: and amateurs,
    32; and broadcasters, 35–46,
    61–62, 72–73, 77–85, 180; and
    FRC, 12, 107, 110–12, 124,
    127, 144, 171; and Radio Act of
    1927, 94–106; and regulation,
    8–9, 10–11, 47–59; program for
    Commerce Department, 28; and
    Washington Conference, 108,
    122. *See also* Department of
    Commerce; Secreatary of
    Commerce

Hours of operation, 40, 116–17,
    124, 134
Howard & Shelton, 158
Hughes, Charles Evans, 88
Huston, Claudius H., 37, 53
Hutchins, Robert M., 164

IAGCB. *See* Interdepartmental
    Advisory Committee on Govern-
    ment Broadcasting
Inspectors, FRC, 139–40
Institute of Radio Engineers, 31, 134
Intercity Radio Company, 53–54, 101
Interdepartment Advisory Committee
    on Government Broadcasting
    (IAGCB), 41–44
Interdepartmental Board of Wireless
    Telegraphy, 20, 28, 29, 44–45
Interdepartmental Radio Advisory
    Committee (IRAC): creation, 9,
    44–46, 106; and FRC, 51, 52;
    and government channels, 58,
    99; on radio conference, 79; shares
    authority, 162
Interference, signal: discussed, 56,
    75, 80; occurrence, 36, 38
    101–02, 124, 126; reduction, 40,
    58, 98, 128, 134, 137, 139;
    stimulus for regulation, 10, 54,
    78, 133
Interior Department, U.S., 169
International Radio-Telegraph Con-
    vention, 54
Interstate commerce, 141
Interstate Commerce Commission,
    162
Ipana Toothpaste, 155

Jameson-Davis, Henry, 18
Jenkins, Elliot, 63–64
Jolson, Al, 157

Jones, H. F., 154
Joy, Henry B., 97
Judson, Arthur, 119, 121, 149–50

Kaltenborn, Hans von, 88
KDKA, 7, 15, 17, 66, 152
Kellog, Frank, 49
Kerwin, Jerome G., 168
Kesten, Paul, 155
KFKB Broadcasting Association, Inc.
    v. FRC, 142
KGO, 66, 142
King, Edward J., 32
"King's Henchman, The," 121
Klugh, Paul B., 99
KMOX, 155
KOA, 66
KSD, 63, 89
KTM, 139
KYM, 66
KUOA, 169
KWY, 152

Labor, organized, 85
Lafount, Harold A., 125, 131, 132
Lahback, Frederick P., 104
Lazaro, Ladislas, 104
Legislation, radio: need for, 94–106
    process of enacting, 48–55,
    81–85, 177–8; proposals for, 44,
    46, 73–74, 77, 80, 129–30, 170
Levy, Issac, 120, 121
Levy, Leon, 120, 121, 147
Licenses: assignment, 38, 40, 54, 82
    95, 98, 101, 109, 123, 133,
    136; fees, 73, 88, 170, 175; re-
    vocation, 53, 73, 79, 80, 83,
    105, 129, 137, 141
Listeners, 3, 42, 52, 67, 69, 103,
    108, 136

Lord, Thomas and Logan (adver-
    tising agency), 156, 164
Louchheim, Jerome H., 121, 146–47
Loudspeakers, 87, 114, 115
Lucky Strike Cigarettes, 157,
    164–65. See also American
    Tobacco Company

McDonald, Eugene Jr., 10, 63–64,
    78, 93–98, 132, 178
McLean, Ridley, 64
McPherson, Aimee Semple, 63
Mann, James R., 23
Manufacturers, 62–63, 86, 89, 150, 151
Marconi, Guglielmo, 18, 24
Marconi Wireless Telegraph and
    Signal Co., 18, 23, 24–25, 68
Maritime communications: early,
    5–6, 18–22, 35; international,
    123; naval, 21, 29, 36, 37; re-
    allocation of channels for,
    56–57, 75
Marketing, of radio, 154
Marsh, Francis, 119
Maxim, Hiram Percy, 37
Maxwell House Coffee, 118
Maxwell, James Clark, 17
Medical shows, 139, 142
Merrill, H. M., 85
Millay, Edna St. Vincent, 121
Millikan, Robert A., 170
Mills Brothers, 149
Modernization, 137
Monopoly: charges of 30, 62,
    119–20, 151, 163; governmental,
    8, 21–22, 23–24, 25, 27, 168,
    170, 175; oposition to, 73,
    83, 105
Morgan, Joy Elmer, 175
Morse, Samuel F. B., 18
Municipalities, 63

NAA, 43, 86
NAB (National Association of Broad-
casters): congressional activities
of, 83, 97, 99; formation of,
63–64; in government confer-
ences, 79, 134; on self-regulation,
102; survey results, 155
Nally, Edwin J., 24–25
National Advisory Council on Radio
in Education, 164, 166
National Child Welfare Association,
165
National Committee on Education by
Radio, 169–170, 175
National communications com-
mission. *See* Commissions,
national communications
National Farm and Home Hour, 169
National Food Products Protective
Committee, 165
Nationalization. *See* Monopoly,
federal
National Lumber Manufacturers
Association, 118
National Radio Club, 163
National radio commission. *See* Com-
missions, national radio.
National Radio Conferences: as basis
for law, 82; First, 39–41, 48,
87; Fourth, 79–81; Second,
55–59; Third, 74–76
National Security, 23, 42, 171, 173
Naval Communications Service, 3,
24, 28–29, 29–30. *See also*
Bullard, William H. G.; Hooper,
Stanford C.
Navy, U.S.: criticism of, 20, 24,
29–30, 32; effects of broad-
casting on, 15, 58; opposition
to broadcasting, 4, 8, 23, 35;
political maneuvering of, 21–22,

28–29, 37, 40, 42–43, 45,
51–52, 59, 99
NBC: criticism of, 163, 164–65;
development of, 10, 89–91,
116–19, 145, 169. *See also*
Red Network; Blue Network
*Nelson Brothers Bond and Mortage
Company* v. *FRC*, 141
Networks: criticism of, 13, 165–67;
development of, 11, 65–66, 89,
116–21, 145–60; and finances,
12, 116, 148, 155; and regulation, 12, 75, 104, 125–26.
See also Blue Network; Red
Network
Newspapers, 63, 89
New York University, 166
Noncommercial broadcasters: educational, 9, 13, 52, 63, 84,
99–100, 133, 136, 140, 166,
168–71, 175, 177; municipal,
9, 13, 64, 133; problems of, 13,
128, 133, 134, 139–40, 166;
protest by, 13, 161–71, 177;
religious, 9, 13, 63, 133, 136,
170, 177

Opposition: to the Commerce Department, 94–98; to federal control,
37, 50, 74, 78, 84–85
Our Master's Voice, 167

Paley, Samuel, 147
Paley, William S., 12, 145, 147–50,
181
Paramount-Famous-Lasky Corpora-
tion, 148
Patents, 24, 64–65, 82
Payne Foundation, 169
Pearl, Jack, 157
Pearson, Drew, 175

Pepsodent Toothpaste, 156, 157, 159
Perrill, H. P., 55
Pickard, Sam, 125, 131, 132, 169
Philco, 150, 151
Politics, presidential, 10, 96, 106
Pontiac, 158
Post Office Department, U.S.: Air
    Mail Service, 26, 44; inter-
    departmental relations of, 40,
    43–44, 45–46, 162; on mon-
    opoly, 8, 25; radio system of,
    26, 29
Power, of transmitters: classifi-
    cations by, 56, 135, 136; in-
    creases in, 69, 112–13; regula-
    tion of, 40, 75, 78, 80, 124
President, office of, 45, 109, 162
Priority of service, 99, 102–03
Programming: criticism of, 164, 168;
    development, 72, 121, 149,
    158–59; regulation of, 138–39,
    158–59; rights to, 146, 148, 152,
    153
Promotion of broadcasting, 98, 146
Protests, 140–42, 164, 168
Public interest, convenience, and
    necessity: as basis for licenses,
    11, 95, 105, 134, 138; evolution
    as standard, 40, 83, 133, 141;
    standard contested, 140
Public relations, 42–43, 55, 135
Public service broadcasting. See
    Broadcasting, public service
Public service standards, 158
Pupin, Michael I., 98

Racism, 157
Radio Act of 1912: circumvention of,
    9, 57; interpretation of, 101;
    provisions of, 9, 21, 54; repeal,
    105

Radio Act of 1927: confirmed 13, 128,
    140–43; enacted, 94–106,
    129–30, 173, 181; implemented,
    109, 111, 137–42; provisions of,
    11, 107, 143
Radio bands. See Radio spectrum
Radio Broadcast Central, 66
Radio broadcasting. See Broadcasting
Radio commissions. See FCC; FRC;
    Commissions, national com-
    munications; Commissions, na-
    tional radio
Radio Convention of 1912, 122
Radio Corporation of America. See
    RCA
Radio group, 10, 64–69, 86–91.
    See also General Electric; RCA;
    Westinghouse
Radio League of America, 103
Radio Manufacturers Association,
    102, 134
Radio Omnibus Bill, 170
Radio Program Corporation, 119
Radio programming. See Programs
Radio Protective Association of
    Chicago, 163
Radio Protective Committee, 102
Radio Service Laboratory, 139–40
Radio sets. See Receivers
Radio spectrum: allocation of, 20–21,
    36, 78–79, 80, 122, 124; broad-
    casting band in, 56–59, 75, 76,
    124, 135; conservation of, 105,
    172; educational band in, 170;
    supervision of, 54, 82. See also
    Frequencies
Radio stations. See Stations
Radio telephony, 7, 20, 37
Radio telegraphy, 5, 18, 20, 37, 86
Rates, 117–18, 120
Ratner, Victor, 155

Rayburn, Sam, 175, 177
RCA: business relations of, 10, 25, 64–69, 81, 86–91, 145, 150–52; creation of, 24–25, 29–30; monopoly charged, 163, 167; and regulation, 10, 31, 53, 129
Receivers, 69, 86, 87, 89, 113–16, 136
Redfield, William, 27
Red Network, 116–17, 154–55
Reduction of stations, 127, 135–38, 139–40, 141, 163
Regulation: by Commerce Department, 27, 31–33, 35–41, 61–62, 72–75, 77–86; domestic measures, 21, 108, 162; efforts for, 4, 5, 7–8, 10–11, 94–106, 133; by Federal Radio Commission, 123–44, 172; interdepartmental contest for, 9, 15–34; by Interdepartmental Radio Advisory Committee, 45–46; international, 30–31, 108, 121–23; legislation for, 48–59, 176–78; by U.S. Navy, 8–9, 20–23, 28; proposals for, 8–14, 20, 25–27, 80, 167; protests of, 5, 13, 140–42
Remington Rand, 118
Rensselaer Polytechnical Institute, 168
Revolt of noncommercial broadcasters, 37, 161–71
Ricketts, Palmer C., 168
"Rise of the Goldbergs, The," 156
Robert Burns' Cigars, 157
Robertson, Andrew W., 151–52
Robeson, Paul, 157
Robinson, Ira E., 125, 131, 132
Robinson, Joseph T., 96
Rockefeller, John D., 166
Roosevelt Board Report of 1904, 20, 28, 29, 44–45

Roosevelt, Franklin D., 174–78, 181
Roosevelt, Theodore Jr., 29
Roper Committee, 174–76
Roper, Daniel C., 174, 177
Rorty, James, 167
Royal, John, 157

Saltzman, Charles, 174–75
"Sam 'n Henry," 157
Sarnoff, David: biography of, 147; criticism of, 29–30, 167; and industrial development, 10, 87, 89, 119; role at RCA, 25, 66–68, 145, 151–52; on regulation, 172, 173
Scheverin, P. R., 74
Scientists, 9
Scott, Frank D., 104
Secretary of Commerce, 49, 54, 57, 83, 77–85, 94–106. See also Commerce Department; Hoover, Herbert C.
Self Regulation, 36–38, 59, 76, 102
Series, radio, 156–58
Shared time, 142
Signals, radio, 113. See also Frequencies
Specialization of stations, 116
Spite franchise, 119
Sponsors, See Advertisers
Staff: FRC, 131; FCC, 182
Standard Brands, 159
Standards, 128, 138–39
Starbuck, William D. L., 144
State Department, U.S., 162
Stations: affiliated, 86, 146, 149; classification of, 56, 75, 79, 135; clear channel, 134, 135, 136, 153, 163; crowding of, 101–02, 124; geographic distribution of, 40, 104, 105, 127,

134, 135; improvements in, 113;
portable, 124, 135; reduction of,
125, 127, 139–40, 141, 163;
specialization of, 66
Stewart, Charles, 74
Stock, 148
Stokes, Harold Philip, 78
Stoopnagle & Budd, 158
Stratton, Samuel W., 39–40, 41
Studies of communications, 171
Studios, 118
Swift and Company, 159
Swope, Gerald, 152
Sykes, Eugene O., 110–12, 125, 182,
130–31, 132

Talent, 118, 119, 146, 149, 157–58
Taylor, Deems, 121
Technology: effect of on spectrum,
56, 58; improvements in, 108,
112–16; promoted by Post
Office, 26; and regulation, 5,
137, 138
Telephone group, 10, 64–69, 86–91.
See also AT&T; Western Electric
Terrell, William D., 124
Texaco, 157
Titanic, SS, 20
Todd, David W., 22
Trade Association of Schenectady, 85
Transmitters, 69, 113, 125, 129, 135
Tubes, 7, 69, 82, 87, 113, 114
Tuning, 113

Umberger, Harry J. C., 84
Underwood, Oscar W., 52
United Independent Broadcasters,
118–21
Universal Electrical Communications
Union, 30–31

University broadcasters. See Noncommercial broadcasters,
educational

Vallee, Rudy, 157
Victoria (queen of England), 18
Victor Talking Machine Company,
120, 151
Violations, 93, 109

WABC, 148, 155
Wagner-Hatfield Bill, 170
Waller, Judith, 166–67
Walsh, David I., 103
Warburton, Clyde W., 100
Washington Radio Conference,
121–23, 137
Watson, James E., 96–97, 104, 132
Wavelengths. See Frequencies
WBU, 63
WBZ, 152
WBZA, 152
WCAP, 90
WCAU, 120, 121
WCBQ, 63
WCCO, 110
WDAF, 63, 89
WDM, 6
WEAF, 65, 66, 87, 88, 90, 138–39
WEAP, 89
Webster, Bethuel M., 112
Western Electric, 10, 64, 115
Western Union Telegraph Company,
68
Westinghouse: government relations,
10, 31, 129, 163; industrial
relations, 10, 25, 64–69, 86–91,
145, 150–52, 167; innovations,
15, 114
WFAA, 63

WGES, 102–03
WGN, 63, 102–03, 157
WGY, 66, 142
WHA, 136
WHAS, 89
WHAZ, 168
White Dill Bills, 94–106
Whitehurst v. *Grimes*, 141
White, J. Andrew, 120
White-Kellogg Bills, 48–50
White, Wallace, 48–49, 50–53, 73–74,
    77–85, 94–106, 129
WHN, 88
Wilkerson, James H., 93
Wilson, Eugene S., 74
Wilson, Francis, S., 102–03
Wilson, Woodrow, 21, 22, 23, 32
Wireless, 17–21, 25, 162. *See also*
    Radio telegraphy; Radio
    telephony
Wireless Ship Act of 1910, 21, 27
Wire Services, 162
WJAZ, 63, 93–95
WJY, 66, 67
WJZ, 66, 81, 116

WMAF, 66
WMAQ, 63, 89, 157, 166–67
WMBI, 63
WMBO, 139–40
WNAC, 66
WNYC, 63
WOC, 63
WOR, 120, 166
Work, Hubert, 44, 45–46
WRR, 63
WSB, 63
WWI, 63
WWJ, 39, 63, 89
Wynn, Ed, 157
WZY, 116

Young, Owen D.: government re-
    lations, 30, 50, 167, 173;
    industrial role, 25, 87, 152, 159

Zenith Radio Corporation, 93–95,
    101, 150, 151. *See also*
    McDonald, Eugene Jr.
Zukor, Adolph, 120, 148

ABOUT THE AUTHOR

PHILIP T. ROSEN is Dean of Continuing Education and Associate Professor of History at Marygrove College located in Detroit, Michigan. His articles on modern American history have appeared in several scholarly publications.